D0791080

City and Regime in the American Republic

Property of Textbook Services
University of Wisconsin-River Falls
410 S. 3rd St., River Falls, WI 54022
Loaned subject to purchase in case of loss or damage
Due by closing time on the last day of finals
Due immediately if class is dropped or upon withdrawal
No highlighting, underlining, or writing in texts
Fines will be levied for infractions

Stephen L. Elkin

City and Regime in the American Republic

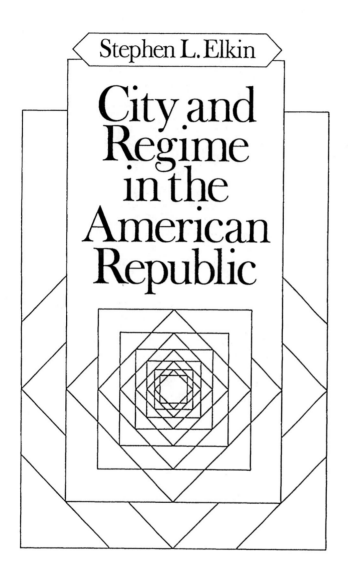

The University of Chicago Press

Chicago and London

The University of Chicago Press, Chicago 60637
The University of Chicago Press, Ltd., London
© 1987 by The University of Chicago
All rights reserved. Published 1987
Printed in the United States of America
96 95 94 93 92 91 90   5432

Library of Congress Cataloging-in-Publication Data

Elkin, Stephen L.
   City and regime in the American republic.

   Bibliography: p.
   Includes index.
   1. Municipal government—United States. I. Title.
JS341.E44   1987   352'.0072'0973   87–5964
ISBN 0–226–20465–0
ISBN 0–226–20466–9 (pbk.)

Stephen L. Elkin teaches political science at the University of Maryland, College Park. He is the author of *Politics and Land Use Planning* and the coeditor of *The Democratic State*.

For D, my teacher

The role of reason in politics is now generally obscured by the popularity in our time of political science as the study of power.

Charles E. Lindblom, *The Intelligence of Democracy*

Fruitful social science must be very largely a study of what is *not,* a construction of hypothetical models of possible worlds which might exist if some of the alterable conditions were made different.

Friedrich Hayek, *Law, Legislation and Liberty*

Contents

Preface

This book grows out of several intellectual impulses. One of these is the attempt to discover how political science can guide political practice. As are many other political scientists, I am embarrassed by the paucity of guidance for practical affairs that political science presently offers. I do not mean to imply that political science should be a kind of nuts-and-bolts enterprise that could serve to train the new recruit to a government bureaucracy, for example, although I confess to thinking that this might be a good deal more intellectually valuable than developing the propositions offered by many parts of the discipline. Instead, I am thinking of the intelligent citizen who might be gratified to gain a deeper understanding of what is required to create and maintain a political way of life that he considers worthy. Political science as it now stands has far too little to offer such a person. This book is, in part, designed to prompt the kind of thinking that will help to remedy this deficiency.

A second impulse is to nudge political science away from what might be called the "organ" theory of politics—that is, that there are only parts and no wholes, that, in the happy (and somewhat altered) refrain of the popular song, we ain't got no body. This emphasis on parts leads to detailed and often very fine studies of the Congress and political parties, to take two examples, but surprisingly little attention is given to what the studies are for. Sometimes the more sophisticated practitioners of this approach make the claim that such studies are designed to determine how we match up against some normative standard. But what is puzzling about such claims is that they do not go far enough. After all, we as Americans are not pursuing an abstraction called liberal democracy but are trying to conduct a political life that is built on a specific institutional inheritance and on an inherited political vocabulary. Thus, political wholes, properly understood, seem to me to be tied to circumstance and history as much as to philosophy.

The other impulses can be more briefly described. I have long been interested in cities—and now I know why. There are two reasons, both of which are displayed in this book. One reason is that the study of cities affords an intimate appreciation of how state-market relations operate in a liberal democracy. Students of cities are less likely to believe that businessmen are simply another, albeit powerful, interest group. This is a useful foundation on which might be built more comprehensive thoughts about the place of business corporations and property in our national political life. The second reason is that the political institutions of the city are potentially crucial in helping to prepare the citizenry to operate the commercial republic that the founding fathers set in motion. Cities are an organ of a particularly important kind in the larger political whole.

The shape of the book reflects an amalgam of these impulses, and thus it is inevitably a compromise. Its organization and emphasis reflect the diversity of the intellectual starting points. Just as I have learned much from trying to marry the various themes, so I offer the results in the hope that others will gain something from its eclecticism. The book is in the nature of a theoretical essay. The test of a good essay is whether it can build on what is widely believed to be true—and present it in illuminating ways. This is what I hope to have achieved.

Acknowledgments

This is a democratic story of liberal politics and as such it is in many ways an odd and difficult undertaking. I have, therefore, incurred many debts, and I wish here to thank those who have helped me understand what is at issue; they are Fred Alford, Charles Anderson, Diana Elkin, Judy Garber, David Greenstone, Russell Hardin, Jennifer Hochschild, Jenny Nedelsky, Joe Oppenheimer, Martin Shefter, Karol Soltan, Clarence Stone, Todd Swanstrom, and Catherine Zuckert.

Above all, I wish to thank Ed Haefele. Were others to benefit as much from his teaching as I have, contemporary American political science would be a different and markedly better discipline.

For research assistance, I wish to thank a long list of graduate students, many of whom must have wondered what could possibly be the connection between the various bits and pieces that I sent them after; these students are John Rohrer, Nancy Petrovic, Alice Krupit, Valerie Lehr, Paul Parker, Greg Lockwood, and, in particular, Cindy Burack, and Patty Davis, who also undertook the tedious task of getting the footnotes and bibliography straight. For yeoman service in typing and retyping, I am particularly indebted to Gale McNelly and Carol Bellamy.

1
Introduction

Alexis de Tocqueville and John Stuart Mill approached the study of politics in cities and towns as part of a more general inquiry into the possibility of popular government. In this they distinguished themselves from most of their successors. For these later theorists, the study of city politics has become a specialization based on abstracting city politics from the larger political order and any assessment of its promise. Tocqueville, in a widely quoted comment, said that "municipal institutions constitute the strength of free nations. Town meetings are to liberty what primary schools are to science. . . . A nation may establish a free government, but without municipal institutions it cannot have the spirit of liberty."[1] Mill shared these sentiments and himself commented that "free and popular local and municipal institutions" are part of "the peculiar training of a citizen, the practical part of the political education of a free people."[2]

In their various discussions of these matters, Tocqueville and Mill emphasized three themes: (1) that the study of local politics should be normative, (2) that it should be normative not just in an evaluative sense but in a way that pointed to political practice, and (3) that this normative focus should chiefly concern the contribution that local political institutions could make to a desirable political way of life.[3] Echoes of these themes can be found in the major works that started the resurgence of urban political studies in the 1950s, but, for the most part, such concerns have faded as this subdiscipline has developed.[4] In its place grew up a resolute empiricism that at various stages concerned itself with such matters as ethnic voting behavior in city elections and the effects of political structure on policy outcomes.

1. *Democracy in America*, 1: 63 (Vintage ed.).
2. *On Liberty*, 181 (Penguin ed.).
3. For a more modern statement, see John Dewey, *The Public and Its Problems*, esp. 143–84.
4. See esp. Edward C. Banfield and Martin Meyerson, *Politics, Planning and the Public Interest;* Norton Long, *The Polity;* and Robert A. Dahl, *Who Governs?*

Much effort was devoted to tying these studies to general theoretical arguments about the workings of city politics. But there was limited success, and, not surprisingly, such studies faded—and, with them, some of the interest in cities. This empiricism coexisted with the more normative community-power studies, as if the two efforts had little to contribute to one another. The community-power studies were animated primarily by the question of how to describe the distribution of power in American localities—and secondarily by the significance of such a distribution for American democracy. In the most sophisticated hands they thus came closer to the themes set down by Tocqueville and Mill. But again a great deal of success could not be claimed, for the effort, for the most part, dissolved into a dispute about methodology. Even now, there are some who are fighting rearguard actions in the methodological wars, trying to salvage positions argued twenty-five years ago and neglecting the significance of any research findings for a well-developed conception of a valued political way of life.[5]

More recently, a normative focus in the study of city politics has had something of a resurgence in the work of such urban theorists as Peterson and Katznelson.[6] Peterson's work is the most wide-ranging, advancing a general theory of how city politics works and of its limitations for pursuing various kinds of egalitarian goals. Katznelson's work is essentially a theoretical case study that is particularly concerned with the prospects of leftist political movements for remaking the face of city politics. While these two authors have different substantive concerns, they do share the sense that the principal normative focus of urban political study should be a concern for the way in which city politics advances or retards equality and/or promotes some conception of efficiency.[7]

The studies by Peterson and Katznelson (especially that of the former), as well as those by their less-sophisticated counterparts, are part of a widespread current interest in the relation between equality and efficiency in political life. Perhaps the most widely cited contemporary

5. Nelson W. Polsby, *Community Power and Political Theory*, 2d ed.

6. Paul E. Peterson, *City Limits;* and Ira Katznelson, *City Trenches.* See also Todd Swanstrom, *The Crisis of Growth Politics;* Douglas Yates, *The Ungovernable City;* and Martin Shefter, *Political Crisis/Fiscal Crisis.*

7. There is one other body of normatively oriented literature on cities, viz., the public-choice literature. See, e.g., Robert L. Bish, *The Public Economy of Metropolitan Areas;* Gary J. Miller, *Cities by Contract;* and Robert Ellickson, "Cities and Homeowners Associations," *University of Pennsylvania Law Review* 130, no. 6 (June 1982): 1519–1608. The critique of these views is a complex undertaking and is, in any case, outside the mainstream of political scientists' discussion of the city. This is not to say that they can be dismissed, and I pick up, in chap. 10, some of the themes raised in these discussions.

statement of this interest is the work of Arthur Okun.[8] These studies reflect the generally held view that the promise of liberal democratic politics is (1) for the establishment of some kind of political and economic equality and (2) for an increased ability to use resources efficiently both to advance material well-being and to cope with policy dilemmas.

A principal difficulty in these studies, even in the sophisticated ones, has been to develop a view of the relation between equality and efficiency that gives due regard to each. In the case of a study such as Peterson's, an insensitivity to how urban politics may institutionalize the advantage of some interests over others exists alongside a complex understanding of the efficiency dimensions of urban politics. Katznelson succumbs to the opposite difficulty, treating city politics as if it were essentially a contest for power between class and racial groupings and neglecting its problem-solving or efficiency dimensions.

A second difficulty is the more subtle one of not fully sharing Tocqueville's and Mill's interest in the larger political whole. Again, the examples of Peterson and Katznelson are instructive, since both, unlike many other students, make the effort. In the case of Peterson's work, one is left with the impression that the larger political order is much like a factory that has two principal tasks—distributing goods and services and efficiently allocating resources for a variety of policy purposes. There is little effort to see what else may be at stake and, in particular, what role city politics might play in any more complex understanding of the national political order. There is presumably some reason why we have both a polity and an economy. Politics may be deeply involved in economics, but there is good reason to doubt whether the former is or ought to be merely an extension of the latter by other means—and presumably a less appealing one at that. Katznelson's sophisticated treatment of why class and racial conflict look as they do in American cities leaves the impression that a good political order would be one in which the tables were turned, and those who currently lose out for systematic reasons would be systematically advantaged. To be sure, there is a kind of rough justice in this view, compensation often being appealing where there are those who have been illegitimately shortchanged. But compensation and turning the tables are not the same things as institutions and rules that are at the core of any political order in which conflict is expected to occur.

A third difficulty is in the development of normative arguments that will be helpful in guiding political practice. Once again the examples of Peterson and Katznelson are suggestive. Being accom-

8. *Equality and Efficiency: The Big Trade-Off.*

plished theorists, they concern themselves with the question of good practice. However, their efforts are not very self-conscious, tending toward conclusions and advice rather than analysis of the kinds of arguments that underlie their advice. In their different ways, they illustrate the most common versions of commentary on political practice: (1) using causal analyses of how some political domain currently works to argue that efforts to make it work in any other fashion ought not to be made and (2) focusing on disadvantaged actors and attempting to discover what steps might be taken to improve their lot. Both types of commentary are necessary parts of any broad version of political practice, but any useful conception must surely include some view, however tentative, of the principal features of the desirable political order toward which such practices are directed.

Studies such as those of Peterson and Katznelson point the way to a recovery of a normative conception of city politics, in the manner of Tocqueville and Mill. But they also suggest that, for such an effort to be successful, it must not only treat the equality and efficiency dimensions of political life in a balanced fashion but must rest on a more complex conception of the larger political whole, a conception that is not confined only to these two dimensions.

CITY, REGIME, AND JUDGMENT

The themes of equality and, to a lesser degree, efficiency, also guide the following pages, particularly the four chapters that follow. I pursue the equality theme by asking whether popular control in cities is characterized by systematic bias such that some interests are systematically favored over others. The absence of such systematic bias I shall call political equality. If the agenda of what gets discussed in the city regularly reflects the preferences of some political actors more than those of others, and if the results of policy decisions reflect the shape of the agenda, we can safely infer that there is systematic bias at work; in other words, popular control[9] in cities would be flawed, a shortcoming that might be characterized as a serious departure from political equality.

I pursue the efficiency theme by asking whether city political institutions are organized to promote social intelligence. The premise of this discussion is that these institutions affect not only the distribution of benefits and burdens but also how well problems that city residents face collectively are dealt with. This is a matter of social

---

9. By "popular control" I mean the effort to connect the use of public authority to the opinions of the citizenry.

problem solving—and a key to it is, again, the shape of the public agenda. If the content of the agenda is substantially restricted to the proposals of only some political actors in the city, then so is social intelligence restricted.[10] In this sense, the roots of political equality and social intelligence are the same.

My general conclusion concerning political equality and social intelligence is that on both counts there are significant failures of popular control. In particular, popular control is unduly hospitable to the preferences of businessmen concerned with land use (or to what public officials consider to be their preferences). The result is systematic bias and shortcomings in social problem solving. Moreover, precisely because the roots of political equality and social intelligence are the same, the widespread effort to consider the trade-offs between equality and efficiency is misplaced. There is good reason to believe that systematic bias leads to poor social intelligence: there is no trade-off, only cumulative loss.

My concern in these beginning chapters is not to present new data on city politics but to offer an interpretation of how the workings of city political institutions affect systematic bias and social problem solving. Also, as I shall say below, these chapters present evidence on how city political institutions contribute to the character of the urban citizenry, evidence pertinent to the Tocquevillean theme of the type of citizenry necessary for a liberal political order to flourish.

The study of American city politics has matured to the point that it is possible to present a comprehensive understanding on the basis of what is already known. A list of the major features of city politics for which there is substantial supporting evidence would include the following:

1. *Electoral contests* in city politics typically do not involve extensive discussion of public issues, especially when contrasted with national elections. Electoral competition is principally between those committed to the defense of existing administrative and electoral arrangements and those committed to "reform." This competition is not manifested in each election, since city politics is characterized by long periods of dominance by one coalition or another. When ethnicity is important in city politics, its principal manifestations are electorally based. Ethnic groups differentially distribute themselves between reformers and those committed to existing arrangements.[11]

---

10. Readers familiar with the work of Charles E. Lindblom, most notably *The Intelligence of Democracy* and *Politics and Markets*, and, more distantly John Dewey, will recognize the sources of these formulations.

11. Edward C. Banfield and James Q. Wilson, *City Politics;* Peterson, *City Limits;* and Shefter, *Political Crisis/Fiscal Crisis* and "Party Organization, Electoral

2. *Interest groups* operate in city politics, and the actions of city bureaucracies in particular are shaped by their activities. In general, conflict over the behavior of public agencies can be observed in which interest groups play a major part. On occasion, such conflict involves many participants and generates intense emotions.[12]

3. *Businessmen* are the most extensively organized of the various interests in the city. A variety of businessmen's organizations operate in city politics, often with substantial resources of expertise, money, and access to public officials. The views of such organized businessmen are widely disseminated and receive a respectful hearing both in the media and from public officials. Among organized businessmen, those concerned with the central business district of the city are particularly well organized.[13]

4. *City governments* are interested in the economic performance of the industries that operate within their borders and in attracting new investment. The management of their external economic relations is a central concern of city officials, and, as a consequence, there is extensive contact between public officials and local businessmen on the subject of the state of the local economy and how to keep or make it healthy.[14]

5. *Bureaucracies* are central actors in city politics. Such agencies have a good deal of autonomy in the day-to-day running of the city and can have significant influence on major policy and budgetary decisions. Mayors are either content to live with such autonomy or find it politically costly to redirect agency activity.[15]

6. *Federal and state governments* have had a powerful—and, in the case of the former, an increasingly powerful—impact on city politics. Political activity in the city is significantly influenced by legislation and

Mobilization, and Regional Variations in Reform Success," Working Papers on Urban Political Economy, Program on Urban Studies, Stanford University.

12. Dahl, *Who Governs?;* Raymond Wolfinger, *The Politics of Progress;* and Alan Altshuler, *The City Planning Process.*

13. John Mollenkopf, *The Contested City;* Peterson, *City Limits;* and Clarence N. Stone, *Economic Growth and Neighborhood Discontent.*

14. Stephen L. Elkin, "Cities Without Power," in Douglas Ashford (ed.), *National Resources and Urban Policy;* R. Scott Fosler and Renne A. Berger, *Public-Private Partnerships in American Cities;* Mollenkopf, *The Contested City;* Harvey Molotch, "The City as Growth Machine," *American Journal of Sociology* 82, no. 2 (September 1976): 309–32; Peterson, *City Limits;* Wilbur R. Thompson, *A Preface to Urban Economics;* Charles M. Tiebout, "A Pure Theory of Local Expenditures," *Journal of Political Economy* 64, no. 5 (October 1956): 416–24; and Stone, *Economic Growth.*

15. Wallace S. Sayre and Herbert Kaufman, *Governing New York;* Theodore Lowi, "Machine Politics—Old and New," *The Public Interest* 9 (Fall 1967): 83–91; John P. Crecine, *Governmental Problem-Solving;* Arnold Meltsner, *The Politics of City Revenue;* and Yates, *The Ungovernable City.*

grants that originate in these other levels of government. Especially in the case of the federal government, these ties of authority and money have become increasingly complex and important to both public officials and citizens of the city.[16]

7. *Racial division* is a pervasive and endemic feature of city politics. It has manifested itself in violence between the races, rioting, and conflict over participation in and receipt of the benefits of city politics.[17]

The one new body of data presented here is a case study of politics in Dallas. This case study is included for two reasons. The first of these is a need to guard against the possibility that the interpretation of the workings of city political institutions that I offer here—and the conclusions that I draw from it—will be biased toward older, northern and midwestern cities. These cities have been the subject of most of the empirical studies to date, and I wish to establish that the interpretation and conclusions of the present work hold across all regions. The second reason is that it will be helpful to have an illustration of those crucial features of the analysis that appear in chapters 2 and 3. Since the present work is a general interpretation, some of the formulations will inevitably tend toward the overly abstract and can therefore benefit from being fleshed out in a case example.

The conceptual foundation on which my comprehensive interpretation rests is the division of labor between state and market as it has become manifest in cities.[18] The interpretation attempts to move beyond the now sterile debate between elitists and pluralists that has characterized community-power studies—and takes seriously what common sense tells us, namely, that city politics is a profoundly economically oriented enterprise. It is bound up with economic matters in direct and powerful ways, so that there can be no study of city politics without the study of city economy. Moreover, the nature of the city's concern with its economic destiny, the extent of its public powers and their internal organization—in short, the principal features of the state-market division—are all historically shaped. Not only must there be a political economy interpretation of city politics, but any such interpretation must be historically informed.[19]

16. Peterson, *City Limits;* and David B. Walker, *Toward a Functioning Federalism.*

17. Harold F. Gosnell, *Negro Politicians;* Katznelson, *City Trenches* and *Black Men/White Cities;* James Q. Wilson, *Negro Politics: The Search for Leadership;* and Arthur Waskow, *From Race Riot to Sit-In, 1919 and the 1960s.*

18. For my earlier efforts to formulate the argument, see "Cities Without Power" and also "Twentieth Century Urban Regimes," *Journal of Urban Affairs* 7, no. 2 (Spring 1985): 11–28.

19. For some excellent studies that are both, see, in addition to the studies by Katznelson and Peterson cited above, Shefter, *Political Crisis/Fiscal Crisis;* Swanstrom, *The Crisis of Growth Politics;* and Molotch, "The City as Growth Machine."

The political economy impulse displayed here is one that is common to both public-choice and Marxist analyses. I seek, however, to avoid the reductionist trap of much of the work in the former vein. In such work, political action is explained largely by reference to the incentives generated by political rules in light of given preferences, and the economic and political context drops from sight. I also try not to fall into the corresponding error of much Marxist work, which sees politics as a deduction from economic structure.[20] As is the case with Marxist analysis, the explanations that I offer are structural in the sense that the choices open to political leaders are understood to be constrained by the economic arrangements in which the city is situated. But, not only do I argue that political leaders have choices in how to respond to this economic context; I contend that they also have other considerations in mind, most notably how to pursue their political ambitions and how to get and continue to be elected. The structuralist analyses offered are not presented as being economically deterministic. The result of these various factors, I argue, is that there is a strong tendency for political leaders and businessmen, particularly those concerned with land-use matters, to find themselves in tacit or open alliance. The results of this, in turn, are the foreshortened public agenda alluded to above, the corresponding problems of systematic bias and ineffective problem solving, and a citizenry ill suited to the running of the sort of republic that we wish to be.

One additional feature of the state-market interpretation should be noted: it focuses on what is common to cities and sees historical and regional differences as variations on common themes. There are also undoubtedly variations by size of city, but, again, these are best understood as variations. The interpretation offered here is meant to apply to all cities with at least approximately 50,000 population and may apply to smaller ones as well. Those larger than this admittedly arbitrary size have sufficient economic and social complexity to sustain the sort of political life that I describe. This focus on commonalities follows from the state-market focus and is at variance with much work in city politics, inasmuch as that work looks to differences.

Formative Institutions and the American Regime

Even sophisticated studies of efficiency and equality—and of political institutions as allocative and distributive mechanisms—do not exhaust what we want to say about the workings of popular control

20. For more extended comments, see my two papers "Castells, Marxism, and the New Urban Politics," *Comparative Urban Research* 2 (1979): 22–32, and "Between Liberalism and Capitalism," in Roger Benjamin and Stephen L. Elkin (eds.), *The Democratic State.*

in cities. Urban political study has overwhelmingly followed the emphasis in political science generally: that the principal subject of liberal democratic politics is economics, that is, the efficient use of resources and their distribution. This emphasis reflects the reality that these are indeed prominent concerns in contemporary political debate and struggle. In market-dominated mass democracies, concern with material well-being—its overall level and distribution—is virtually certain to be central.[21] Neither virtue nor honor is the defining concern of such polities. But liberal democracies are unlikely to flourish if they rely on the view that politics is simply economics carried out in nonmarket settings. Something is missing in this view, and, to the degree that it is also missing in urban political study, these analyses are radically incomplete.

It is difficult to overestimate how strongly political science is gripped by the view that the fundamental facts about society and polity are economic ones. This is not an exclusively Marxist view, for although Marx was perhaps its foremost exponent, believers in free markets are often at least fellow travelers in this regard. Still, it is hard to suppress the feeling that there is more to the story, if for no other reason than the inkling that there must be *some* reason to have a *political* science. After all, if the principal subject matter of contemporary politics is economics, why should political scientists not confess to having chosen the wrong discipline? Of course, this would imply that contemporary economics is well equipped to understand how resources get distributed, which it plainly is not, since it is largely uninterested in the connection between political struggle and economic distribution. But even this sizable lacuna in economic theory does not seem a large enough intellectual space in which to sustain a political science: it would still be a subspecialty—the study of distributive processes—within the larger edifice of economic analysis. Again, more is wanted, and a principal task of the present undertaking is to suggest some of its content.

In contrast to the discussion of systematic bias and social intelligence, new ground must be broken here both empirically and conceptually. There are few studies, and certainly none of cities, that are self-consciously trying to look beyond the efficiency-equality/allocative-distributive conception. Any such study must be much more of a bootstrap operation, one that tries to make sense of what else is at

21. Ronald Inglehart, "Post-Materialism in an Environment of Insecurity," *American Political Science Review* 75, no. 4 (December 1981): 880–900, points out that Americans who give priority to policies concerning income growth and economic stability are three times as many as those who give priority to policies concerned with other values.

stake in the workings of popular control and analyzing city politics in light of it.[22]

Again Tocqueville and Mill are helpful. They suggest that, in addition to seeing political institutions as vehicles for distributing valuable outcomes and for solving social problems, they are also formative of the citizenry. Tocqueville says that municipal institutions can bring liberty "within the people's reach, they teach men how to use and how to enjoy it," [23] while Mill, as noted, talks about these same institutions as parts of the "peculiar training of a free people." [24] While this is not, as we shall see, the only meaning to be given to "formative," both men point away from a conception of political institutions as tools and suggest the centrality of a noninstrumental aspect of political institutions, and of the concomitant importance of certain kinds of political experience. We who come after them may well use different language to point to these noninstrumental aspects of political institutions, talking, as we are likely to do, about their symbolic importance or perhaps about their intrinsic moral significance. There is a family of ideas here that, in one way or another, indicates that how we carry on our political life helps to define us. The language that presents political institutions as formative is perhaps the most direct expression of this idea.

The idea of political institutions as formative is no longer a prominent theme in contemporary theorizing about politics. Nor is this surprising, since it smacks of a kind of moral coercion that seems to be at variance with the central tenets of liberalism.[25] Yet, Tocqueville and Mill imply that a certain sort of citizenry is needed if liberal democracies are to flourish. I contribute to the discussion that they helped to set in motion by considering how a certain organization of political institutions in the city is important and by examining whether the present political institutions of the city help to constitute us in the appropriate manner. Here is where the evidence presented in chapters 2–4 concerning the present workings of city political institutions is reinterpreted. The first interpretation (particularly in chap. 5) is in the service of the arguments about systematic bias and

22. For some pioneering empirically minded efforts that focus on political units other than cities, see Philip Selznick, *Law, Society, and Industrial Justice;* and Clifford Geertz, *Negara: The Theatre State in Nineteenth-Century Bali.*

23. Tocqueville, *Democracy in America,* 1: 63 (Vintage ed.).

24. Mill, *On Liberty,* 181 (Penguin ed.).

25. Cf. Walter Lippmann's comment that "the liberal democracies of the West became the first great society to treat as a private concern the formative beliefs that shape the character of its citizens." (*The Public Philosophy,* 100).

social intelligence. The reinterpretation is intended to further the argument concerning city political institutions as formative of the sort of citizenry that is necessary if a commercial republic is to flourish.

This commercial republic defines the heart of our aspiration to achieve a particular political way of life, that is, a political regime that is worthy of us. Our fundamental aspiration is to establish a popular regime, but one that rests on and promotes a commercial society. Given the present workings of the political economy, if this aspiration is to be served, there must be a citizenry with a lively sense of what I shall call the commercial public interest. A concern for the commercial public interest means, among other things, that popular government should be directed at promoting material well-being by harnessing market forces, but that businessmen's views of how this is to be done should not have a privileged hearing. To have a citizenry with a sense of the commercial public interest requires, in turn, that city political institutions be organized so that citizens are inclined to reason about its content. To the extent that these institutions are not so organized, there is another sort of failure of popular control in the city, a failure to help constitute the citizenry in a manner consistent with our aspirations.

It will help to emphasize at this point that the idea of the regime does not enter my analysis until after the discussion of the formative nature of political institutions. I can best indicate why in the following way. The discussion of the need to eliminate systematic bias and foster social intelligence is, in a particular way, not substantive. Political equality and effective social problem solving are desirable features of *any* popular government. Plainly, popular control in cities should also work then so that it is not characterized by systematic bias and lack of social intelligence. But when the discussion turns to the formative impact of political institutions, the need for something more substantive is apparent: what *kind* of popular government is wanted? To answer this question invites a discussion of our aspirations for a political way of life.

An additional and even more important feature of the organization of the book must also be emphasized. My interpretation of how city political institutions work, discussed in chapters 2–4, is presented largely with an eye toward questions of systematic bias and social intelligence. I have already indicated that the evidence analyzed there can be used to establish how city political institutions help to form us as a citizenry, but the few comments I make on these matters at that point are incidental to the flow of the analysis. I have proceeded in this way and, in particular, have waited until a later chapter (chap. 8) to reinterpret the evidence about city political institutions because I wish to emphasize that we are interested in political institutions not only because they are formative but for reasons of equality and capable problem solving. I also wish to emphasize not only that there are these different dimensions of political institutions but also the possibility of tensions among them. To accomplish both these purposes requires an extensive separate discussion of political institutions as distributors of the benefits and burdens of collective life and as vehicles for collective problem solving. Hence the strong emphasis in chapters 2–4 on arguments pointing toward political equality and social intelligence and the extended statement about these matters in chapter 5. This plan of organization has the additional powerful advantage of giving special emphasis both to the analysis of political institutions as formative and to the place of their formative impact in our attempt to be a commercial republic. These themes are separated from the arguments about systematic bias and social intelligence because they have been little appreciated and understood. Yet, it is also important not to neglect the more conventional analysis of political equality and social problem solving for which the study of city politics has prepared us.

The discussion in the book might have been organized in a different way. The arguments about political institutions as formative and the place of city political institutions in the American regime might have come first. Because this material constitutes the most significant thematic departure in the book, it might have been given the most prominent place, with the discussion of problem solving and equality serving simply to round it out. The dominant theme of the book would then have been the necessity of constituting a certain sort of citizenry in order for us to be a fully realized commercial republic. While there are obvious advantages to this way of proceeding, the disadvantages are greater. Again, I believe that it is fundamental that readers be reminded that we care as much about whether our social problem solving is adequately organized and whether some of us are systematically shortchanged in political life as we do about the kind of relations between people that define us as a citizenry. The organization of the book is best understood as itself making a point—namely, to juxtapose a more conventional political science, with its concern for political equality and social problem solving, to a less conventional one, with its concern for the form of the citizenry and for our aspirations for a political way of life. This means starting with the more common concerns of political study, paying them due regard, and then turning to the less common.

By emphasizing the distinctiveness of the parts of the book, I do not, however, mean to convey that they are wholly separate enterprises. The very organization of the book invites discussion of how the various pieces are to be brought together. That is the purpose of the last chapter, a matter to which I will turn in a moment. Also, as mentioned above, the evidence presented in chapters 2–4 is necessary (in a reinterpreted form) to the subsequent discussion. In addition, the analysis of the plausibility of the reforms contemplated in these later chapters depends on understanding whether the economic facts of city life will inevitably defeat such reform efforts. One of the tasks of the early chapters of the book is to show in what sense this is not so.

Political Judgment

If political equality and social intelligence are desirable features of any popular government, they must also be part of our particular aspirations. Our aspirations, then, are complex. One way to characterize this complexity is to say that the institutions of popular control that are central to our aspirations have several dimensions. They shape the distribution of valued outcomes; they organize social problem solving; and they (potentially) help to form the citizenry in ways that are necessary if our aspirations are to be realized. The formative impact of political institutions can be more generally defined. Our aspirations, I will argue, can be said to include the desire to be constituted in certain ways. How we are constituted may be thought of as a moral concern, since it involves how we shall stand in relation to one another, that is, what we shall expect of one another in our political relations. Political institutions, then, also help to define what may be thought of as our procedural morality.

To realize our aspirations requires an understanding of how to combine the various dimensions of political institutions. This is a task of political judgment. What is wanted is a theory of political judgment to guide those devoted to the purposes of the regime, whom I shall call friends of the regime. The arguments that I present in the present book are the first steps by such a friend of the regime toward developing such a theory of political judgment as it concerns cities. It is offered to others who are themselves willing to present reasoned accounts of regime purposes and how they may be reached.

This tentative account of political judgment is best viewed as part of an increasingly common effort to turn political science into a practical science.[26] What the theorists engaged in this effort are attempting to do, in their various ways, is to discuss public affairs systematically, showing a healthy respect for facts and logic. They also seek to avoid essentially technical views—for example, the conception of governments as giant factories with production functions—and the empty formalisms of a good deal of moral and political philosophy in which the fact that we are a particular society with a particular political tradition and circumstances is accorded too little weight. We need both technique and morals, they suggest, but the real problem is the proper understanding of each of these requirements and of the appropriate way to join them.

Such efforts (my own included) may be thought of as attempts to recapture part of the original impulse behind the creation of political science and to move it beyond its present resolutely empirical/explanatory bent. These efforts are also presented from what Ronald Dworkin calls the internal point of view, that is, from the perspective of someone who wants to make good arguments about how some enterprise to which he or she is committed can be made to flourish. Dworkin contrasts this with the external point of view, which he says is concerned with explaining why certain patterns occur.[27] The latter has been the dominant concern of contemporary political science, and its most devoted practitioners have on occasion gone as far as to deny that an internal point of view is possible. They have attempted instead to look for causal factors that help explain the views of those who purport to argue from an internal viewpoint. This is causal science with a vengeance and can only leave a reader wondering what the value of the external theorists' own arguments are supposed to be.

By saying that political science needs to be a practical science I do not mean to argue that its explanatory pretensions are wrong headed. It is entirely possible that both an explanatory and a practical political science can be developed and that they need each other to be successful. What I do mean to say is that, without political science as practical science, the field will be left to those who offer debased and truncated views of political judgment. Current specimens of such views are being offered by antipolitical theorists who think that politics is, at best, simply an inconvenience and, at worst, a tyranny to be suffered. Political judgment for them (if they would use the term at all) is prophylactic, designed to

26. See, among others, Lindblom, *The Intelligence of Democracy* and *Politics and Markets;* Charles Anderson, "Pragmatic Liberalism: Uniting Theory and Practice," in Alfonso J. Damico (ed.), *Liberalism: Essays in Renewal;* Karol Soltan, *A Causal Theory of Justice;* and Paul Diesing, *Reason in Society.*

27. Ronald Dworkin, *Law's Empire*, chap. 1.

extirpate any moral claims made in behalf of political life. This is not comforting for the rest of us who must live by politics.[28]

There is also a question of self-respect here. When great political questions arise, especially when citizens run around in the streets raising them, it would be pleasing if political science offered something more than what a newspaper columnist well versed in recent polling data and electoral statistics can muster.

The conclusions to which the exercise of political judgment has lead me may occasion some unease. In particular, the idea that we aspire to be a popular regime that serves the commercial public interest may cause some dismay among those who count themselves as part of the left. But there is a sting to this view that those who think of themselves as being on the right might also find unsettling. For even a "conservative" account of our aspirations, if taken seriously, is sufficiently radical to point to significant alterations in our political institutions. In particular, for us to be the commercial republic that we say we wish to be requires both substantial democratization and significant alteration in property rights. More generally, a commercial republic is not the same thing as a republic dominated by businessmen. Once this is understood, much in the way of institutional change is called for. In this sense, the dispute between left and right is less important than the dispute between those who are willing to take *any* account of our aspirations seriously and those who are not. Much of what passes for conservative thought in contemporary American political debate is simply an unwillingness to provide a serious account of what is required to achieve the sort of political life to which such conservatives say that we are dedicated. But this self-interested intellectual lethargy should give little comfort to those on the left, who are more often than not offering a vision of a political way of life that bears little resemblance to what thinking Americans appear to want. They do this, one supposes, with the thought that such advanced ideas are required to justify any significant reforms. In believing this, they, too, in their way, are unwilling to contemplate what is implied in our aspirations and unwilling to pay them their just regard.

Conclusion

There are, then, four basic themes in this book: (1) the workings of the political institutions of the city, (2) the several dimensions of

28. A classic of this genre is James M. Buchanan and Gordon Tullock, *The Calculus of Consent.* Also see the discussion in chap. 10 below.

of political institutions, (3) the political way of life to which we aspire, and (4) the political judgment necessary to guide the reform of our institutions of popular control in ways that will serve our aspirations. The book is designed to be read as building toward the discussion of political judgment in chapter 10. The evidence and arguments on equality and problem solving offered in chapters 2–5 are not only a necessary preface to the discussion of formative institutions and political aspirations in chapters 6–9 but are meant to have equal weight. The discussion of political judgment is designed to draw the themes together, albeit in a provisional manner.

One ideal reader of the book would be a person who has hitherto understood politics as a matter of conflict of interest and the organization of social problem solving. For such a reader, the discussions of institutions as formative, of democratic citizenship, and of the character of the American political economy in light of our aspirations will all strike new notes. For this reader, the value of the book is likely to lie in its analysis of the different roles that political institutions play in a democratic polity.

Another ideal reader would be someone who has thought about what else political institutions are in addition to being engines of conflict and ways of organizing problem solving. This reader will probably wish to test his or her sense of the content of this additional dimension of political institutions against the one offered here. Such a reader will, without prompting, be drawn to the question, How shall the various dimensions of political institutions be drawn together in statements about desirable political practice? For this reader, political science is fundamentally a practical enterprise, designed to help create and maintain desirable political ways of life. The topic of good political judgment will seem to such a person to be the natural focus of political inquiry.

Two final introductory remarks are necessary. First, while the arguments that follow are framed in terms of central cities, it is possible that they will need to be expanded to include all local governments. I will take up this question in chapter 8, particularly in the context of whether citizens are likely to have the motivation to focus on the commercial public interest in localities other than cities. Here I only want to emphasize that this book is not an exercise in urban studies and is thus not obliged to talk about metropolitan areas, suburbs and all. It is a study of political institutions, and those of the city are sufficiently distinctive to be singled out.

Second, by concentrating on the shortcomings of city political institutions I do not mean to imply either that cities are badly governed through and through or that the republic is in immediate danger. Lest the message come out unbalanced, let me say here that, for the most part, cities have done routine things reasonably well. This is consistent with the relative autonomy of the functional bureaucracies that I discuss in the following four chapters. And, considering the possible difficulties, the fact that such a large variety of racial and ethnic groups have managed to live together at all says something positive about the way in which city politics has been carried on; this has indeed been the traditional strength of city politics.

My interest is in shortcomings, however, because my deepest concern is whether a regime dedicated to both popular control and a property-based market system can thrive. Or is it an oxymoron, as some have argued? And so the underlying questions of the book can be taken to be, What is implied by our aspirations, and is it possible to achieve and sustain them? The analysis that I present and the conclusions that I reach might be characterized as an attempt, built on the study of city politics, to marry a strong democratic sensibility to a Madisonian account of the American regime.

2
City, State, and Market

The way in which popular control operates in contemporary cities is largely a consequence of the division of labor between state and market as that is manifest in cities. This division, which stems from the corresponding arrangement of the national political economy,[1] means that ownership of productive assets in the city is largely placed in private hands. Public officials share responsibility for the level of citizen well-being with these private controllers, but these officials cannot command economic performance, only induce it.[2] The concern of public officials with citizen well-being stems largely from their being subject to election or appointment by those who themselves have been elected.

The particular form that this division of labor has taken is the consequence of the structural factors that give city politics its underlying continuity and specific character. Political actors in the city have strong incentives to act in particular ways because of these structural factors and are constrained in various ways from taking actions that they might otherwise contemplate. Of special importance among these structural factors are (1) the definition of the prerogatives of those who control productive assets vis-à-vis the prerogatives of city authorities, (2) how public authority is to be organized, and (3) the external relations of public authorities to private controllers of assets, relations that are in part a manifestation of a federal division of governmental power that largely leaves to cities the task of competing for private resources.

POWERS AND ORGANIZATION

City authorities are not recipients of broad grants of power but have only limited specific powers to set the rules for and otherwise regulate the conduct of the urban citizenry. Conversely, private controllers of

1. See chap. 7 below.
2. See, generally, Charles E. Lindblom, *Politics and Markets*, esp. pt. V.

assets have substantial prerogatives vis-à-vis city governments. Those who wield what powers cities have are the product of electoral contests that typically turn on the creation of complex coalitions or some substitute for them. The most important elected figures are city executives and their appointees, but they must share the wielding of city powers with organized functional bureaucracies that are largely responsible for the day-to-day administration of the city. These structural features of city politics have a common historical origin, being the product of the remaking of urban government in the later nineteenth and early twentieth centuries. It was then that the modern municipal corporation took shape, in a protracted effort to create city governments that suited the political actors who had emerged on the stage of the industrial city.[3]

Dillon's Rule

The contemporary city is not a sovereign body, and in law its limited powers are understood to be the powers that are specifically granted to it by state governments. Cities are understood to be creatures of states. This status of municipal corporations has been essentially accepted since the early part of the twentieth century, when the views developed by the jurist John Dillon came to be widely employed by the courts.[4]

Dillon's views on the status of the municipal corporation can be understood as an attempt to resolve the dilemma of what to do with corporations in a liberal polity. Although early colonial towns and cities were, for the most part, not formally granted charters as corporations, they did exercise powers as a particular kind of association. They were "bodies politic" and as such were quasi corporations. The difficulty for a liberal polity was that, whereas corporations of any sort might, on the one hand, be counted as bulwarks against state power in protecting individual liberty, they also had powers of their

3. As will be apparent, the analysis will focus on the older cities of the East and Midwest and indicate variations for newer cities. The variations have to do not with the structural features themselves but either with the timing of their creation or the character of the political responses to them.

4. The following account of John Dillon and the legal development of the city is drawn from the following sources: Gerald E. Frug, "The City as a Legal Concept," *Harvard Law Review* 93, no. 6 (April 1980): 1059–1154; Edward A. Gere, Jr., "Dillon's Rule and the Cooley Doctrine: Reflections of the Political Culture," *Journal of Urban History* 8, no. 3 (May 1982): 271–98; Henrik Hartog, *Public Property and Private Power;* Frank I. Michelman, "States' Rights and States' Roles: Permutations of 'Sovereignty' in *National League of Cities v. Usery,*" *Yale Law Journal* 86, no. 6 (May 1977): 1165–95; and Anwar Syed, *The Political Theory of American Local Government.*

own that could be used against individuals. They were neither state
nor individual, but intermediate entities. The neatest resolution of
the difficulty would be to assimilate corporations that somehow could
be construed as "private" to the role of individuals in society and to
assimilate others, somehow "public" in character, to the role of the
state. If this could be accomplished, the standard liberal ideas of
individualism, rights, and restraint of state power could be applied.
Short of this, there would remain an anomalous, undigested entity
whose status was difficult to describe and evaluate.

The municipal corporation, with powers as he defined them, was
an attempt by Dillon to resolve this dilemma. The first step, taken by
other jurists before him, had been to define the municipal corporation
as a public corporation having, as it were, a counterpart in the private
business corporation. This helped to resolve the difficulties by con-
signing cities to the state side of the liberal equation. But historically
the municipal corporation also exercised proprietary functions involving the ownership of various kinds of property that enjoyed the
protection of property rights. This raised the question of whether
such functions were appropriate, given the increasing desire on the
part of the politically active to restrict public activity in favor of private
activity. The issue was further complicated by the question of whether
the powers of the city were to be understood as springing from a
right of association on the part of the people who composed the city:
if they were, there would be the danger that the exercise of such
popular sovereignty would jeopardize property rights. In short, the
question was, Is it possible to have city governments that are not
anomalies in a liberal polity—that is, that do not themselves exercise
property rights or exercise state power in a manner that threatens
individual property rights? Dillon built on the public-private distinction concerning the corporation and provided the rationale for the
limited city implied by a restriction on proprietary functions and the
protection of property rights.

Dillon wrote the first and most important treatise on municipal
corporations in 1872. In presenting his views, he did not seek to hide
his underlying purposes. He defended the need to protect private
property and indicated his reservations about the kind of democracy
developing in the cities. His was not a crude defense of the rich and
propertied, however, but a case for rational government in which the
best in the nation might be attracted to city affairs. He hoped to
achieve this by preventing in the city that mix of public and private
functions that made for inefficiencies and extravagancies and that
invited the domination of the public sphere by the private. In addition,
Dillon hoped that the possibilities of class legislation—whether in

behalf of the rich or the poor—could be diminished, so that the talented would be attracted to municipal life. His vision was of a city government that was wholly public and run by those fit to do so.

For Dillon the two keys to achieving these ends were judicial supervision and control of cities by state governments. In his treatise, he said that the power of the state government "is supreme and transcendent: it may erect, change, divide, and even abolish, at pleasure as it deems the public good to require."[5] Dillon succeeded in providing what Hendrik Hartog says judges of the time needed: "doctrinal language that could be used as a wedge to split apart the cozy relationship between municipal action and political sovereignty."[6] It is the task of the courts, said Dillon, to enforce the following view of the relationship between city and states: "It is a general and undisputed proposition of law that a municipal corporation possesses and can exercise the following powers, and no others: First, those granted in express words; second, those necessarily or fairly implied in or incident to the power expressly granted; third, those essential to the accomplishment of the declared objects and purposes of the corporation—not simply convenient, but indispensable. Any fair, reasonable, substantial doubt concerning the existence of power is resolved by the courts against the corporation, and the power is denied."[7]

The result of this rule, which has been used by the judiciary right up to the U.S. Supreme Court, has been to construe the city's ability to regulate private activity as being more like that of an administrative agency than like that of a state government. Cities, then, are likely to be prevented from any regulation of private controllers of assets except for cases in which they have been expressly authorized to do so. They are unlikely to be allowed to rearrange land use in the city for purposes other than those expressly defined by states, and they are similarly likely to be restricted from undertaking commercial ventures that, while they might serve the public good as the city government understands it, have not been authorized by state legislation. Cities, in short, are understood to perform largely a "welfare-improving regulatory service" and have no "general authority to define rights."[8] Concomitantly, private controllers of assets are assured of a substantial sphere in which their ability to shape the life of the city will be largely unrestricted and unchallenged.

5. Quoted in Frug, "The City as a Legal Concept," 1111–12.
6. Hartog, *Public Property and Private Power*, 222–23.
7. John Dillon, *Commentaries on the Law of Municipal Corporations* (5 eds., 1872–1911), 1: sec. 237 (1911 ed.).
8. Michelman, "States' Rights and States' Roles," 1170.

The Organization of Public Authority

As the post–Civil War period turned to late century, the industrial city was becoming fully visible. All of the enormous activity of money-making, building, and the settling down of immigrants that characterized the explosion of the city was being played out within a characteristic set of political arrangements. Industrialists and commercial entrepreneurs, saloon keepers and workers, homeowners and utility magnates, all dealt with each other through a set of political institutions that were both expensive to operate and ramshackle. Governmental authority was exercised through a wide array of boards and commissions as well as through city councils and mayors.[9] City councils of the period were very large by contemporary standards and were commonly bicameral. Mayors were weak, most often having few appointive powers and little else in the way of authority. Executive budgets were unknown, and city governments typically had little idea of their expected revenue or of how much they were actually spending. City legislative authority was dominant, but as often as not it was exercised either through committees that city councils set up or through the special boards and commissions whose members it had a hand in appointing. Appointments to schools, police forces, and the various administrative agencies were made on the basis of patronage or acquaintance with the appointing agent.

The various officials were typically products of a highly factionalized politics. The most notorious of these factions was the Tweed Ring in New York. One acute student of the Tweed era described it as a period of "rapacious individualism." [10] The major political formations of the time are best understood as combines designed to enrich their members as quickly as possible, or as unstable coalitions put together to advance the careers of particular individuals. These formations were often short-lived, having little means of internal discipline. More important, perhaps, they had weak ties to the electorate. The Tweed Ring, for example, was essentially an *intragovernmental* formation that was set up once its members had achieved positions of authority. In short, such organizations were not essentially political parties.

9. See Morton Keller, *Affairs of State;* Jon C. Teaford, *The Unheralded Triumph: City Government in America, 1870–1900;* Ernest S. Griffith, *A History of American City Government: The Conspicuous Failure, 1870–1920;* Kenneth Fox, *Better City Government;* Martin J. Schiesl, *The Politics of Efficiency;* and Michael H. Ebner and Eugene M. Tobin (eds.), *The Age of Urban Reform.*

10. Martin Shefter, "The Emergence of the Political Machine: An Alternative View," in Willis D. Hawley et al., *Theoretical Perspectives on Urban Politics.* The following paragraphs follow Shefter's analysis.

At any particular election the factions and combines could, of course, recruit voters, but their ability to sustain such efforts over time was weak and so new combines and factions soon took over. The key figures in these organizations often were saloon keepers and other small-scale local businessmen with wide acquaintanceship, who were able to capitalize on friendships to build political followings that they either could use themselves or rent out. George Washington Plunkitt, the noted raconteur of how to build a political following, is a prototypical figure here in this respect.[11]

As the century progressed, the combines and factions gave way in some cities to organizations more nearly resembling political parties. Here the ward bosses and saloon keepers came into their own as they managed to establish the ability to deliver voters. Again, the case of New York during the 1870s and 1880s is suggestive. Tammany Hall, Irving Hall, and the County Democracy all conducted primaries and had assembly-district and city committees as they contended for power inside the Democratic party. The party was a confederation of these and other factions that, in fact, fought mightily over who would dominate. But the factions did have strong connections to the electorate, unlike the strict intragovernmental combines.

Although cities varied in the extent to which their politics revolved around combines or competitive party factions, to take the two extremes, the overall effect was a shifting, unsteady set of arrangements. The sheer array of independent authorities and the factionalized nature of electoral and intragovernmental formations made for a highly permeable and expensive politics. Each group of politicians had their expenses (electoral and organizational) to meet and, as often as not, their pecuniary ambitions to fulfill. They were inclined to serve these needs by putting up for sale their ability to facilitate or prevent various forms of business activity in the city. The difficulty from the point of view of local businessmen was that the bargains struck often had a short lifetime. Either politicians became greedy (and, short of a major scandal and the threat of jail, there was no political leadership to stop them from becoming so) or a different group of politicians would come along and require money for what had already been paid for. The costs of running an electoral

11. See William L. Riordan, *Plunkitt of Tammany Hall;* Samuel P. Hays, "The Changing Political Structure of the City in Industrial America," *Journal of Urban History* 1, no. 1 (November 1974): 6–38, and "The Politics of Reform in Municipal Government in the Progressive Era," *Pacific Northwest Quarterly* 55, no. 4 (October 1964): 157–69; and Diane Ravitch, *The Great School Wars.*

system, choosing and electing candidates, and organizing city governments, all of which were the essential functions of these politicians, were great indeed.[12]

In much the same way, the drain on the public treasury of such an unsteady politics was also considerable. Without a political leadership able to impose sufficient discipline, the danger was that the public treasury would be looted sufficiently to cause major scandal and bring an end, at least temporarily, to this source of income. Moreover, without leadership of some kind it was unlikely that intelligent use would be made of public resources. As it was, the typical result was that city expenditure and debt increased more quickly than seemed warranted by population growth and improved service levels.

It is not easy to say how much of the increase disappeared into private bank accounts, how much went into building political followings through patronage, and how much reflected increased provision of services. For as interested as politicians were in advancing their own interests, they also understood that their hold on office would be more secure if the increasing numbers of voters who owned no property and had little wealth were helped in various ways by the provision of city services.[13] Boston serves as an example. From 1850 to 1900 its per-capita expenditure on health, education, and welfare doubled.[14] The extent of the financial undertaking across the range of cities is indicated by the following statistics for the thirteen largest cities for the period 1860–75. Population rose by 70 percent, taxes by 363 percent, and debt by 27 percent. Philadelphia's debt burden, for example, increased from $20 million to $70 million between 1860 and 1880.[15]

The local taxation system that was supposed to finance these undertakings was almost as precarious as the unofficial taxation system of the combines and factions. Almost the entire revenue of cities was raised through property taxes that were designed to tap both personal and real property. Not only was the former virtually impossible to enforce, but the latter barely creaked along because of enforcement problems and the difficulties of assessment.[16]

12. See C. K. Yearley, *The Money Machines*.
13. The Twelfth Census reported that in Manhattan less than 6 percent owned their own homes, in Philadelphia 22 percent, and in Boston not quite 19 percent. See Yearley, *The Money Machines*, 27.
14. Yearley, *The Money Machines*, 25. See, generally, Teaford, *The Unheralded Triumph*, chap. 10.
15. Charles N. Glaab and Theodore A. Brown, *A History of Urban America*, 191–92.
16. Yearley, *The Money Machines*, esp. pt. I.

These were the political arrangements through which the building of the post–Civil War industrial city was transacted. They linked neighborhoods and their politicians looking toward the bigger city-wide prizes with a considerable array of businessmen who were engaged in either the actual physical creation of the city or financial speculation on how this would occur. But fewer and fewer of those actively involved in the city's political economy were satisfied with existing arrangements. Consider first city businessmen.

For businessmen, the city is a pattern of access—to workers, suppliers, markets, services, etc. In pursuing efficient access, devising strategies to shape it, or betting on its direction, businessmen require varying amounts of fixed assets. Additionally, the extent to which the city is the principal market as well as a base of operations varies. We may suppose that, depending on what sort of access is most problematic, the extent of fixed assets, and the location of markets, businessmen might have greater or lesser problems with the sort of political relationships that obtained during the last decades of the nineteenth century.

For the larger industrial firms a regional or even large base of operations was characteristic. A localized, highly corrupt politics was, at a minimum, no advantage to such operations. Indeed, politicians with a neighborhood view might prove positively meddlesome and expensive for a corporation competing in national markets.[17] Political arrangements with a citywide reach, capable of enforcing agreements, and not outrageously expensive to run were best suited for such businessmen. If, in addition, city governments could also be induced to be efficient by utilizing budgeting and accounting methods, so much the better. As a result, then, across the range of American cities industrialists supported efforts to strengthen the mayor, promote at-large or enlarged council districts, improve budgeting, and institute similar efficiency-oriented improvements. Major industrialists such as Rockefeller and Carnegie went so far as to support what rapidly became a national reform effort in the guise of the New York Bureau of Municipal Research, one of whose principal concerns was the improvement of fiscal management.[18]

Not only did the scope of their operations incline industrial leaders to support reform; so did their worries about industrial strife, broader forms of class conflict, and political radicalism. Major industrial violence was occurring, anarchists were feared to be at work, and radicals

17. Shefter, "The Emergence of the Political Machine"; and Hays, "The Politics of Reform."
18. Fox, *Better City Government;* and Schiesl, *The Politics of Efficiency,* 112–20.

had made strong runs for municipal office. City governments that were in a position to help enforce industrial peace and a city politics that did not focus on class issues were clearly desirable. The desire for the former probably inclined many industrialists to support the strengthening of mayors, whereas desire for the latter probably led to support for those electoral schemes—for example, at-large electoral systems that require money and publicity for success—that make it more difficult for radicals to find platforms.[19]

If we turn to businessmen with large fixed assets and markets within the city, we get a different story. If New York is at all representative, among the principal supporters of a strengthened machine politics were utilities that needed a good deal of political stability. A fragmented politics composed of politicians all trying to pluck the goose was an unsettling climate in which to do business. But where else could the utility go? Cooperation was possible with bosses trying to organize citywide machines, since they might be willing to regularize the informal fiscal arrangements with utilities in the course of curbing the tastes of their lieutenants for independent income opportunities.[20]

Merchants and those in the construction business are more difficult to sort out. In Philadelphia, at least, large-scale merchants were one of the principal supporters of reform efforts,[21] but it is easy enough to suppose that in other cities an emerging boss who was able to inject order into the chaos and corruption would prove attractive. Similarly, those in the construction business—paving contractors and builders—were, at the century's turn, very likely tied to operating in particular cities. Presumably the biggest of them were dissatisfied with a fragmented politics, but it is difficult to say what possible remedies might have occurred to them.

Although many businessmen had fairly specific worries about the existing political arrangements, a more diffuse set of concerns characterized many members of the middle class. It is easy to imagine modest merchants and members of the established professions being worried, on the one hand, by the rise of the great corporations and the great rich[22] and, on the other hand, by the depredations of politicians whose principal support came from the waves of immigrants filling up the cities. They might perceive their status to

19. For the background, see Robert H. Wiebe, *Businessmen and Reform;* and Gabriel Kolko, *The Triumph of Conservatism.* More generally, see James Weinstein, *The Corporate Ideal in the Liberal State, 1900–1918.*

20. Shefter, "The Emergence of the Political Machine."

21. Philip Benjamin, "Gentlemen Reformers in the Quaker City, 1870–1912," *Political Science Quarterly* 85, no. 1 (March 1970): 61–79.

22. Richard Hofstadter, *The Age of Reform,* pt. IV.

be eroding on all sides. But worries about city politicians pandering to the working class by giving out jobs and services also had a quite practical side to it. Middle-class holders of real property were the principal legal sources of income for financing these public activities. Business enterprises large and small might contribute money illegally to politicians, but the tax system of the city ran on real property. It was *supposed* to tax personal property, but this it largely failed to do, and, as a result, the rich went largely untouched in terms of their real wealth. The poor, of course, owned nothing; and the taxation of corporate wealth had yet to emerge.

One response of middle-class people to the unsatisfactory state of city affairs was to support municipal reform efforts. The hope of some was that people like themselves would be able to gain public office and displace the existing set of politicians. But mixed in with these overt political concerns was dismay at the supposed moral corruption of the ward-based politics, disdain for the immigrants and their politics, and anger at the inefficiency, disorganization, and waste in the conduct of city affairs.

For those whose principal worries were political corruption, the assertion of political claims by immigrants, and the perceived decline in their own status, the favored remedies were nonpartisanship and the devising of political machinery that would make an assertion of citywide interests likely. Political parties in city government were the enemy here, since parties were the principal vehicles by which the new groups were making their claims, graft was organized, and the supposed moral corruption was occurring.

Others found the administrative side of city affairs particularly dismaying. How could so complex an organization run without a strong executive figure? So either the mayor's powers needed strengthening, or professional managers should be employed. In much the same way, the city lacked expertise to carry on many of its functions in areas such as public health, housing, and education. In general, this was the period in which great public and private organizations were being created, and the people who were emerging to staff them were particularly concerned that cities utilize their expertise. If worries about corruption and ward bosses were defensive and backward looking (in being concerned about old privileges), these champions of the use of technical expertise were looking toward the future.[23]

23. Otis A. Pease, "Urban Reformers in the Progressive Era," *Pacific Northwest Quarterly* 62, no. 2 (April 1971): 49–58; Robert H. Wiebe, *The Search for Order, 1877–1920*, 111–71; and Ravitch, *The Great School Wars*, 161 ff.

There were yet others among the broad range of the better-off city dwellers who supported reform efforts. The casualties of the industrial city were their concern. These were the social workers, the builders and managers of charities and settlement houses who worked for new tenement and public-health laws and set up private charitable institutions. For them, ward politicians were an obstacle to any scheme of substantial social reform.[24]

It is too simple to say, then, that the dominant worry among the better-off city dwellers was the protection and enhancement of their material wealth; but such sentiments were far from unknown. Among the anxiety-ridden, such worries issued in the specter of popular rule gone riot and prompted comments by people such as Brooks Adams, who said that "the most difficult problem of modern times is unquestionably how to protect property under popular governments." [25]

This ferment of reform enthusiasm among the better-off city dwellers was echoed by the more farseeing and ambitious among factional and party leaders. Two intertwined matters were of principal concern to them, and both dealt with the political lifeblood that was money. A fragmented, corrupt politics was dangerous because corruption could and did get out of hand. Creating a citywide organization could provide the means for disciplining the overly greedy and prevent businessmen and outraged citizens tired of too much graft from inviting the judiciary to put the municipal house in order. In addition, even the legitimate monetary requirements of competing for the large number of offices were growing increasingly large, and unless some way of maintaining a substantial flow of money for electoral purposes was found, professional politicians might find themselves out of jobs.[26]

The beneficiaries of the existing arrangements were no match for this whirlwind of dissatisfaction, reform proposals, and political energy. Saloon keepers, skilled artisans, and politicians anxious to stick to ward affairs were in no position to mount a compelling defense of political institutions that were often visibly corrupt, inefficient, and a severe drain on the pocketbooks of substantial citizens. The mix of moral outrage, concern for property and efficiency, the search for material advantage by businessmen and aspiring citywide bosses, and worries about immigrants not only had behind

24. Allen F. Davis, *Spearheads for Reform.*
25. Quoted in Yearley, *The Money Machines*, 18.
26. Shefter, "The Emergence of the Political Machine"; and Yearley, *The Money Machines*, pt. I.

them the force of numbers and resources but it also touched some of the deeper themes of American political life, including both a search for a more effective democracy and a concern for the protection of property. The serious question, then, was not whether significant changes would occur but what form they would take.

With the array of proposals directed at a variety of concerns, broad agreement among the politically active on how to proceed was not possible. What suited the aspiring citywide boss was unlikely to suit the reformer trying to promote nonpartisan government.[27] The difficulties in agreement were compounded by the fact that what was really at issue was the invention of new political arrangements for cities. This was not just struggle for advantage within the existing arrangements but an effort to lurch forward into something new.

What emerged out of the complex maneuverings was not what any group—whether reformers, businessmen, or machine politicians—would have wanted if it alone could have dominated the proceedings. Reformers, however, could do little on their own without the support of businessmen, party politicians, or both. And in different cities they were, in fact, allied with one or the other, or both.[28] Nor could businessmen hope to dominate party politicians who controlled votes and therefore could affect the exercise of political authority. Party politicians, in turn, needed the cooperation of a variety of business enterprises—for example, utilities and contracting firms—as sources of revenue to finance their operations. The resulting institutional arrangements reflected the range of concerns of the politically most active.

Probably the most common result across the range of cities was that mayors received more powers. They now were able to make appointments of department heads and could therefore exert some influence over them. They also began to have a substantial say in city fiscal affairs as executive budgeting emerged. The balance of authority began to shift markedly from council to mayor. The executive departments of the city were also strengthened by being given permission to undertake more services and by being staffed

27. Steven P. Erie, however, notes that on some matters a community of interest between reformers and party politicians existed. Neither was interested in upsetting city businessmen by mobilizing a working class that might be inclined to radical politics. See Steven P. Erie, "Rainbow's End: From the Old to the New Urban Ethnic Politics," in Joan W. Moore and Lionel A. Maldonado (eds.), *Urban Ethnicity: A New Era.*

28. See Wiebe, *The Search for Order, 1877–1920.*

with increasing numbers of professionals. Consolidation, centralization, and efficiency were the bywords. Citywide school districts were created, police chiefs were appointed by mayors, and larger public health departments and finance departments were brought into being. At the same time that executives were being strengthened, so, in many cities, were party leaders and party organizations. In place of the often chaotic and rapacious politics of the preceding several decades, there grew up party organizations able to exert some discipline in at least some wards of the city or even, on occasion, across the whole city. The support of these more stable confederations was needed by those seeking city office.[29]

These reforms defined the organization of public authority for the contemporary city. Mayors were now on their way to being the key elected officials; complex party-based coalitions—or, in their absence, coalitions of some sort based around mayors, professional politicians, and neighborhoods—became crucial for election to office; and city agencies began to be staffed by increasingly professional administrators anxious to avoid control by elected officials and determined to find allies among the clientele groups that they served and other groups interested in their services.

EXTERNAL RELATIONS

The division of labor as it is manifested in cities involves not only the prerogatives of the private controllers of assets and the organization of public authority but also the external relations of such authority with such controllers of assets. These external relations depend on a number of contextual factors in addition to the prerogatives and powers of the actors involved. Three contextual factors are of particular note: (1) cities must raise funds in a private credit market; (2) there is no national location policy aimed at inducing businesses and populations to move to declining economic areas; and (3) the national system of aid to cities is not meant to guarantee the financial solvency of cities, and thus cities may default and even go bankrupt. Each of these factors is, in part, a manifestation of a federal system that has come to define city governments as independent governmental units whose general vitality may be the subject of federal government concern but not of federal guarantees. Federal involvement can extend to encouragement, monetary subventions in return for certain kinds of

29. Teaford, *The Unheralded Triumph*, chap. 7.

promised performance, and some general financial aid but not to the provision of resources or to policies that will shift the burden of competition for private resources from the shoulders of city governments.[30]

Undoubtedly the most important of these contextual factors is the need for cities to raise credit in private markets. The effects on city politics are substantial and little appreciated by students of city political affairs. The shape of city public policy, the access of certain kinds of businessmen to public officials, and the latter's consuming interest in economic growth all are greatly affected by the city's reliance on private credit.

The credit needs of cities are, for the most part, met by issuing bonds that are then sold by underwriters to various private investors.[31] Involved in this process are three sets of private actors, all of whom need to be convinced that buying a city's bonds is a good risk; they are (1) the underwriters themselves, who invest their own money, (2) the purchasers of the bonds, who are typically commercial banks, certain kinds of insurance companies, and wealthy individuals, and (3) the bond-rating agencies, which tell investors how great an investment risk is involved.[32] Although there are undoubtedly differences between the actors, they all hold to one axiom: invest in cities that are growing economically and be wary of ones that are stagnant or declining and, from the latter, demand a risk premium in the form of higher interest rates. The result is that, for a city to market its bonds at reasonable interest rates, it must be attentive to what the bond "community" thinks of its economic prospects. This, in turn, means that city officials must be deeply attentive to demonstrating that they are fiscally conservative and interested in stimulating local growth and in presiding over a city that will continue to be economically vibrant. A reputation for being antibusiness, for not listening to

30. Even a compressed historical account of the development of the federal system, designed to parallel the emphasis in the preceding pages, would substantially divert the present discussion. Relevance will be best served if the necessary points are, instead, treated analytically.

31. For two useful discussions of the bond market, see Alberta M. Sbragia, "Politics, Local Government and the Municipal Bond Market," in Alberta M. Sbragia (ed.), *The Municipal Money Chase;* and Thomas M. Boast, "Urban Resources, the American Capital Market and Federal Programs," in Douglas Ashford (ed.), *National Resources and Urban Policy.*

32. Since the New York City fiscal crisis, the monopoly of the two big rating agencies has been broken as commercial banks have begun to develop their own research services to better protect themselves against the misjudgments that they felt they made in the New York case.

local businessmen's schemes for making a greater city, is an invitation to fiscal trouble that even the hardiest progressive politicians are unlikely to be anxious to accept. As the New York City case suggests, officials may expend a good deal of effort finding ways to rig the credit system to keep the flow of money continuing, but in the end they do not control the tap. It can and will be cut off. Cleveland during the Kucinich era is probably more typical. Local officials quickly found that the financial tap was not under their control and that there was little they could do about this situation.[33]

A comparison with England highlights the consequences of the private bond market as it works in the United States. English cities are a good deal less worried about attracting and keeping local business within their boundaries than are their American counterparts. There are many reasons for this, including the fact that businesses are less mobile and simply have fewer suitable places within the country to which they can move. But, of at least equal importance, English local authorities need not be so concerned with private lenders' perceptions of the financial health of the local economy. For a start, in England private lenders know the financial condition of local authorities much better. There is a standard auditing procedure at work there that is generally believed to be both accurate and revealing. In contrast, in the case of many American cities, private lenders must rely on local accounting systems that look like nothing so much as the household accounts of a large family that only intermittently makes entries into its checkbook. Moreover, English lenders know that borrowing by local authorities has to be centrally approved, so again they have some assurance that trouble is not immediately at hand. But, most important, local authorities can borrow from the central government, which means both that private lenders are guarded against defaults, since the deficit will be made up centrally, and that projects for which private finance cannot be found can still be undertaken. Simply put, English local authorities worry more about how central authorities view them than they do about how private lenders rate their economic prospects. The result is that they have to be less dutiful in seeking out and attending to the desires of local businessmen.

The existence of federal aid to cities in the United States does little to alter local officials' attentiveness to the perceptions of pri-

---

33. See Martin Shefter, *Political Crisis/Fiscal Crisis;* and Todd Swanstrom, *The Crisis of Growth Politics.*

vate lenders and to the proposals of local businessmen, who are in effect the stand-ins for those advancing the money. Although federal money is available to cities and can free local officials from the chase after private credit, the level of such aid is never high enough to allow them to relax. More important, not only are high levels of aid of recent origin but the level itself is too variable to be relied on, as recent experience with the Reagan administration has made painfully clear. Most important of all, however, federal aid does not mean that private lenders can be sure that they will get their money back. Although the existence of direct aid to cities suggests that federal authorities have some commitment to the well-being of cities, there has never been any indication of a national policy to guarantee the latters' fiscal integrity. Quite the contrary: federal authorities seem prepared to let cities default on their bond notes, at least if a national financial panic is unlikely to ensue—or if one is, in any case, underway.

National policy with regard to location also makes local officials attentive to the concerns of private asset holders in the city. Were it the case that local businesses contemplating a move from a declining area had to forgo nationally provided incentives aimed at getting them to remain—or that businesses committed to moving discovered that there were bonuses for moving to economically weak areas—then local officials might be able to relax their vigilance in the economic growth wars. But neither is the case in the United States. Indeed the reverse is more nearly the case, since federal policy in effect encourages movement by means of, among other things, a tax system that allows rapid depreciation allowances.

CONCLUSION

Understanding contemporary city politics is largely an exercise in grasping the implications of the structural factors that define (1) the powers of cities, (2) the prerogatives of asset holders, and (3) the relations between them. Once these structural factors are in place, the dynamics of contemporary city politics are set. All of them were at work by the post–World War II period, and most were in operation earlier in the century. Once this occurred, the daily rounds of individual actors exercising power and jockeying for profit and position were given definition. Henceforth, city politics was to revolve around three principal axes.

1. There is a strong tendency for public officials and local businessmen, particularly those with fixed assets, to regard each other with fond interest. Public officials know that they cannot command the economic activity that they need but can only cajole. They also know that they have few powers of their own to stimulate economic growth, that capital is mobile, that the city's creditors are deeply interested in whether economic activity is on the upswing, and that, if credit dries up, default and bankruptcy are possible. Local businessmen, being as alert as public officials, also know these things. Under these circumstances it would be amazing if local officials and businessmen were not deeply interested in finding ways for cooperation to blossom.

2. City officials running for office need to put together coalitions of diverse interests and find a sufficient flow of benefactions of various kinds to keep the coalitions intact. Either that or they must find some substitute for these complex coalitions, a conspicuous possibility being an alliance with local businessmen who are sufficiently resourceful to have found a way to shape the electoral process to their taste. The most important of these elected officials are mayors, in terms of both the powers that they wield and the visibility of their activities. Again, variations are possible, with some cities opting for professional managers. But even in these cities, mayors are more important than their fellow council members. Some cities, Dallas being a notable example, have combined these two variations. But the more common form is one in which mayors are at the center of complex electoral coalitions. Because local officials need a flow of benefactions, they are drawn to public policies that are likely to provide them, and particularly to policies in which the inducements are tangible and divisible.

3. Functional bureaucracies that seek to expand and maintain their autonomy are important actors in shaping a city's policies. The preferences of these bureaucracies regarding how their administrative domains shall be organized and what sorts of policies shall be pursued within them have become increasingly influential as these bureaucracies have gained some measure of independence. The result is that their actions and preferences impinge on the efforts of the alliance between public officials and local businessmen to promote city growth, with resulting coordination problems arising.

My next tasks are to give additional content to these axes and to bring them together into a coherent framework. Doing so will provide a fuller picture of contemporary city politics. Postwar urban politics is much of a piece, the result of the same structural factors operating throughout the country. There have been and are variations over time and region, but these largely concern either the timing of the introduction of a structural factor or variations in responses to one or more of them.

3

Urban Political
Economies

There are only certain kinds of politics that can flourish given the
particular form that the division of labor between state and market
has taken in cities. The structural factors that define that division are
most likely to facilitate a politics that revolves around the following
axes: (1) efforts by public officials and local businessmen to construct
an alliance focused on promoting economic growth in the city; (2)
efforts by local politicians to organize electoral coalitions and the
inducements necessary to sustain them, and (3) efforts by city bureaucracies to gain autonomy in the shaping of the policies that guide
their bureaucratic domain. These axes, it should be emphasized, are
only analytically distinct. In practice, they are so closely intertwined
that in describing any one of them it is necessary to bring in one or
both of the others. Indeed, in the discussion below the axes will be
brought together in descriptions of what I shall call urban political
economies, which are the types of stable political patterns to be found
in cities. But first each of the axes needs to be discussed in greater
detail.

GROWTH POLITICS

Promoting economic growth in the city has come to mean viewing
the city as a pattern of land use.[1] This is the case because when a
growth-oriented alliance between city officials and businessmen is
consumated, rearranging land-use patterns is typically a central feature of its activities, and because the principal businessmen involved

---

1. For earlier statements of the arguments presented here, see my "Cities
Without Power," in Douglas Ashford (ed.), *National Resources and Urban Policy*,
and "Twentieth Century Urban Regimes," *Journal of Urban Affairs* 7, no. 2
(Spring 1985): 11–28. For a parallel argument, see Todd Swanstrom, *The
Crisis of Growth Politics*.

in the alliance are those whose business activities are deeply concerned with the city's land-use patterns.

The first thing that public officials in the city, as officials elsewhere, must do is get elected. If they cannot achieve this they have little else to worry about. As do officials at other levels of government, city officials believe that their electoral prospects are markedly improved if they can secure a reputation for promoting innovative policies and if, in general, they are associated with publicly visible activities of almost any sort. Those who seek office live off publicity, unless they have contrived ways to make the preferences of voters largely irrelevant to the electoral process. What is at stake here is not stands on issues, for, as we shall see, city politics is only intermittently concerned with officials' stands on public controversies. Rather, it is reputation that is of concern, and, while officials are concerned with their reputations for electoral reasons, reputation building is not essentially a matter of directly appealing to voters. The audience for their efforts is, in significant part, other officials, powerful private citizens, and groups in the city whose support would be useful for gaining and holding office. For example, a mayor who is seen to be active in shaping the city's affairs and who is associated with new ideas is likely to find it easier to convince neighborhood leaders that he has good prospects for holding onto or gaining public office. He is also likely to be seen as a good bet for dealing effectively with other levels of government on the city's behalf.

One of the easiest ways for public officials to gain the necessary reputation for innovation and to achieve visibility is by association with major land-use projects. Such projects have one supreme advantage over most other public decisions: by definition they produce something new. Adding to the budget of the police department may be a useful thing to do, but it is less likely to be seen as innovative. By contrast, a major downtown mall or convention center can be advertised as taking the city into the new metropolitan age. Such projects are also visible in a way that few other things that happen in cities are, and such building is taken to be a sign that much else of note is going on in the city—even if it is not.

Equally important, major land-use projects generate a stream of benefits that can be used to build public support by those seeking to hold onto or achieve city office. The most effective kinds of benefits for building electoral coalitions are those that are material and divisible.[2] They do not stimulate controversy over policy decisions and can be targeted to specific persons. The ideal political inducement

2. See Edward C. Banfield and James Q. Wilson, *City Politics*, chap. 9.

from the point of view of gaining someone's cooperation is monetary. Major land-use projects—and high levels of development in general—generate flows of money and other material benefits in the form of jobs and contracts that are relatively easy to transfer to the campaign treasuries and the personal pocketbooks of officials. The expectation on the part of some businessmen of direct material gain from land-use changes is matched by that of some politicians, and the more assiduous among the latter are not above pointing out their requirements to developers. Also, the continuing difficulties of maintaining electoral organizations are alleviated by the flow of campaign money, contacts, "honest graft," and jobs that attend major development efforts. Mayors, elected officials generally, and those concerned with electoral matters are likely to find a sympathetic audience among development interests. And the latter will equally suppose that those who hold public office will have inferred that long careers are facilitated by making it possible for development interests to flourish.[3] Politicians anxious to reward their present or prospective followers find development interests a ready source of cash and favors.

The attractions of rearranging land use also follow from the city's relation to the private credit market. In their quest for high bond ratings, cities expend a good deal of effort lobbying the bond rating agencies, attending luncheons and dinners with members of bond underwriting firms and banks, giving seminars for the financial community, and hiring consultants with good contacts in the world of municipal bond underwriters and buyers.[4] In these various efforts, being able to point to large-scale development projects and generally high levels of investment in development efforts is a decided advantage. Banks and underwriters, like other observers of city affairs, are

3. What little evidence there is about campaign contributions in city politics supports the proposition that a substantial portion of the money comes from such sources. Most cities lack serious campaign-financing laws—and so either no data is collected or evidence is fragmentary and anecdotal. See, e.g., the comments by Robert Caro on William Zeckendorf in *The Power Broker*. Boston has a campaign-finance law that does seem to require serious reporting and records show that in 1982 Mayor Kevin White raised $374,120, "most of it from real estate developers and property interests." *The New York Times*, January 13, 1983.

According to a report in the *New York Times* (December 23, 1986), thirteen of the top twenty campaign contributors to the three principal citywide officials in New York were involved in real estate. For the period reported (Jan. 1, 1981, to Oct. 31, 1986) the contributions to individuals ranged from a high of $189,000 to a low of $5,000, with all but a few over $40,000.

4. See the account by Alberta M. Sbragia, "Politics, Local Government and the Municipal Bond Market," in Alberta M. Sbragia (ed.), *The Municipal Money Chase*.

likely to be impressed and take this to be an indication of underlying economic strength. They are also likely to take it as a sign that public officials have the right attitude toward businessmen, being attentive to their interests and respectful of their plans for the city. These signs are especially important given the complications of getting reliable data on many cities' financial situation and long-term economic prospects.

The impact of the private credit market is likely to be especially great in cities that rely heavily on local banks' buying their bonds. They may turn to local banks because they have trouble marketing their bonds at decent rates in the national market, and local banks may be willing to take them because they themselves have a large stake in the city's prosperity. But, whatever the reason, in such situations, an interest in large-scale development projects and an attentiveness to land interests is likely to be even more prominent than it is in cities with wider access to credit.

Finally, the limited powers of cities and the prerogatives of private controllers of assets also direct the attention of city officials toward rearranging land-use patterns. As I have already said, the division of labor between state and market means that public officials cannot command investment. This would cause little difficulty if the desired level of investment were forthcoming without any prompting. Unhappily for officials, the scale of investment wanted, the degree of risk, and the penalties of failure are all sufficiently great so that even the prospect of substantial gain is often not enough to bring forth the desired activity. In short, the combination of limited city powers and private prerogatives means that city officials must seek to induce investment. There are a variety of ways in which this can be done, and each of them either reduces risk, decreases costs, or increases the likelihood of profit. The inducements include (1) provision by the city of capital assets, such as roads and parks, necessary to a development, (2) help in seeking investment funds, (3) tax incentives of various kinds, (4) waiving or otherwise helping with municipal regulations, including zoning requirements, (5) developing an educational system that will produce an attractive mix of work skills, and (6) help with land assembly. City officials can and do attempt all of these and other ways of inducing investment. But the most important are the first and last—that is, those that focus directly on land use.

There are several reasons for this. Some of the forms of inducement noted are difficult to pursue very far. Substantial efforts to train an appropriate labor force, for example, are limited by knowledge of how to do so and by the fact that those trained can easily leave the city. Cities can, indeed, only help in the search for funds; they typically can provide little themselves. Tax breaks, if extensively used, are likely to be self-defeating to a city needing to keep a close watch on its coffers. More important, none of the forms of inducement mentioned confront the major difficulty, at least for many large-scale investments in the city: the problem of land assembly and satisfactory access patterns. Whatever the investment, it is often accompanied by new building, and the problems of creating a satisfactory site and easy access to it for both people and services are central. The difficulty, of course, is that in built-up areas where land is not uncommonly owned by several parties, both of these are often complex problems. Controllers of assets are unlikely to make major investments in cities unless the considerable risks associated with securing adequate sites and access are reduced. The penalties for starting to invest and being unable to complete land assembly are too great. Officials, then, are drawn to land-use matters because they understand that reduction of the major source of risk associated with land use is crucial to inducing investment. Facilitating negotiations about site assembly, using what legal powers the city has, providing public facilities, and altering road patterns are the staples of such inducement. If we set aside investment that does not require land-use changes, then we can simply say that, for any significant investment to take place at all, the principal form of inducement by officials will be help in arranging land-use patterns.

Many city officials are also drawn to promoting city growth because they are genuinely dedicated to the well-being of its citizenry and believe that economic growth is the key to enhancing citizens' lives. Moreover, they believe that new development projects are a fruitful way to pursue this end. As a result of this happy coincidence of the public interest and their own interests, the most energetic of them become tireless promoters of development in the city. But, however vast and deep their commitment to city growth as the definition of the public interest, for many politicians this is too long term a proposition. Politicians are not noted for their ability to defer gratification, whatever they may commend to others, and so for many their commitment to growth and particularly to rearranging land use is more likely to come from the near-term incentives of coalition building, meeting the city's requirements to market bonds, and the difficulties of pursuing strategies other than rearranging the city's land-use patterns.

In their efforts to encourage growth by offering a variety of inducements to city businessmen, officials are, to a large extent, preaching to the converted. They have particular allies among those businesses with large fixed assets in the city and those whose revenues depend on the level of economic activity in the city and metropolitan region.

These are enterprises whose health is most directly tied to the economic vitality of the city—banks, newspapers, large stores, developers, real estate agencies, real estate law firms, property management firms, utilities, and the like. Their behavior is best understood as an effort to enhance the value of their fixed assets by attracting mobile capital to the city. Since many of these fixed assets are themselves parcels of land, such businessmen are naturally drawn to land-use schemes, and thus a community of interest with officials is born. Not only will they encourage officials in their efforts to induce investment through rearranging land use, but they will also propose projects that the city should undertake. And since they themselves control large parcels of land, many of the projects that they propose will be ones from which they will benefit directly. These land interests, as they may be called, will also work to put in place institutional arrangements that will facilitate inducement of city growth and, to this end, will often cooperate with city officials in securing the necessary powers from state and federal governments. More generally, these businessmen are, by and large, receptive to any schemes—including tax incentives, revenue bonds, and other sorts of inducements—that they expect will enhance the worth of assets whose value is heavily tied to location.

Officials, in their turn, are likely to be deeply attentive to what those with large fixed assets say about attracting mobile capital. Even if they find it difficult to move their capital, such businesses can, at a minimum, reduce their investment in the city and, in the worst case, simply abandon it. They are unlikely to continue to sustain substantial losses over long periods of time and will, if they must, use their capital for other purposes and in other places. Officials know that if those who have strong reasons to invest in the city cut back or quit, it will be doubly difficult to attract new investment to what will now be perceived to be a sinking ship.

The desire to induce investment by facilitating land-use changes is one thing; having the institutional arrangements to do it is quite another. A good deal of growth politics consists of efforts to create the institutional context that will facilitate the inducement process. The institutional arrangements range from those that affect who runs for office and gets elected to the creation of special authorities to undertake development projects. These institutional arrangements form the context in which development interests decide to undertake specific projects and in which negotiations with city officials occur. In the language of theories of power, we are talking here about the creation of the second face of power:[5] the institutional structure that

5. See Steven Lukes, *Power: A Radical View.*

will help set the public agenda for development of the city both by regular efforts to stimulate growth and by the selection of particular projects that will be pursued by private and public parties.

In addition to those already mentioned, the pertinent institutional arrangements constitute a lengthy list; they include (1) the creation of city planning and economic development agencies that will promote the desirability of development as well as provide expert assistance in land assembly and financing, (2) institutional arenas, most importantly special authorities, in which public and private actors can meet, free from extensive public scrutiny, to discuss and coordinate projects,[6] (3) coordinating mechanisms for the variety of local permissions and publicly provided capital works necessary for any significant development effort, (4) agencies that will funnel private money aimed at promoting development into public educational efforts (such as exhibitions) and that will promote newspaper stories, (5) agencies to provide insurance—that is, guarantees of tax waivers or public purchase of sites—if development schemes fail to materialize on schedule, and (6) regular links to other levels of government that control resources and dispense permissions and expertise.

It is important to emphasize what is being claimed up to this point. To see the politics of growth as an exercise of power by businessmen manipulating public officials is to miss the sense in which it is a product of mutuality of interest. And that mutuality grows out of the structural features that define the city's political economy. Given the manner in which officials get elected, the prerogatives of private controllers of assets, the limits on a city's ability to affect and exercise property rights, and the need for cities to raise money in private credit markets, city officials will naturally gravitate toward an alliance with businessmen, particularly land interests, and such an alliance will naturally be devoted to creating institutional arrangements that will facilitate investment in the city.

One characteristic feature of growth politics has been established. Cities typically have in place a set of institutional arrangements aimed at facilitating development and other inducements to investment. As a consequence, promoters of development have significant advantages in pursuing their purposes and they have a receptive audience in public officials, who themselves often have worked to create the institutional arrangements. If this were all there were to land-use politics, then promoting city growth would simply involve a cozy

6. Special authorities have additional advantages: they can be used to handle financial burdens for the city that might impair its bond ratings, and their revenues can be used to finance development that can serve as the core of larger projects. See Charles J. Orlebeke, *Federal Aid to Chicago*, 14–20.

relationship between businessmen—particularly land interests—and officials. Either could take the lead, and by and large officials would find it easy to be guided by the knowledge and preferences of private controllers of assets, simply facilitating the choices that they make in the marketplace. Two considerations strongly militate against such a conclusion and point to a second characteristic feature of land-use politics.

First, facilitating land assembly and site access is a peculiarly direct and public form of inducement to invest, for although the inducements can be screened until the last moment, that moment is inevitably public. The buildings come down or the foundations get laid. The comparison to tax incentives, for example, is instructive. While the incentive may be a matter of record, unless an official or developer takes on himself to make an announcement, its appearance on a form may constitute the full extent of publicity. In land-use matters, protest is possible simply because of the tangibility of what is being done.

Second, significant alteration of land-use patterns in the city means that substantial costs are imposed on a portion of the local citizenry.[7] The reason is simply that no one wishes to have altered the terms on which he or she lives his or her life, and that is precisely what major land-use schemes do. Jobs are lost or made more difficult to reach. Homes become more expensive or disappear. Settled ways of living are disrupted. If the means are at hand to prevent it—that is, to constrain the reach of the market, resist public facilitation of market choice, and use public authority to provide compensation for loss—these paths will be pursued. Perhaps it is the notion of a "free market" that blinds us to what is otherwise obvious. Having a choice between alternatives is serving one's interests. Indeed, this is what the marketplace offers. But being able to keep one's life circumstances as they are is also to serve one's interest. This the marketplace does not offer. No substantive claim is being made here about what people's "real" interests are, only the more modest assertion that, whatever their interests, they will care about having the ability to choose and protect them. They will therefore be upset if someone else makes important choices for them.

Land-use changes and other efforts to promote investment are likely to prompt sufficient dissent to turn the thoughts of at least some citizens to political action. What happens to this impetus to mobilization? Is the prospect of quiet negotiations between officials and land interests dramatically reduced? Here is where the disposition of officials to induce investment and the importance of

7. See the more extensive discussion in chap. 5.

institutional arrangements become manifest, for they both work to forestall protest in the first place, for example, by screening development decisions from public view. And when protest emerges, land interests are advantaged. Those who wish to stop a particular project must not only stop it this time but, ultimately, must stop the institutional machinery designed to facilitate a continuing stream of proposals. Or, what may amount to the same thing, they must overturn the institutional arrangements that generate the flow of proposals in the first place.

Protestors are not without resources, and they do succeed in stopping development projects and the dispensing of inducements. But they are running a more difficult race than development forces. They are often without adequate information about the prizes being contested and face referees—which is to say, public officials—who are not, by and large, neutral. In addition to these burdens, protestors must deal with the problems of collective action, problems that developers, being already organizations, have partly solved for them.

Of course, none of the preceding implies that on any given project there is homogeneity of opinion. Some businessmen will gain and others will lose, just as some officials will be against a particular change. Extreme division on a project coupled with mobilization of those adversely affected may bring a development project to a halt more or less permanently. But the forces at work promoting development are wide and deep enough that this is unlikely to be common.

It should also be clear that none of the preceding discussion of the characteristic features of growth politics means that cities inevitably engage in extensive development. Many do, but others languish. Rather, the argument indicates how it will be politically organized if it is undertaken. More important, the argument suggests that if extensive efforts at altering land use do not occur, this will typically *not* be because of extensive protest. Lack of activity is more likely to stem from the failure of the natural alliance between officials and land interests to come to fruition. It is by no means impossible that officials will devote considerable energy trying to induce investment in their cities and find little forthcoming. Similarly, prodevelopment forces may not be able to find officials who, however interested in new investment, are willing to go far enough in offering inducements.

Considering the regular efforts to reshape city land-use patterns, we might suppose that development efforts would be a major electoral issue, but this is less often the case than its importance would seem to warrant. Candidates do campaign on progrowth platforms, and so development matters are raised in a general way. But, for all the reasons discussed above, it is not surprising that candidates should do so. Nor, for the same reasons, is it surprising that few candidates will argue for long that development efforts generally ought to cease or not be undertaken in the first place. Indeed, there is little cost to politicians in saying that they prefer growth to stagnation, industry to indolence, and prosperity to poverty. A much more interesting question is why particular large-scale projects and the overall process by which investment in the city is induced do not become subjects of electoral controversy. The stakes are sufficiently important to invite speculation about the relative paucity of discussion.

That such matters are not regularly raised is best understood as a result of the structural arrangements that arise out of the natural alliance between development interests and officials. It is easy to see that if the use of land assembly, zoning changes, access improvement, and the like to induce investment were regularly raised at election time, investment in the city would be substantially slowed. In most cities no set of actors needs to work very hard, however, to filter out what, from the alliance's point of view, is best kept from the public's gaze. It will help to distinguish at least two broadly different kinds of situations.

In the first, the natural disinclination of office seekers to argue against particular development projects or the general process of inducement is sufficient. Land interests thus can rely on broadly sympathetic candidates, and the distinctions between them are not large enough to warrant great investments or the possibility of unwanted publicity. In other cities, the electoral agenda is more directly controlled. Land interests display a deep interest in who gets selected to run for office and in some cases go so far as to actually screen the candidates and run the campaign. The reasons for such emphatic interest vary from those cases in which there is little risk in such involvement to ones in which the risk is greater but the rewards large enough to warrant it. The first occurs in cities such as Dallas, where other interests are too unorganized to mount much in the way of electoral effort, publicity is easy to avoid, since local newspapers are supportive or timid, and business involvement in public life is held in high repute.[8] The second occurs in cities such as the Pittsburgh of the postwar–mid-sixties period. Extensive help was given to selected candidates, probably because they were seen as likely to be sufficiently more energetic and imaginative in

8. See the discussion in chap. 4.

redevelopment efforts. Since so much private money was at stake in redevelopment efforts, a form of insurance that public cooperation would be forthcoming was no more than prudent.[9]

The decisive point in understanding growth politics in the city is that public officials choose—and feel obliged—to consult land interests. These businessmen are not, however, simply another group whose interests must be consulted. They are instead privileged:[10] officials believe that their cooperation is necessary and that their own electoral prospects are tied to the benefits engendered by development efforts; and businessmen believe that they rightfully have a special place in the city's politics. Much of the flavor of the alliance is captured in the remarks of a recent head of the Philadelphia Development Authority, a man not noted for his attachment to the well-being of developers and other land interests. He commented that "we need developers for revenue and growth. They lie at the base of promoting social well-being and so we must seek their cooperation. But too often this is done on the backs of the poor. The developers we deal with are often not interested in neighborhoods. We play a reactive role since development is going where it is economically viable. Developers working in affluent areas use our resources and our help very well. But so far we have not been very successful in getting development into areas where it otherwise would not occur."[11]

ELECTIONS

If elections are not centrally concerned with growth issues and land-use matters—and thus settle little of consequence in this regard— what are they about? It is important to understand that issues of *any* kind are typically not central. Certainly there are, at a minimum, questions of police protection and education policy that might be expected to engender campaign interest. Candidates for office, in

9. On the occasions when a citywide campaign critical of city development trends is mounted, prodevelopment forces may need to take a much more overt role and thereby run the risk of adverse publicity and harm to their case. These sorts of challenges typically occur in cites dominated by major universities, where a pool of antibusiness, energetic recruits is available. Other cities must rely much more on those who have a material stake, with the consequences we have been addressing.

10. Cf. Charles E. Lindblom, *Politics and Markets*, chap. 13.

11. The remarks are from a statement made by Richard Bazelon to a conference on "Equality in the City" sponsored by the Public Interest Law Center, November 1984, Philadelphia.

fact, do get drawn into controversies over such matters as schools and police if they cannot avoid it. But unless there are strong reasons to enter such stressful and uncertain terrain, city politicians will attempt to stick to what concerns them most: who shall wield city powers in the negotiations over inducing growth, with the attendant personal, organizational, and electoral advantages; and who shall control city jobs and for what purposes (e.g., as patronage) they are to be used. Not all of these matters are central in all cities, but one or a combination of them defines what most interests candidates for office. To maintain electoral coalitions of which they are a part it will help politicians to control the city's part in pro-development efforts, and to maintain their own organizations it will help to control a large number of city jobs. In the end, jobs and the powers to facilitate growth are simply the most important ingredients in helping to create and cement the alliances that city politicians need to gain office.

The contestants in electoral contests are, then, coalitions anxious to control the sources of the benefits noted. A campaign that re-volves around politically conflictual matters such as police protec-tion and education can only upset what are likely to be complex and perhaps painfully negotiated alliances. The temptation is, how-ever, present for each side to attempt to gain an advantage over its opponents by making such appeals. No doubt this occurs. But, setting aside many intricacies, we can say that the opponents are involved in a kind of prisoner's dilemma. Each may gain from a broader appeal if the other does not make one—but if both try, the field may be opened to new contestants and both the existing alliances may lose. In reality, what occurs is often a kind of tacit collusion in which one coalition dominates at the polls for long periods and makes side payments to the losers.[12] In some cities, however, collusion is unncessary, since a single coalition simply dominates, with others leaving the field. In these cities, the temp-tation to raise and discuss major issues declines accordingly. Both reformed and party-dominated cities can fit into this category.

As has just been implied, the coalitions that we have been dis-cussing have often traveled under the banner of "reform" and "party."[13] The reform/party distinction probably simplifies too much,

12. Stephen L. Elkin, "Political Structure, Political Organization and Race: English-American Comparisons," *Political Society* 8, no. 2 (1978): 225–251.

13. Martin Shefter, "Party Organization, Electoral Mobilization, and Re-gional Variations in Reform Success," Working Papers on Urban Political Economy, Program on Urban Studies, Stanford University.

however, since, in some cities, electoral coalitions probably bear only a tenuous resemblance to either sort of coalition. In such cities, they may be shifting alliances of racial, ethnic, and neighborhood groupings loosely tied to remnants of party organization or to a newly arisen or rapidly disappearing group of reformers. In any case, reformers have most often claimed that reform must occur in the staffing of government offices and that the grip of party must be broken. At other times they have restricted themselves to party reform that would allow them more influence within party circles and more access to the benefits of electoral success. In either case, they are not unmindful that reform will place them in positions of influence within city government. But reformers are not tied together merely by self-interest, sharing, as they typically do, views about the proper conduct of public affairs. Party men, in their turn, have defended the existing party and administrative arrangements of which they have been the principal beneficiaries. They too presumably share a view that the commonwealth is at least not a great loser if they control public affairs. Popular lore has it, however, that party men tend to be more cynical in these matters.

An image useful for representing the preceding discussion of land-use politics and city elections is that of a political order with a public and a private face. Although this is a considerable simplification, what is visible is the world of elections and the struggle over the benefits of office. Here are the contests between reformers and party politicians that are the familiar staple of the newspaper column and editorial. At the same time, there is the world of negotiation about land-use changes and the structural arrangements that underlie it. This world is more removed from public gaze. Mayors are likely to be key figures in each, which is why analysts focus their attention on them; but the roles that they play and who their allies are vary in each case.

GROWTH POLITICS AND OTHER POLICY ARENAS

Land interests have three major concerns in city politics in addition to those that we already have discussed. These additional concerns all rest on their desire to ensure that the city is a hospitable environment for investment. First, they care about budgets. A city with strained finances will have trouble in the municipal bond market and thus have difficulty building the capital works necessary to keep and attract business investment. Similarly, a strained budget will make problematic the delivery of the kind of services that are thought to make investment more attractive. Second, land interests are interested in taxes, and for much the same reasons that budgets concern them. Low taxes are better than high taxes. And if that is not possible, tax levels should at least be competitive with those of other likely competitive locations. Finally, land interests care about the impact of city services and related matters on the prospects for investment. They therefore have some interest in the quality of schooling, the degree of racial turmoil over schools and police protection, and the degree and persistence of corruption. For much the same reason, land interests prefer an allocation of police services to those parts of the city where investment is to take place and where new managers of expanding firms are likely to wish to live.

On these matters, as with more direct efforts to induce growth, land interests can reasonably expect to find a sympathetic ear among elected officials of the city. They, too, may be expected to see the connections between investment decisions and such matters as budgets and police allocations. Although officials may be broadly sympathetic, however, they cannot be as accommodating in this regard as they are in land-use matters. This may be seen by considering the consequences if development interests were to shape all of city politics to their tastes. A principal result for city politicians would be an increase in the difficulty of creating and maintaining the political alliances that are, in the end, the center of their concern. Once again, it will help to distinguish two cases.

The first case is characteristic of the politics of older eastern and midwestern cities. For politicians in these cities, having the city's finances and the management of its services run only with an eye toward making the city attractive to investment would mean substantial loss of control over offices, perquisites, and other benefits that make coalition building possible. For example, the parceling out of sections of the city bureaucracy to allies, whether reformers or the more predatory minded, would be curtailed. And, crucially, the benefits that flow from land development, while considerable, are not themselves enough to maintain complex political alliances. Politicians in these cities would find it difficult to operate under such circumstances. They know it—and resist when necessary.

In the second case, the results and motivations on the part of politicians are similar, but the specifics differ. The cities under consideration tend to be newer and to have experienced substantial doses of reform—and thus to have more professionalized administration and nonpartisan political structures. In such cities, of which

Dallas is a good example, politicians are ambivalent about attempts by development interests to directly shape the full course of city government. On the one hand, they are themselves usually strong advocates of city growth. Indeed, since land interests typically play a strong role in elections, these politicians probably have been screened for just such enthusiasm. But, on the other hand, if development forces were to attempt regular intervention into city departments, making staunch allies of agency heads and influential personnel, elected officials would fear loss of the city's reputation for efficient, noncorrupt government. A second consideration follows naturally from the first. The professionalized city administration is likely to resist regular incursions into agency routines and decision making. If any significant attempt were made, this might well precipitate public struggle and many elected officials would side with professional administrators in an attempt to preserve the sort of city government that they believe ensures the city's prosperity.

We may say, then, that although prodevelopment forces have wide-ranging concerns in city government, their concerns are unlikely to dominate across the full range of policy arenas. They do not control, in part because they cannot. But *need they* make such attempts in the first place?

The short answer is no. They need not attempt to duplicate the close accommodation with public officials that is characteristic of growth politics. One obvious reason is that most day-to-day actions of city governments have little direct bearing on land use and investment matters. But, more important, much of what development interests care about, especially with regard to fiscal matters, is already in place. By the beginning of the twentieth century, a number of fiscal requirements that constrain the financial behavior of cities in ways congenial to development interests (but not completely, as we shall see) already had been established by courts and state governments.[14] These include the requirement of balanced budgets, restrictions on how cities can raise money, strict construction of grants of taxing authority, and restrictions on borrowing for other than capital works. These restrictions were part of the larger, successful effort to define the city as a creature of state governments, one with no basis for local autonomy in popular sovereignty. To these fiscal constraints we must also add the creation of executive budgets and of executive powers in general, which also increased the possibilities of fiscal control. In some cities, moreover, even more of the matters

14. See Susan MacManus, "State Government: The Overseer of Municipal Finance," in Sbragia (ed.), *The Municipal Money Chase.*

of concern to land interests were historically settled in ways that they undoubtedly find congenial. After the turn of the century, they were likely to be at least satisfied with a city administration that delivered services in a noncorrupt and efficient manner. Setting aside many complexities, there is a widespread sense among many city political actors that those contemplating investment will be attracted to an efficient, business-like city government.

The links then between land-use politics and the politics of the rest of the city are complex. They are comprised of a mix of overall fiscal constraint and of city agencies that can act relatively autonomously within those constraints (but not without particular efforts by land interests to shape agency conduct). The importance of these constraints having been noted, it is important to recognize that they can be sorely tested and even evaded, with consequent fiscal stress and crisis. Especially in cities where reform has not been pervasive, using control of agencies and city jobs as matters to be bargained over in coalition building for elections simply means that it is difficult to enforce fiscal discipline. The temptation to evade limits on borrowing for operating expenses is substantial if allies who are well entrenched in some part of the city bureaucracy proclaim it as necessary. Land interests and particularly banks who hold city bonds ultimately do attempt to see that the built-in fiscal restraints are obeyed, but the struggles are often bitter, and, again, the various actors do not always get what they want. Politicians desire to be elected, and that leads them to resist severe fiscal discipline; but their ability to resist ultimately is circumscribed by the city's need for credit.[15]

FEDERALISM AND RACE

Where do the roles of the federal government, of state governments, and of racial conflict—all of which are major aspects of city politics—fit into a politics that revolves around the three axes that we have been considering? Each of these subjects merits substantial attention, but all that needs to be indicated here is how the view of urban politics that we have been developing can accommodate some essential facts about each.

First, let us consider the impact of federal involvement in cities. The discussion up to this point suggests that a useful way to view

15. Sbragia, "Politics, Local Government and the Municipal Bond Market," in Sbragia (ed.), *The Municipal Money Chase.*

it is to start with its effects on the natural alliance between public officials and land interests, in particular on whether it draws mayors closer to the concerns of such interests or helps to loosen the ties. It is easy enough to see that mayors (and officials generally) who are recipients of substantial and continuing sums of money from the federal government will feel at least marginally bolder in their dealings with development interests. They will likely be somewhat less interested in the connection between investment and city budgets. In much the same way, mayors will be less anxious to deflect protest about land-use decisions and may even encourage and attempt to capitalize on it. Indeed, we may speculate that the rather bold courting of the poor by some big-city mayors during the mid 1960s can be explained partly by increased feelings of independence stemming from large increases in federal revenues. Conversely, as federal expenditures become more uncertain and/or decline, mayors are likely to grow more cautious and thus more sympathetic to proposals about city redevelopment.

The behavior of the other half of the alliance, land interests, is also likely to be affected by federal expenditures. Prodevelopment forces seem likely to be more or less indifferent to federal expenditure in the city except as it makes investment less attractive by complicating land-use matters or threatening the city's finances. For example, a reduction in the growth of federal expenditures that leaves the city committed to a variety of programs that must be paid for out of its own revenues is likely to prompt progrowth interests to work for retrenchment. In some cities, a few of the progrowth forces may have the foresight to argue that the city government ought not to get involved in federal programs in the first place, since inevitably it will increase demands on the city's own resources. As for land-use matters, here the point is simply that development forces will likely resist adoption of federal programs that increase the participation in and the visibility of land-use decisions. If the program cannot be staved off, their interest is likely to turn to evading the entirety of the federal requirements.

Federal funds also affect the politics of the functional bureaucracies. To the degree that agency heads and/or professionals inside agencies can establish close links with federal agencies providing money and other resources, their independence from city politics is increased. There is much reason to think that this has happened already, making it more likely that development interests will hesitate to intervene and increasing the likelihood that they will not succeed in reorienting agency activity. Mayors are also likely to be more chary about pushing for major changes. Declines in federal funding should reverse the process.

A parallel analysis will illuminate the connections between city and state politics. A number of plausible links are immediately apparent. Once again, we may suppose that outside sources of funds will make mayors more independent of land interests. In the case of state funds, however, land interests are likely to have more say about how those funds are to be given out and used, and mayors are thus less likely to make bold moves away from their natural allies. As at the federal level, development interests will be concerned with the impact of state action on the city fisc, and, since the city is a legal creature of the state, they will often find it advantageous to pursue their visions of fiscal discipline in the state arena. State scrutiny and state assumption of fiscal powers over the city is a not uncommon result. Finally, city agencies and their panoply of groups will find allies and adversaries at the state level, and thus the politics of the functional bureaucracies will reach outside the city. Again, the degree of relative autonomy will be affected.

As for racial politics in the city, after the central features of the division of labor between state and market were largely in place, the increasing concentration of blacks in the city was the principal source of political disruption. Their presence increased the difficulty in creating stable political patterns around the three principal axes that we have discussed. At first, the possibility of disruption in northern cities turned on how to link the increasing number of black voters to the political patterns being established. This effort to link black voters to the developing political order had to be accomplished in the context of white violence against blacks. In southern cities, the problem was not the challenge of possibly disruptive voting but that of maintaining a system of racial subordination. After World War II, in both northern and southern cities the problem became one of black political mobilization. It is difficult to assess whether the situations before and after World War II had real potential for substantially altering the basic pattern of city politics. In retrospect it is easy to see that in neither instance did this occur. The black mobilization of the 1960s in northern cities and in some southern ones had the principal impact of altering both the players in the politics of the functional bureaucracies and the pool from which the public side of the politics of growth was drawn. The principal features of the axes that define contemporary city politics remained intact, however. And that is the essential point in this context. Although race has been a significant factor, we will understand more about the overall shape of city politics if, instead of seeing race as its center, we view it as revolving around the three axes that have been postulated above.

URBAN POLITICAL ECONOMIES

A variety of political economies can, in principle, be constructed around the three axes that we have been considering. Electoral coalitions may be put together in different ways, or substitutes may be found, for example, in the form of local businessmen creating organizations that dominate the electoral process. The alliance between land interests and officials may have a number of forms, one of the principal reasons for this being variation in the organization of the local business community. And city bureaucracies may be more or less professionalized and thus more or less able to resist incursions by political leaders and development forces. Moreover, the links between growth politics, electoral politics, and the policies of the functional bureaucracies can vary. Urban political economies are defined by this variation—both around the axes and in the links between them. An exploration of several types of urban political economies can elucidate both the variety of political patterns that gives particularity to the political life of cities, and their important commonalities. Being a bureaucrat or an advocate of minority interests in contemporary Dallas or postwar Chicago is to have fundamental things in common but also to be different in ways worth noting.

Examination of two types of urban political economies will illustrate something of the range of variation possible. One, which characterized the larger cities of the Northeast and Midwest during the 1950s and early 1960s, I shall call a pluralist political economy. The second, which succeeded the pluralist version in the same set of cities after the political mobilization of the mid and late 1960s, I shall call a federalist political economy. A third type, one that has characterized many of the newer cities of the Southwest during the postwar period and that will be considered in the study of Dallas in the next chapter, I shall call an entrepreneurial political economy. These urban political economies do not exhaust the types of political patterns that have characterized postwar city politics, but they do capture a good deal of the variation that actually occurred.

Pluralist Political Economies

Pluralist political economies were at work during the 1950s and early 1960s in the largest cities of the Northeast and Midwest.[16] These political economies were created in older industrial cities with ethnically and racially heterogeneous populations whose politicians had sufficient organizational resources to be independent figures. The primary feature of pluralist political economies was an inclusive coalition that dominated land-use matters, particularly those linked to the economic vitality of the downtown. These political economies are enshrined in the urban politics literature of the period, a literature that has a pluralist emphasis. Hence the name given here.[17] The coalition's principal concerns were to reshape the land-use patterns of the downtown and to improve transportation into the business district. Coalition partners aimed to bolster a declining tax base, principally by improving the city's attractiveness as a business center and as a place for middle-class citizens to live.[18]

The land-use coalitions were the most important actors in the pluralist political economies. They were more able to influence events in other policy arenas than the dominant actors in these other arenas were able to influence land-use policy;[19] however, the coalitions were by no means able to determine decisions in those other domains, and, indeed, a principal feature of the pluralist political economies was the relative autonomy of the functional bureaucracies and their associated interest groups.[20] Here was the pluralism of these political economies.

The coalitions typically had numerous partners, among whom the most important were the principal elected officials. Elected officials included both reformers (e.g., in Philadelphia, St. Louis, and Detroit) and regular party politicians (e.g., in Chicago and

16. See my discussion in "Cities Without Power."

17. See Robert Dahl, *Who Governs?;* Edward C. Banfield, *Political Influence;* Banfield and Wilson, *City Politics;* Raymond Wolfinger, *The Politics of Progress;* and Wallace S. Sayre and Herbert Kaufman, *Governing New York City.*

18. See Edgar M. Hoover and Raymond Vernon, *Anatomy of a Metropolis;* Roy Lubove, *Twentieth-Century Pittsburgh;* and John Mollenkopf, "The Post-War Politics of Urban Development," *Politics and Society* 5, no. 3 (1975): 247–295.

19. See Mollenkopf, "The Post-War Politics of Urban Development," and Theodore Lowi, "Machine Politics: Old and New," *The Public Interest* 9 (Fall 1967): 83–91.

20. See Lowi, "Machine Politics"; and Sayre and Kaufman, *Governing New York City,* esp. chaps. 8 and 11.

Pittsburgh), who, in spite of their differences, shared an uneasiness over fiscal difficulties and the loss of middle-class citizens. In general, the mayors either were elected on a platform of revitalization and reform or realized the soundness (in terms of insuring future success at the polls) of being a willing party in such efforts.[21] They also played the principal broker's role of assembling the relevant actors and inducing compromises. In some cities businessmen were more or less equal partners with mayors and their lieutenants (e.g., in Pittsburgh and Philadelphia), whereas in others elected officials were more powerful (e.g., in Chicago).[22]

The electoral base of the political economy—and particularly the support for downtown revitalization—was comparatively broad and stable. Support came from middle- and upper-income homeowners for whom increases in the tax base held the promise of both steady (or even reduced) property taxes and a halt to what was felt to be the deterioration of the city. Liberally inclined voters also were a major source of support, since renewal promised an improved housing stock. This was especially true in the earlier years of the political economy, before it became clear that the principal burden of renewal was being borne by the less well off.[23] Those who most suffered from the reshaping of land use, largely lower-income minorities living at the edge of the central core, provided substantial passive support by continuing to vote for party candidates or reformers bent on renewal. This was sometimes in exchange for the favors and friendship traditionally provided by big-city parties. Others were excluded from even the minimum participation of voting and thus from the political economy.[24]

The case of Philadelphia suggests that an important ingredient in bringing the coalition partners together in the first place was private money, typically raised from local businessmen.[25] Research efforts could be financed and forums provided, all in the context of very limited public funds. Agreements about particular projects were also easier to reach through the vehicle of essentially private development corporations with some public membership.[26] The

21. See Banfield and Wilson, *City Politics*, esp. chap. 9.
22. See Banfield, *Political Influence*; Dahl, *Who Governs?*; Lubove, *Twentieth-Century Pittsburgh*; Kirk Petshek, *The Challenge of Urban Reform*; and Wolfinger, *The Politics of Progress*.
23. See Herbert Gans, "The Failure of Urban Renewal," in James Q. Wilson (ed.), *Urban Renewal: The Record and the Controversy*.
24. See Frances Fox Piven and Richard Cloward, *Regulating the Poor*.
25. See Conrad Weiler, *Philadelphia: Neighborhood, Authority and the Urban Crisis*.
26. Petshek, *The Challenge of Urban Reform*, and Jeanne Lowe, *Cities in a Race With Time*.

extreme example of the importance of private money and private organization was Pittsburgh, where the Mellon interests, with the cooperation of the mayor and the Democratic party, managed to invest and attract enough private money to rebuild a substantial portion of the central business district.[27]

Whereas the cases of Pittsburgh and Philadelphia taken together, suggest one version of the general theme sketched above, Boston represents a different emphasis. If the pluralist political economy in Pittsburgh was relatively stable and achieved great renewal successes with a modest amount of public furor, the pluralist pattern in Boston, while it too had major renewal successes, was subject to significant stress. Some of the requirements of a stable political economy—for example, a stable electoral organization—were not met, and the day-to-day politics of land use accordingly differed from that in Pittsburgh.[28] Chicago, with the core of its pluralist political economy provided by the Cook County Democratic organization, represents yet another emphasis—as does New York, with the formidable Robert Moses and his mastery of money, laws, publicity, organizational resources, and land-use expertise.[29]

Federalist Political Economies

The mid-1960s brought struggles over land use and the public bureaucracy that disrupted efforts to facilitate city growth. The mobilization of neighborhoods made the quiet bargaining of pluralist political economies harder to achieve, and councilmen and neighborhood party leaders found it increasingly difficult to speak for neighborhood interests. These changes affected projects in the neighborhoods as well as those in the central core, especially those perceived as diverting resources from residential areas. Equally important, conflict over the behavior and staffing of public bureaucracies meant that policy matters previously treated as peripheral by those concerned with land use could no longer be seen in this way. The alliance between businessmen concerned with land use and city politicians came under strain. Organizing major land-use projects now meant that businessmen needed to commit themselves to trying to ensure the civic tranquility necessary to major undertakings, and many businessmen hesitated to become involved in explosive areas—for example, school politics—about which they knew and cared little. In many cities the intricate pattern of co-

27. Lubove, *Twentieth-Century Pittsburgh.*
28. See Stephan Thernstrom, *Poverty, Planning and Politics in the New Boston;* Edward C. Banfield, *Big City Politics;* and Walter McQuade, "Urban Renewal in Boston," in Wilson (ed.), *Urban Renewal.*
29. See Caro, *The Power Broker.*

operation fell into disrepair as the politics of service delivery, city jobs, and neighborhood assertion took over.

The problems presented by the rise of new claimants in city politics were quickly compounded by the severe fiscal stress felt by many cities during the early 1970s. Fiscal uncertainty further reduced the incentives for major business interests concerned with land use to keep the alliance with local politicians in good repair. To be sure, fiscal stress itself provided a way for those concerned with promoting investment in the city to discipline the political enthusiasms of city employees and minority groups. But, by itself, the prospect of municipal bankruptcy was not a strong enough foundation on which to build a vigorous reassertion of the alliance between land interests and city politicians, since the prospective losses—to both minority groups and city employees—incumbent on strong fiscal discipline were great.

New, federalist, political economies were, however, created in many cities. The key in the creation of these federalist versions was the availability of federal dollars. From 1970 to 1978, for example, direct grants to cities increased sixfold. There was, moreover, a shift from categorical aid to block grants, which enabled local politicians to use substantial portions of federal money for coalition-building efforts.[30] Federal dollars were used either to prevent or to cushion substantial cutbacks in employment, benefit, and service levels.[31] Continuing turmoil over the number and remuneration of city jobs and over city support for social services was thereby forestalled. This, in turn, made it possible for mayors to negotiate the necessary electoral alliances, particularly with minority groups and city employees. Minority-group leaders, moreover, had something to show their followers in the way of continuing social services, many of which had been won in the political struggles of the previous decade. If federal dollars had not been available to keep minority leaders engaged in the politics of the service bureaucracies, it is not inconceivable that they would have turned to matters closer to the heart of the land-use interests and city politicians anxious to see a continuing stream of investment in the city.

Federal money was also of more direct use in the rebuilding of the alliance between land interests and local politicians. Urban-development action-grant (UDAG) and community-development block-grant (CDBG) funds became available for reworking the land-

30. See James W. Fossett, *Federal Aid to Big Cities.*
31. For federalist political economies, see Thomas J. Anton, *Federal Aid to Detroit;* Henry J. Schmandt et al., *Federal Aid to St. Louis;* and Orlebeke, *Federal Aid to Chicago.*

use patterns of the central core of the city. While not all such federal
money could be used in downtown and surrounding areas, a noticeable portion has gone to support neighborhood gentrification
near the downtown core and to facilitate investment in the business
district itself.

Disruptions of pluralist political economies did not occur in all
cities, a conspicuous example being Chicago,[32] where the pluralist
pattern gradually evolved into a federalist pattern as federal money
became available to deal with fiscal stress and with increasingly
assertive minority groups. Fiscal stress was less acute[33] and minority
mobilization less powerful[34] there than in other older cities, and so
federal money was less important in the continuation of the alliance
between land interests and city politicians. As a recent study puts
it, "Chicago has tended to absorb new federal programs into a
relatively stable city government structure."[35] In the case of cities
such as Chicago, the underlying continuity of city politics is particularly apparent.

The principal difference between the federalist political economy
and its predecessor is that in the former the alliance between land
interests and city politicians is more difficult to keep in repair. City
politicians have become more factionalized as local parties have
weakened. Land interests worried about the fiscal conditions of
cities—and enticed by possible investment opportunities in the outer
reaches of the metropolis—have found the hard work of negotiating secure working arrangements with local politicians less appealing. The accomodations are reached, but now they may turn
more heavily than before on great public inducements offered by
city officials, on businessmen being particularly loyal to the city,
and on a mayor of great tact and energy. The flow of federal dollars
and federal relationships into the city, even if now on the wane,
have also affected the autonomy of functional bureaucracies. These
bureaucracies are more capable than their predecessors of fending
off importuning mayors and developers by pointing to federal
regulations and the need to continue federal funding. Their autonomy vis-à-vis mayors and land interests is further enhanced,
because, at least for the social service bureaucracies, strong links
to clientele groups are now common. Bureaucratic chiefs can now
claim that they must first attend to the needs of their (often largely

32. See J. David Greenstone and Paul E. Peterson, *Race and Authority in
Urban Politics;* and Orlebeke, *Federal Aid to Chicago.*
33. See Orlebeke, *Federal Aid to Chicago.*
34. See Greenstone and Peterson, *Race and Authority in Urban Politics.*
35. See Orlebeke, *Federal Aid to Chicago,* 66.

minority) clientele, and mayors are unlikely to strongly resist the claim when minority voters can punish them. Finally, the electorates of federalist politicial economies are harder to organize than their predecessors, since the inducement of patronage is less available and appeals to city growth and renewal are less likely to be attractive to poor and working-class minority populations—who, it may be added, have come to understand that the burdens of altering land use often fall heaviest on them.

Still, federalist political economies represent a strong reassertion of the underlying continuities of city politics. This has been made possible by the availability of federal dollars; and it is the federalist pattern of politics that is at work in a large number of cities today. The inclination to seek ways of accomodating the mutual concerns of politicians and land interests in reworking city land-use patterns (especially as these relate to the central core and the means of access to it) remains. For the moment, federal money makes continuation of federalist political economies possible, but marked cutbacks in federal funds may yet force a break in the continuities that we have been describing.

Not only do urban political economies, beneath their diversity, have in common the three axes of a land-use alliance, a complex electoral coalition, and relatively autonomous bureaucracies. But, not surprisingly, the results of these shared features are similar. In each case, political institutions work to produce systematic bias and failures in social problem solving. Equally important, in each case, political institutions help to define the citizen's primary attachment to city political life as a bearer of interests, a client of a bureaucracy, or both. Systematic bias is just as evident in contemporary Phoenix as in present-day Philadelphia, and the inadequacies of social problem solving have not changed all that much in the progression from a pluralist to a federalist Boston. In much the same way, the manner in which city political institutions help to form the citizenry does not vary a great deal from San Francisco to Houston. But before turning to these themes, we must complete the task of demonstrating that there are substantial commonalities in the workings of city political orders. For this, we turn to Dallas.

4
An Entrepreneurial
Political Economy

We need to look beyond the pluralist-federalist political economies because these occur in a particular kind of city, and, if any general conclusions are to be reached, we must look at a wider range. We need not look, however, at all types of urban political economies. It is enough to extend the range by looking at southwestern cities and the entrepreneurial political economies characteristic of them during the postwar period. In contrast with the approach taken in the discussion of the pluralist and federalist political economies, however, the best way to understand the features of the entrepreneurial version is through a case study. Although enough is known about its central features, the necessary detail is, by and large, lacking, and any sketch of these features would thus be unconvincing. Dallas is a particularly useful case to consider because the defining characteristics of the entrepreneurial political economy are strikingly evident, especially the natural alliance between local businessmen and public officials.

Other southwestern cities differ from Dallas in various respects, reflecting, among other things, that Dallas is a city-manager system. But all entrepreneurial cities have in common a relatively unimpeded alliance at work composed of public officials and local businessmen, an alliance that is able to shape the workings of city political institutions so as to foster economic growth. In each, moreover, electoral politics is organized so that businessmen play an important role, and urban bureaucracies are adept at organizing their domains so that they are neither dominated by elected officials nor in the service of local businessmen. In short, just as much as do pluralist and federalist political economies, entrepreneurial ones reflect the structural factors that define the shape of city politics.[1]

1. For other examples of entrepreneurial political economies, see Richard M. Bernard and Bradley R. Rice (eds.), *Sunbelt Cities: Politics and Growth since World War II*; Susan A. MacManus, *Federal Aid to Houston*; Carl Abbot, *The New Urban America: Growth and Politics in Sunbelt Cities*; Amy Bridges, "Boss Tweed and V. O. Key Head West," in Clarence Stone and Heywood Sanders

The analysis of Dallas politics serves, then, several purposes: to emphasize the variety of types of political economies built upon the structural factors shaping city politics; to show the underlying continuities among the same varieties; and to pave the way for an analysis of the consequences of the features that city politics have in common.

THE PURE ENTREPRENEURIAL POLITICAL ECONOMY

Subsequent to the creation of the city-manager system, the politics of Dallas has fallen, historically, into two parts, which may be termed the "pure" and the "complex" entrepreneurial political economy. The first characterized the politics of the city from the late 1930s until approximately the mid 1970s. The latter has taken shape since that time, and to understand this present political economy, the essential features of the pure variant need to be described.[2]

From the late 1930s until the mid 1970s the broad purpose of city politics in Dallas was clear to anyone who paid attention to local affairs—it was to promote the growth of the city, particularly its economic growth. And what voices were heard with any force loudly proclaimed that Dallas was a businessmen's city. The links between public officials and business leaders were extensive and well developed. They were in evidence in the full range of city affairs, from specific civic projects to bolstering the city-manager form of government, from guiding the capital works agenda passed through bond votes to affecting who got elected to office. The extensiveness of the links is suggested by the fact that, for a substantial portion of the period of the pure entrepreneurial political economy, leading business figures were also the principal elected officials. Much more than is the case in older cities, the alliance was dominated by business figures. Public officials did not have the independent basis of support characteristic of their counterparts in many cities; and, more important, both those who were elected and those who were appointed had views

(eds.), *The Politics of Urban Development;* John Stuart Hall, "Case Studies of the Impact of Federal Aid on Major Cities: City of Phoenix"; and Steve B. Steib and R. Lynn Rittenoure, "Case Studies of the Impact of Federal Aid on Major Cities: City of Tulsa."

2. Unless otherwise stated, the analysis presented here draws on some fifty hours of interviews with a wide variety of local officials and political activists. For the most part, the interviews were conducted during the spring of 1982, with some completed earlier. For a more extensive discussion of Dallas politics, see my "The 'Real' Dallas," in Stone and Sanders (eds.), *The Politics of Urban Development.* The following pages draw freely on this paper both for language and analysis.

in common with leading businessmen. But it was *business* views that were shared, not vice versa.

The way to begin understanding the alliance is to consider the extensive efforts that business leaders made to ensure that elected officials shared their views on what they considered a fundamental aspect of local politics—namely, the protection of the council-manager system and, with it, the reputation of Dallas as an honest and efficient city. From 1907 to 1931 Dallas was governed under a commission form of government that had come into being largely as a result of efforts to find a form of government that would run in a businesslike manner. By the late 1920s, however, the city government was thought to be dominated by officials who were pursuing personal political ambitions in a way no longer suitable for fostering economic progress.[3] Many of those who had previously supported the commission form of government now switched their allegiance to the city-manager system. The efforts of local business elites in behalf of the council-manager system resulted in the creation of the Citizen Charter Association (CCA). To sell the city-manager system to the electorate, the CCA orchestrated a campaign that included hiring a professional director and clerical staff and creating neighborhood organizations. These efforts were crowned with success in 1930 when the citizenry voted in a council-manager form of government.

From the beginning the city-manager system was seen by leading local business figures as a form of government that would best suit their concerns. Local business leaders were willing to see that some sustained effort was made to recruit candidates for office who would be committed to the perpetuation of a local government that was efficient, professional, and administered by experts. This commitment to the city-manager system was at the core of a more general judgment that Dallas would best prosper under honest professional government: new investment would more likely come to the city if investors knew that they did not have to engage in corrupt negotiations with public officials for whom politics was a livelihood.

In addition to looking toward an honest and professional city government to promote the economic growth of the city, business leaders also saw the importance of fiscal restraint. A city government that kept its revenue demands to a minimum would be a city government that also would have high bond ratings and little trouble raising money in the bond market. In turn, this would enhance the city's reputation as a good place to do business. The city would be seen as capable of

3. The best source on this early period is Harold Stone et al., *City Manager Government in Nine Cities.*

providing the necessary infrastructure without imposing a heavy tax burden on business enterprises. Beyond the commitment to fiscal restraint, leading businessmen also believed that a lively civic and cultural climate was necessary if Dallas was to grow. The city needed to be attractive as a place to live for those who would manage its new and expanded firms.

To understand this commitment to growth on the part of leading businessmen, it will be helpful to specify in some detail just who they were. First, there were bankers. The commitment of the banks to a growing Dallas is easy to understand, since a bigger city meant more business for them. This was true not only because of increased deposits and loans but also because expansion meant that their own investments would prosper. Beyond that, a growing city meant more city funds to be put into their coffers. But the motives were not only monetary; the heads of the banks had a good deal of civic pride. This was their city, and they wanted it to be a great one. To be head of a bank in a modest provincial city was one thing, to be a bank president in a great city was quite another. The motives of the other business leaders involved were not very different. These leaders ranged from downtown merchants to heads of the big corporations doing business in the city, including as well a few developers. Perhaps most important was the head of the local morning newspaper, G. B. Dealey, whose commitment to preserving the city-manager system was widely evident.

The CCA was the principal means by which leading businessmen sought to ensure that elected officials shared their views on the importance of city growth and how it was to be fostered. The organization only supported candidates who were committed to the continuation of the council-manager system. What the CCA wanted were amateurs who would be happy to leave the day-to-day running of the city to the city manager and his staff. Whether through party organization or personal followings, full-time politicians would seek and require independent bases of support in the electorate and thus likely would be independent of businessmen's counsel. The ideal elected officials would be business executives who would take time out from their principal careers in order to serve in a civic capacity. If full-time businessmen could not be found, then other people sympathetic to clean, honest, growth-oriented government would do, as long as they, too, saw politics as an avocation. Middle-class women in pre–women's liberation days nicely fit the bill. If appropriate candidates could be found and elected, appointed officials—especially the city manager— would then be appointed by and broadly responsive to the right sort of people. These appointed officials might then be expected to be attentive to the concerns of the business elite. An additional advantage of part-time nonprofessional politicians was that they were less likely to be drawn to expensive ways of running a city, for it was just such demands on the city fisc that leading businessmen wished to avoid.

In all these efforts the CCA—and thus the business elite—proved eminently successful. When business leaders came to discuss city affairs with elected officials, they were largely engaged in intramural discussions. Moreover, they faced officials who had no independent political base from which to raise a dissenting voice. And when business leaders came to discuss city affairs with the city manager and his staff, they dealt with someone whose elected bosses were not inclined to push him in directions that would make it difficult for him to listen sympathetically to business concerns.

The sources of the CCA's success are not difficult to discern. Consider the case of George Allen, a black candidate for city council who initially ran twice for city council, in 1963 and 1965, without the endorsement of the CCA and lost both times. In the 1963 race he spent about $6,000, of which about $4,600 came from his own pocket. He was endorsed by two slating organizations, but neither of them had any money to give him. In 1965, the slating organizations did manage to come up with a little money but most of the financing came from a loan that he took out. This race cost him about $9,600. By one estimte, it would have taken approximately seven times that much to get elected.[4] In 1968, Allen was appointed to one of the new seats created by the expansion of the city council.[5] He was at that point the preferred candidate of the black leadership of the city. This endorsement by the black leadership and his appointment to the city council paved the way for his endorsement by the CCA. This time he won without a runoff, whereas in the two previous elections he had not managed to get even that far. He was subsequently reelected twice, each time with CCA endorsement.[6]

Evidence of the CCA's prowess in getting its candidates elected is provided by its record between 1959 and 1973. According to one calculation, during this period the organization endorsed 75 candi-

4. See the testimony of Dan Weiser, a local elections analyst, in *Albert Lipscomb et al. v. Wes Wise,* U.S District Court for Northern District of Texas, Dallas Division, July 1974, vol. 4:56 ff.

5. From 1931 until 1968 the city council was elected entirely at large and contained nine members, six of which had to reside in a designated district. In 1968 the number of city councillors was increased to eleven and again a residence provision was employed.

6. See the testimony of George Allen, given in the case of *Lipscomb v. Wise,* 3:89 ff.

dates and got 64 of them elected, making its success rate 82 percent. The organization was thus far from invincible, but it surely must be counted successful, especially since its candidates during this period always constituted at least a two-thirds majority on the council.[7] Perhaps the high point of the CCA's strength was in 1955, when its ticket ran unopposed. The turnout in the election was remarkably low, 2.5 percent of registered voters. In general, voting turnout was modest at best during this period. In part, this reflected the perceived dominance of the CCA and the lack of attractive alternative candidates. But whatever the reasons, the low turnout worked to the advantage of the CCA, since the vote was highest in the more affluent districts of the city where the CCA's strength was greatest. This increased the organizational advantages that it enjoyed vis-à-vis possible competing slating organizations.

At the CCA's zenith, the candidates that it endorsed did not need to raise any money on their own. In an at-large system, such money raising can be a substantial burden. In 1971, for example, the CCA raised about $70,000 dollars and incurred additional debts on the order of $14,500. None of its candidates reported any other source of money than CCA support. In addition to financing campaigns, the CCA also organized all the publicity for the candidates and went so far as to do the filings required of each candidate by the campaign law.[8] The association was also able to enforce a policy of supporting candidates for only two terms. In this way, the CCA itself—not particular elected officials—was the preeminent electoral force.[9]

Among elected public officials, the mayor, being the principal link between elected officials, the city manager, and business leaders was the most important figure. This was reflected in the fact that leading businessmen were more anxious that he be one of them than they were that ordinary council members might be so. Their efforts took the form of seeing that a person of substantial business standing ran for mayor under the CCA banner—and by and large they succeeded.[10]

7. See the testimony of Dan Weiser in *Lipscomb v. Wise*, vol. 4:56.

8. These data on campaign expenditures are from documents on file in the City Attorney's Office, City of Dallas.

9. In addition to interview sources, the material on the CCA comes from Carolyn Jencks Barta, "The Dallas News and Council-Manager Government," M.A. thesis, University of Texas at Austin, 1970. See also the testimony of Tom Unis, head of CCA during the mid 1960s, in *Lipscomb v. Wise*, 4:4 ff.

10. The only exception was Wes Wise, who held office during the early 1970s. Wise was a popular local broadcaster and thus one of the few sorts of people who had a sufficiently large independent reputation to contest a seat on equal terms with CCA-backed candidates.

The other crucial public official in Dallas was, of course, the city manager.[11] His elected bosses, the council, were unlikely to have views very different from those of leading businessmen, and, in particular, they would be unlikely to press on him the competing concerns of neighborhoods or ethnic or racial groups or indeed any other concerns that would make it difficult for him to respond to leading business interests. In effect, he could consult his professional training and his career ambitions and these might reasonably lead him to views not markedly different from those of the business elite. Since Dallas businessmen were anxious that city government be run honestly and efficiently and were by and large drawn to the latest techniques in management, they were likely to give the manager free rein. Beyond that there was certainly little in the training of city managers that made them insensitive to the claims of promoting city growth. Perhaps as important, the manager's own career ambitions might reasonably lead to his favoring rapid growth of the city. After all, it would be good for his career to preside over a booming city where, in any case, he might continue to reside, since there well might be no bigger cities in which to pursue his career as manager. Most important, however, is the consequence of the division of labor between state and market as it is manifest in cities. Given a long time horizon and concern for his professional reputation, the city manager, more than even elected officials, might be expected to understand the necessity of encouraging business activity. Perhaps the most suggestive bit of evidence in this regard is that one of Dallas' early managers became head of one of the city's banks and that another, later manager became an executive in a leading business firm in the city.

The nature of the alliance between business leaders and public officials is best suggested by a brief look at the decisions undertaken by the city in such an important area as capital works. Most capital works in Dallas are financed through a regular bond program approved by Dallas voters. This in itself is significant, since it effectively institutionalizes the business elites' commitment to low taxes and puts the system on a pay-as-you-go basis. In addition, because capital works are a crucial part of the expenditures of any city, this mode of financing means that those who are most influential in shaping the bond program have significant influence over the budget of the city.

Since the capital works must be approved by voters, the crucial question becomes how the bond campaigns were organized. Typically,

11. Dallas is, in fact, the largest city in the United States with a city-manager form of government.

the mayor approached a leading business figure and asked him to head up the bond campaign. He, in turn, undertook to raise the money necessary to present the city's proposals to voters. The actual vehicle for raising the money for the campaign was and remains an organization called the Dallas Citizen Council (DCC), another businessmen's organization, which drew on the same pool as the CCA. No very elaborate theory of influence is required here. If, indeed, public officials harbored any inclinations strongly at variance with those of leading businessmen, they would likely reconsider them in light of the business elite's crucial role in the bond campaign.[12]

The DCC's role was not confined to capital projects connected to bond votes. There were a variety of other capital projects that could not be handled through the bond program. These included those that involved cooperation with other authorities as well as those that voters might find objectionable. In addition, there were projects that involved city resources but were not capital works and that also either required cooperation with other authorities or were particularly delicate and might not flourish if they became the subject of public scrutiny. Such projects ranged from ensuring that Dallas had an adequate water supply,[13] to desegregating the schools, to building a new city library downtown. The existence of a businessmen's organzation[14] able to raise money and other resources meant that when public officials needed to take action in these matters they had at hand help in laying the groundwork for the projects, carrying on delicate negotiations, and generally pushing the project to completion. In this context, public officials could be expected to tailor their views to what they supposed leading businessmen would find acceptable.

The heart of the entrepreneurial political economy was the business elite's ability to create and maintain a political system in which those who held elected and appointed office did not have to be told what to do. They would be drawn of their own volition to particular projects

12. On the DCC, see Carol Estes Thometz, *The Decision-Makers: The Power Structure of Dallas*. See also "The Dynamic Men of Dallas," *Fortune*, February 1946.

13. The solution of the water problem was the first big triumph for the entrepreneurial political economy, and indeed it is a story still regularly told in Dallas when outsiders have to be convinced of the civic-mindedness of local businessmen and persuaded that a strong, well-organized business community is good for the city. The story is one of the civic totems of Dallas and no doubt is also passed on to new members of the business elite to explain why a politically active business community is a valuable thing.

14. In addition to the DCC, leading businessmen would also form special purpose organizations to undertake particular projects.

and general ways of looking at the city that were compatible with the inclinations of business leaders. They were to act in ways that, if the business elite had time and authority, they might be drawn to themselves. The officials were often, in fact, leading businessmen themselves or, if not, were most often people with business backgrounds. Just as important, if they were elected officials, they had no strong incentive to look at matters in ways that would bring them into conflict with leading businessmen. They were part-time officials with no need or opportunity to build independent political followings and whose election depended on an organization that was strongly supported by leading businessmen. It need only be added that the city manager was in a position to act in accordance with the highest standards of his profession. The manager knew to what sorts of projects and policies leading businessmen would be sympathetic—and by and large these were things that he likely would pursue on his own.

Bureaucracy and Electorate

The central fact about the Dallas bureaucracy in the pure entrepreneurial political economy is that it was (and continues to be) highly professionalized. Appointments were made according to civil-service procedures and according to professional criteria rather than as a reward for political service, and the principal administrators were in a position to act, for the most part, according to professional judgment. The character of the bureaucracy stemmed in part from the city's status as a city-manager system. But more important, since legal formalities may be overridden, were two things. First, elected officials had little incentive to interfere with the day-to-day running of the city, since they were not engaged in building political careers. And, second, business leaders wished for a well-administered city and understood this to mean that the manager and his staff must be allowed considerable autonomy. They also believed that the manager shared their views about how the city should be made to grow. In the case of both elected officials and business leaders, it was also generally understood that attempting to extract personal favors or using bureaucratic largesse to advance political careers would make it more difficult to attract competent managers and skilled city administrators. The autonomy of the manager and his staff existed, however, within well-understood (if broad) boundaries. These boundaries were the purposes shared by leading businessmen and elected officials about how to promote the vigorous growth of the city and about the need for fiscal restraint.

The central point about the organization of appeals to the electorate is that there was no serious organizational alternative to the CCA. Thus, any electoral challenge to the alliance between leading businessmen and public officials was effectively precluded. Other slating organizations came and went—or, if they stayed, lacked resources. Neighborhood organizations were too weak to provide an organizational basis for a political career even if the at-large voting system had not effectively made a career rooted in neighborhood appeals very difficult. As for organizations of municipal employees, a source of organizational support in many cities, neither policemen nor firemen were even engaged in collective bargaining, much less an active political force.[15]

The CCA did not, in fact, set its face against accommodating those people who were not themselves local businessmen and who wished to hold office, as long as they were willing to be attentive to the basic purposes of the alliance. So, over time, the association sponsored black and brown candidates who showed that they had wide support. Those who were excluded were simply those who wished to pursue independent political careers or who had doubts about how the alliance was trying to create a greater Dallas. Spokesmen for the poor, minorities, working men, neighborhood interests, or any other views that might complicate the business of creating an attractive expansionary climate faced substantial difficulties.[16]

It only needs to be added that, in attempting to organize the electorate, those contending for office could not rely on a stream of benefits—such as jobs, contracts, and favorable decisions—generated from past or prospective control of the city bureaucracy. Building a political following in the manner characteristic of patronage politics in many other cities was not important in Dallas. In part, this was simply a matter of the council-manager system itself prohibiting intervention of elected officials in the day-to-day decision making of the city and in personnel matters. An electoral politics that protected the integrity of the city-manager system thus served to preclude patronage as a political base.

The outlines of the pure entrepreneurial political economy are now complete. Organized businessmen were able to create and foster a political system that was directed at promoting a greater Dallas. This was done not by corrupting the system but by excluding "politics," by which was meant the pulling and hauling of various interests, and politicians who were spokesmen for these interests and acted to fur-

15. See Richard D. Brown, "Collective Bargaining and Public Employee Strikes," *Texas Business Review* 52, no. 9 (September 1978): 179–81.
16. See the testimony of Dan Weiser in *Lipscomb v. Wise*, 4:90.

ther their own political careers. Instead the aim was to professionalize the city bureaucracy and see that the day-to-day matters of the city were dealt with honestly and efficiently. The complex entrepreneurial political economy of present-day Dallas is in many ways an extension of the pure variant, but it also contains some noteworthy departures from it.

The Complex Entrepreneurial Political Economy

Dallas is now a largely built-up city, confined more or less to its present boundaries and competing in a larger metropolitan region with suburban locations and nearby Ft. Worth. The fact that its land area is mostly filled in is, in part, a testimony to the efficiency of the pure entrepreneurial political economy. Increasingly, city growth will depend on rearranging land use. This will be true regardless of whether it is a matter of investment by those already located in the city or of attracting new investment. One important result is that progrowth activities will increasingly result in direct, tangible, and significant costs to substantial portions of the local citizenry. The most important source of these costs is likely to be improving transportation flows within the city, particularly between the middle-class districts north of the downtown and the central business district. Both new roads and fixed-rail schemes will impose substantial costs on significant numbers of city residents.

Responses to these costs in the form of community organization must be seen in the context of a variety of gentrification efforts in neighborhoods within striking distance of the central business district. Gentrification has brought in its trail a modest level of neighborhood organization where almost none existed before. There are now a variety of neighborhood associations at work protesting new traffic patterns or trying to ease the path of gentrification by having housing inspections enforced or simply protesting new development in areas where development will remove low-income citizens—in short, the usual concerns of citizen associations.[17]

In addition to the physical and economic changes in Dallas, the political arrangements set in motion by leading businessmen, arrangements that were crucial for explaining the community of views of public officials and businessmen, have now altered significantly.

17. See, e.g., the discussion of East Dallas neighborhood organizations and their opposition to the Crosstown Expressway in George Rodrique, "The Best Laid Plans," *D*, December 1981.

Three changes are of particular note: the change in the electoral system to a mixed single-member/at-large form, the demise of the CCA, and the weakening of the DCC. Single-member districts grew out of a suit brought by a black candidate for office who argued that the at-large system effectively discriminated against blacks. The electoral system that emerged from the suit was to have an eleven-member city council, eight members of which were to be elected from districts and three members of which, including the mayor, were to be elected at large. The demise of the CCA had several sources, of which the increasing fragmentation of the business community is one. Probably more important in this regard has been the onset of single-member districts, which significantly reduced the comparative advantage commanded by both the money and the organization that the leading businessmen could bring to bear. At present, there is no single dominant slating organization at work in Dallas elections. The DCC has not disappeared, but it has changed, and the changes have moderately weakened its impact on city affairs. Its principal impact as an organization was on specific projects and on the bond program, where it served as the principal vehicle for raising money for leading businessmen. The latter role has continued. The principal weakening has occurred in the realm of specific projects, where the DCC is now probably somewhat less capable both of carrying out specific projects proposed by public officials and of proposing its own. The basis of the weakening is simply that the organization is no longer a small group of elite businessmen who on their own are able to say yes or no. It is now a larger organization that has a paid staff to facilitate coordination.

Lying behind the demise of the CCA and the weakening of the DCC are significant changes in the business community of Dallas. The leading businessmen of the kind actively concerned with city affairs in the pure entrepreneurial variant are still in evidence. Their concerns are much the same. They wish to see an attractive climate for business investment maintained, and to this end they still work to see that the city-manager system remains, that cultural facilities attractive to middle- and top-level business managers are provided, that housing suitable for the professional classes is widely available, and that suitable schools can be found.

But these business leaders, who are themselves largely not directly concerned with land-use matters, now have been joined by a significant number of developers and others concerned with development and redevelopment projects. Their concerns, while overlapping with those of leading businessmen, also differ: they, too, wish to see a local political order that facilitates investment, but for them this largely means a city government that will facilitate land-use changes and provide the infrastructure necessary for new development. Broadly speaking, they are less interested in honest, efficient government than in government that facilitates good development opportunities.

Not only have major developers become more important in Dallas politics, but the local business elite has itself become more complex. Dallas has grown enormously, and the number of leading businessmen has expanded. Moreover, they do not now come mostly from the same background (some even come from the Northeast) and their business success is as likely to be tied to markets outside of Dallas as to anything going on inside it. Dallas, in short, is experiencing what many scholars have said is characteristic of older cities. Some idea of the extent of the change is suggested by the fact that, in 1960, 69 percent of the corporate headquarters in Dallas were local firms. Throughout the 1960s one of every three new headquarters locating in the city came from outside the state, but in the period 1970–76 the figure rose to eleven of twelve.[18] The result is that it is simply harder for leading businessmen to organize themselves.

The crucial point in all this is that, as Dallas has evolved into a major city with its businessmen and banks conducting business nationally and internationally, the question that increasingly presses on them concerns what incentive they have to remain or take an active interest in city affairs. The businessmen who founded and ran the CCA and DCC during the period of the pure entrepreneurial political economy had strong material and civic reasons for devoting themselves to city affairs. They were engaged in making a city that would make them rich and proud and provide a style of living that suited their tastes. The present generation of business executives are as likely as not to have other interests. Their city is already attractive, its government not corrupt. Moreover, they are as likely as not to seek to advance their careers in the national business arena and to seek entertainment outside the city.

With all these changes in the business elite, it is important to note that candidates—for mayor at least—still can run as *businessmen.* This is perhaps the most suggestive point of all. Business leaders continue to be widely believed to have a rightful, indeed prominent, place in the running of the city. It is no longer possible for elite businessmen to think that they need not explain their claims pub-

18. John Rees, "Manufacturing Headquarters in a Post-Industrial Urban Context," *Economic Geography* 54, no. 4 (October 1978): 337–54.

licly, that if they come out for a candidate or a project that ought to be enough. But, even with the need to argue and struggle in a more public fashion, they need not dress up as politicians who are trying to build political followings. Their claim is that the city's well-being depends on them, and on that basis their views ought to carry considerable weight. In this, they remain persuasive.

The full implications of increasing neighborhood organization, of alterations in the political arrangements earlier created by leading businessmen, and of the increased fragmentation of the business elite are not yet clear. The shape of the political economy, and particularly the organization of the bureaucracy and electorate, is still emerging. But the broad implications can be discerned. Even in the context of more politically difficult land-use strategies for promoting city growth and of changes in the political arrangements, public officials are still drawn to policies that promote the economic growth of the city. They are thus drawn into extensive links with businessmen who share these purposes and whose cooperation is in any case required to pursue them. These links are, inevitably, different from those that existed under the pure entrepreneurial political economy. They are, in fact, more complex—not least because public officials are now themselves more diverse in their incentives and businessmen more fragmented. On balance, the relationship is one in which public officials play a stronger role than previously. This is partly because business interests are, in fact, more fragmented and partly because the problems are more complex and businessmen lack the time to act as civic statesmen thinking through proposals. In general, the relationship between public officials and business is more like a coalition than it is like the alliance characteristic of the pure entrepreneurial political economy.

First, consider elected officials, starting with those elected at large, notably the mayor. Contests for the three seats elected at large still draw significant financial support from leading businessmen and, increasingly, from development interests. The reasons are not far to seek. The mayor, although formally just another member of the city council without additional powers, is the most visible elected official. He is, moreover, more influential in city decisions than ordinary councillors because he spends more time tending to city matters. This is partly because he represents the city in all sorts of negotiations and public occasions. But, even more important, it stems from the fact that he is the principal link between elected officials and the city manager. His acquiescence at least—and, more probably, his active support—is required for pursuing progrowth policies. And, not surprisingly, this is reflected in the amount of money spent on mayoral campaigns.

The size of recent expenditures in the mayoralty campaigns reflects not only the importance of the office but also a decrease in the ease with which someone sympathetic to the business elite's concerns can be elected to office. In retrospect, the turning point seems to have occurred during the early 1980s. The last several races have required the spending of a good deal of money and have been more hotly contested than hitherto has been the case. For example, in the race for mayor in 1983 the candidate most sympathetic to keeping intact the existing arrangements to promote the economic advancement of the city spent on the order of $1 million to defeat a candidate who represented much that the alliance between officials and leading businessmen found objectionable. In the next race, the challenger, a hardware store owner who has served on the city council and has been active in city affairs for many years, raised $20,000, while the incumbent, who had raised large sums in the previous election, again did so, this time spending on the order of $400,000. The turnout was low (about 15 percent of the registered voters) and the race much closer than expected, with the incumbent getting just over 50 percent of the vote and the principal challenger just over 45 percent. The most striking feature of the voting was the decline in support for the incumbent by the north Dallas neighborhoods, whose support is crucial if the alliance between leading businessmen and public officials committed to reworking the land-use patterns of Dallas is to continue. But the feeling among local observers was that supporters of the incumbent, considering the race to be a foregone conclusion, had underestimated the appeal of the challenger and had done little to see that voters sympathetic to their candidate turned out at the polls.[19]

The central point in all this is that although the mayor is very much a public figure on whom the competing pressures will fall and is by no means a creature of businessmen, he is typically a leading business figure himself whose principal financial backers in the election are businessmen and developers. It would, therefore, be surprising if he were inclined to take any tack other than one directed at promoting the growth of the city and facilitating changes in the pattern of land use.

The situation is much the same for the two other members of the city council who are elected at-large. If they are not themselves

19. See the account in *The New York Times*, April 8 and April 10, 1985.

leading business figures, they still draw their principal backing from the same sources as the mayor, and for much the same reasons. But the members of the council elected in single-member districts present a more complicated story.

Single-member districts have substantially reduced the importance of money in getting elected. Candidates who are widely known in their districts now have some chance to get elected even if they are short of funds. Almost as important, Dallas media coverage—which at the height of the pure entrepreneurial political economy was a relatively quiet affair largely supportive of local businessmen and city officials—has now altered dramatically. Gone are the days of Mr. Dealey (and the visit of prospective candidates to his office) and his active role in the DCC. Dallas is now one of the few cities that have two newspapers that really compete. In addition, there are now several local magazines that pay some attention to Dallas affairs. The result is that organized business interests and their allies among public officials can no longer depend on the favorable coverage that Dealey afforded. Quite the contrary, for now the incentives in a competitive system are to ferret out evidence of unfairness, incompetence, and the like. Indeed, as do many other cities, Dallas now has a city magazine covering local affairs that appears to define its mission as bringing to public light what it understands to be the real workings of city politics.

The corollary is that it is now possible for ambitious local politicians to think that they can make up for lack of money with astute publicity. In short, the recruitment process is no longer controlled and there is now evidence, for example, of a variety of minority politicians who are starting to build careers around the single-member districts and the possibilities of media attention.

These changes, however, have not meant that those who hold seats in single-member districts have proved to be a substantial barrier to progrowth strategies. The reason is not far to seek, since a crucial ingredient is missing. Only those who expect to make full-time political careers for themselves would make substantial investments in trying to build up political followings. Resistance to growth strategies—particularly in a context where they mean land-use changes—is most likely to come from citizens adversely affected by the new commercial developments, roads, and the like. To be sure, any elected official from the area affected will pay some attention to such discontent, but it will usually be only those who see articulating the discontent as crucial to a long-term political career who will devote sustained energy to the matter. The part-time politician and the person who (for whatever reason) cannot build a political career are less likely to do so. Elected officials in Dallas lack such incentives.

Crucial here is a 1981 amendment to the city charter that set a limit of three terms for holding office on the city council. When this is added to the fact that members of the city council are still paid only $50 per council meeting, the incentives are small to invest much in trying to build a political following by responding to citizen discontent about development projects or, in general, by not acting to facilitate growth strategies. As a consequence, even though the variety of neighborhood, racial, and other interests that go to make up a city political order now find it easier to gain expression, they are far from having elected officials who will give them significant voice.

Among those holding and seeking office in single-member districts, there is some difference in the extent to which those from more affluent districts and those from poor and minority districts resist progrowth strategies. Those from the former are most likely to be enthusiastic, since their constituents are most likely to be beneficiaries, reaping the benefits of a larger, more vibrant city with better job opportunities for those with high educational attainment and incurring few direct costs from the redevelopment. There is every reason to suppose that such support will continue as long as progrowth policies do not impinge on the tax rate. Dallas still has no income tax, and its property taxes are low by the standards of the rest of the country. The policy of financing capital investment almost entirely by bonds continues. If tax rates were to rise significantly, development strategies might well be attacked. The last time that a significant tax rise was proposed, there was a major uproar accompanied by lawsuits.[20]

In poor and minority districts, residents—and hence council members—are more suspicious of growth strategies, at least of those that involve redevelopment. Such suspicion is manifest, for example, in responses to recent proposals to stimulate commercial and industrial development in the city in areas south of the central business district. The density of development in these areas tends to be low, a characteristic that makes them relatively attractive for redevelopment, but the neighborhoods are also home to a substantial number of minority residents.

There is still, then, a set of elected officials in Dallas that can be relied on to favor policies that facilitate the economic expansion of

20. See the account in John Fullinwider, "Dallas: The City With No Limits?" *In These Times*, December 1980, 17–23.

the city, whether this means fostering a general political environment that encourages investment or helping to rearrange land use.
At a minimum, there is a majority of the city council who will be
drawn to such policies. The new electoral system, the demise of the
CCA, and the other changes have not meant disaster from the
viewpoint of business interests committed to a vibrant business
climate in the city. There have, nevertheless, been departures from
the pure entrepreneurial political economy. Although elected officials are drawn to or acquiescent in growth strategies, they are,
in fact, somewhat freer to offer their own interpretation of what
this entails. They are now more nearly coalition partners than members of the community of interest that characterized the alliance
under the pure entrepreneurial variant—and as such are more
often inclined to take the lead.

The city manager's outlook is also more complicated in the present political economy. But, again, he is drawn to progrowth strategies. In part, this simply stems from the factors already noted:
the division of labor between state and market, the city manager's
professional responsibility for the revenue base of the city, and his
extended time horizon. Even more than is the case for elected
officials, to do his job and secure his professional reputation requires that he take investment in the city seriously.

Just as important, although the manager is drawn to neighborhood, racial, and ethnic groups for reasons suggested above, he is
not faced with elected spokesmen for these interests strongly pushing him to resist progrowth strategies. Essentially, the manager is
as free under the complex as under the pure entrepreneurial variant to pursue his own predilections. But more so than under the
pure variant, he will tend to have independent interpretations of
what pursuing such strategies entails. This is because, even if he is
not under strong pressures from council members and spokesmen
for various citizen interests to resist progrowth strategies, he does
find it useful to accommodate their concerns as the strategies get
worked out. Indeed, the present manager was hired, among other
reasons, to be accommodating in this fashion. Once neighborhood,
racial, and ethnic interests have been politically expressed, it is, if
nothing else, prudent not to ignore them. Thus, an important part
of the burden of arranging the necessary compromises falls—and
will continue to fall—on the manager. In contrast to city business
leaders, he has the necessary time, inclination, and skills to undertake the task. The result is simply that the city manager inevitably
will have a different appreciation of what is entailed in imple-

menting the progrowth strategies. Just as much as to the point, he will be able to tell businessmen that, if they wish to achieve their goals, then they must take account of the political realities and that he knows what these latter are. Thus, as with elected officials, it is again more a case of a coalition with business leaders than of a community of interests. The city manager is, in fact, becoming more like the mayor of a sizable city and less a staff person for leading businessmen.

The conjunction of gentrification, neighborhood organization, the costs of rearranging land use, city councillors elected from single-member districts, and a city manager who is not adverse to paying at least some attention to neighborhood organizations might be expected to complicate development politics. No doubt this has occurred. But more indicative of what is happening are two recent decisions to significantly alter land-use patterns. Both suggest that an alliance around growth is still vital and can engineer significant land-use changes.

Bryan Place was developed under what is essentially a local urban renewal program, but without the requirements of public hearings and other restrictive regulations characteristic of the federal program. The local ordinance making it possible (the Area Redevelopment Plan) was passed in 1975, and in it the city agreed to buy back from developers land that they subsequently could not develop. The ordinance was later amended to reimburse developers for the interest costs that they bore as well as for the original cost of purchase. Only land within a two-mile radius of the center of the downtown is eligible for the program, and the advertised aim is to encourage housing near the central business district. The original funding for the program came from federal revenue sharing, so that the city did not need to commit any of its own funds. All that it committed was its guarantee, which developers could then employ when trying to raise funds from banks. The attractions of the ordinance are obvious. Local public authority is used, but without public scrutiny. As the city manager commented, "this is a private venture and doesn't become a public venture until the city is asked to acquire the property." [21] As it has been completed, Bryan Place is a development of some sixty acres at the edge of the downtown in which a typical house or condominium costs on the order of $100,000 and up. In addition to the guarantee of repurchase, the city also made a variety of changes in fire codes and minimum

21. *Dallas Times Herald,* July 24, 1976.

street lengths and closed some streets altogether. The result is a very appealing development that has already attracted middle- and upper-level managers who work in the central business district.

A further illustration that the alliance between the local business elite and public officials can still engineer significant changes in the look of the city can be found in the recent commitment made by the city and DART, the local transit agency, to widen the major north-south expressway and build sixty-nine miles of light rail above and below ground. In its first phase, the rail system is to have three stations downtown and forty-two stations outside the central business district. The initial commitment is for $1 billion, with a targeted completion date of 1995. Dallas voters have already approved the plan, which is to be paid for, in part, by an increase in the local sales tax, by bonds, and by an additional mode of financing that is suggestive of how local business interests will be able to shape the development of the city even as its politics is growing more complex.

Local business corporations are to be solicited to pay for the cost of some of the stations. In return for their contribution, the stations will be located where the businesses consider them to be most convenient.[22] Under the guise of public-private partnership, local corporations will be in a position to ensure that the route of the rail system will, at least in part, follow their preferences. With a little bit of an exaggeration, we might say that they can simply buy the station locations that they prefer rather than go through the arduous process of translating their money and organization into political influence. Purchasing what they wish is much easier.

The impression of an active alliance around rearranging land use is given added substance by the host of major projects in and near the central business district. Some of these are in the form of public-private partnerships in which, through a variety of land swaps, coordinated investment efforts, and related endeavors, major undertakings have been brought to fruition.[23] Along with the concomitant large-scale private investment, these projects have had a noticeable impact on the downtown. Simply put, there is, a commercial boom that extends to areas outside the central business district. Perhaps most noticeable in all this is a downtown arts district, which contains a new art museum, performance facilities, and a variety of commercial buildings. It covers several square blocks

22. See the account in the *New York Times*, September 8, 1985.
23. See William A. Clagget, "Dallas: The Dynamics of Public-Private Cooperation," in R. Scott Fosler and Renee A. Berger (eds.), *Public-Private Partnerships in American Cities*.

at the edge of the downtown and involved major land clearance. It is not the project of a city in which leading businessmen, developers, and public officials find it difficult to act with force and dispatch. Nor is the office and commercial boom.

Development politics in Dallas occurs in the context of a city-manager system that does little to facilitate the development of political followings by elected officials. Not the least important point is simply that the city charter is designed to dissuade council members from involving themselves in administrative matters. Although the temptation is difficult to resist (and no doubt is given into), the existence of a manager and his staff and of those devoted to protecting the city-manager system make it difficult for any councillor to do this as matter of course. One of the principal sources of benefactions that an ambitious local politician can use, and probably needs, to build a political career is access to local bureaucracy. Here, potentially, can be found favorable decisions for supporters and material benefits, including jobs. If it is difficult to do favors for valued political supporters, then it is difficult to have very many. All this being so, elected officials are much less likely than their counterparts in many other cities to have the skills to seek out discontent and to build coalitions that might draw them into stances critical of progrowth strategies.

CONCLUSION

Dallas illustrates one political pattern characteristic of the entrepreneurial political economies that can be built around the axial principles of city politics. The essential point of difference between this sort of political economy and the pluralist and federalist types is that the behavior of public officials in the entrepreneurial version is not as much shaped by the building of electoral organizations and political coalitions. Concomitantly, public officials are less drawn to land-use schemes to generate the stream of benefits helpful to their electoral careers. Rather, they are drawn to land-use schemes because the political arrangements work to recruit those with a strong disposition to ally themselves with local businessmen. Dallas is perhaps extreme in these regards, but other cities with entrepreneurial political economies display similar features compared with their northern counterparts. Whatever the differences among types of political economies, however, all show efforts to create and maintain growth coalitions. The motivations of public officials may vary, but the results are much the same.

Equally important, in entrepreneurial political economies, insofar as citizens play an active role in political life, they are drawn into politics either to speak for their neighborhood, ethnic group, or some other interest or as a bureaucratic client. There is, to be sure, an effort by some of the participants in Dallas politics to portray it as a search for the best way to make a vital city, a theme echoed in other cities with entrepreneurial political economies, but the reality is that those who get to offer reasoned versions of how this is to be done are very few and their views much of a piece. In this, entrepreneurial political economies are much like the other variants. In all cases, the overwhelming majority of citizens have no part in what is finally not a deliberative effort at all.

5
Systematic Bias and Effective Problem Solving

Although the differences among the types of urban political economies are real, more important are the commonalities in their consequences. This should not be surprising, since they are variations built upon the common axial principles: the natural alliance between public officials and land interests, the importance of coalitions or some functional substitute for them in getting and staying elected, and the relative autonomy of city bureaucracies. Although the types of political economies considered do not exhaust the range of actual or possible variation, they do cover enough ground to allow some general statements to be made about these consequences.

The first set of consequences is suggested by the following outline of some of the central features of city political life as it has been portrayed here: public officials are disposed to favor some actors and some kinds of policies over others, and some political actors are substantially better placed than others to realize their purposes. Two questions naturally follow from this outline. First, does it describe a system of popular control that is systematically biased in its workings? Popular control should not be organized in such a fashion that some actors and some viewpoints are given overwhelmingly favorable treatment such that the benefits of public life are consistently directed one way and the burdens shifted in another. Second, does popular control work in ways that enhance or retard the ability of city residents to deal effectively with the problems that face them collectively? Popular control should not work so as to diminish efforts to improve collective well-being and, if possible, should operate to enhance it. These two features of the workings of popular control are central to any assessment of its success and, conversely, point to any significant kinds of failure. Under a variety of headings—most notably, political equality and efficiency—they have been the staple concerns of those who have studied the politics of cities.[1]

1. What about majoritarianism itself and its possible failure in cities? This question is not directly addressed here because, at least in the study of city politics, the issue of majoritarianism has been merged with or replaced by the study of systematic bias, i.e., the question of whether any group or groups

There is a second set of consequences that arise from what the urban political economies have in common. Although in many ways the entrepreneurial political economies were created by and continue to be run by people who have wished for a city political life unlike that of older northern cities—that is, one that would be characterized by expertise and a larger role for the expression of citywide concerns—in fact, being a citizen of Dallas or San Antonio is, in crucial ways, not very different from being one of Chicago or Philadelphia. In all cases, citizens stand in relation to one another both as potential bargainers in a set of political institutions that work to aggregate interests, and as clients of city bureaucracies. The mix of potential bargainer and bureaucratic client varies between federalist and entrepreneurial political economies, with the range of actors who become active bargainers being more restricted in the latter. Still, when citizens of Dallas enter the political arena, they do so typically as claimants speaking for interests or as bureaucratic clients, just as their counterparts in Chicago do. These commonalities suggest that, concerning the working of city political institutions, there is another set of consequences to consider—namely, the manner in which these institutions help to form the urban citizenry and whether the manner in which they do so is appropriate.

I will start to address the question of city political institutions as being formative in the next chapter. Here, however, I wish to concentrate on the two other common results of the range of urban political economies: systematic bias and failures in social intelligence. These have been widely discussed by political scientists (social intelligence perhaps less so). Therefore, we need not linger as long here as we will in the discussion that considers both political institutions as being formative of a citizenry and the contribution to our aspiration to be a commercial republic of a citizenry appropriately constituted. Still, because systematic bias and social intelligence are important matters, they do need to be discussed, if only to emphasize their centrality for the political judgment necessary to maintain a decent political order. After discussing each in turn, I will briefly consider a generally misunderstood point about the relation between them. If we understand systematic bias as a central aspect of equality and social intelligence as a central aspect of efficiency, then, contrary to the general view, there is no simple trade-off between them.

---

dominate decision making in the city and receive a disproportionate share of the benefits of city political life. This focus on groups and bias is consistent with the more general proposition that simple majority rule is difficult to achieve and not, in any case, desirable. See Robert A. Dahl, *A Preface to Democratic Theory*.

SYSTEMATIC BIAS

It is unlikely that the workings of any political order are neutral if by that is meant that, at any given moment, its configuration advantages no interest or interests. The important question is whether such advantages are general, so that the workings of the political arrangements consistently favor some interests and impede others. If this is so, it is appropriate to speak of systematic bias. Such bias is particularly offensive under popular government since, by its very nature, it promises that the benefits and burdens of political life will not be systematically skewed. What is the case with the operation of popular control in the city?

It is most revealing to address the question of systematic bias by looking at the shape of the public agenda. What gets discussed logically precedes what actually gets decided on. To know which viewpoints are regularly advanced, which find it hard going, and which are not considered at all—as well as why these things occur—is to know a good deal more than how particular decisions are made and how controversies are resolved. For the decisions will reflect the kinds of viewpoints regularly advanced; bias in the agenda will be reflected by bias in decision.

Much political activity is, in fact, not directed at making decisions at all (i.e., at allocating goods and services and issuing regulations) but at maintaining existing patterns of access and excluding formulations of the public's business that will impede policies. Just as much effort is likely to be expended, for example, in ensuring that those neighborhood groups who might resist large-scale growth projects will find it difficult to mount serious electoral challenges as is expended in putting together the political and economic pieces of the project itself. This is the principal point of the Dallas study: virtuoso political talent was displayed in keeping control of the public agenda. Indeed, the premiere form of controlling the public agenda is to establish that the position and benefactions of those who dominate political pathways are not considered a fit subject for public discussion but are instead part of the natural order of things.

Decision making, in the sense of making and/or ratifying conscious choices through formal decision procedures, hardly exhausts what governments do, for much of what they do is routine. Indeed, the cumulation of these routine actions is likely to have marked consequences on the well-being of the urban citizenry, consequences perhaps even more marked than the results of public decision making. Again, a focus on the public agenda will be more revealing than an examination of particular decisions. Much government activity is a matter of following standard operating procedures, rules of thumb, professional practice, and the advice of valued clienteles or other interested parties who are regularly consulted. The attention to bond ratings by city financial officers, and their regular reminders to elected officials of the need to be able to market bonds at reasonable rates, is not a matter of decision making, as this is ordinarily understood. It is simply a matter of professionals doing their jobs. In the same way, much of the effort to facilitate growth in Dallas comes from the city manager and his staff following the canons of good professional practice. The content of the public agenda of course reflects these designations of what is routine and properly a matter for experts and what is suitable for public decision. But to say that something is best decided on by bureaucratic rule does not mean that there are no regular beneficiaries of such practices. Systematic bias may result from the mundane workings of city bureaucracies and the definition of expertise as well as from the more obvious stuff of political struggle.

A comprehensive analysis of systematic bias should not stop with an analysis of the public agenda. To guard against missing something significant, it is important to look at what is known about the actual pattern of results. We want, then, to look at the distribution of goods and services across population groups, for example, or at the direct impact of policy decisions, for example at the number of people displaced by land-use changes. But a focus on such outcomes is not enough for the assessment of systematic bias. Individual citizens will make various kinds of choices in response to their perceptions of how existing political arrangements work. They are likely to believe that the political arrangements that are responsible for the shape of public policy are difficult and expensive to alter. As a consequence they will, for example, sell their houses and change jobs because they sense that the drift of public policy makes this either advantageous or at least prudent. But the ability to adapt is differentially distributed. The result is that some citizens are more at risk from the shape of the public agenda and thus more regularly in need of having to adapt their behavior. These may also be the citizens least well equipped to do so. It is necessary only to add that the effects may well be cumulative. Every effort to adapt and every failure to do so may drain resources and morale. The cumulative effect of having to adapt one's behavior and of occasional or regular failures to do so will also affect the resources available for political activity. In short, the shape of the public agenda can have significant effects on who can participate effectively in the political life of the city.

Given the above understanding of systematic bias and the importance of the public agenda, we are in a position to interpret the analysis presented in the preceding chapters. Its main theme is that certain viewpoints and interests are regularly included on the agenda of city politics, others excluded, and yet others considered routine. What remains to be done is to draw out the implications in terms of systematic bias of what by now should, in any case, be reasonably apparent. For present purposes, the most important consideration is not the variety of urban political economies but their commonalities.

The discussion can be conveniently divided into three parts: city services, land-use control, and city jobs. These are the principal domains in which systematic bias, if it exists, can be expected. The distinction between city services and land-use control reflects the central role that the latter plays in the growth-oriented politics of the city.

City Services

The implication of the analysis in the preceding chapters is that there is no central directing force at work shaping the behavior of city bureaucracies. By and large, elected officials are willing to allow them substantial autonomy—and, in many cases, have no choice—while land-use interests have no continuing need to pay attention to the workings of the police department or the school board, for example. There are two principal exceptions: when major land-use changes require the special attentions of a service bureaucracy, for example, the police department, to make them successful and when periods of intense fiscal strain may prompt the natural alliance between elected officials and businessmen to exert substantial control over the service bureaucracies.

Rather than a central directing force being at work, the politics of most city services is dominated by the bureaucracies themselves, acting in concert with groups that are particularly attentive to their workings. Considerable effort goes into fending off the attentions of outside politicians and businessmen, and, in the manner of bureaucracies at other levels of government, what is sought is a secure environment in which to operate.[2] The agenda of each bureaucracy is likely to be shaped by some combination of professional criteria, the demands of interest groups, organizational maintenance requirements, and the givens of the service area. Although this is likely to mean that some groups are going to be favored by the politics of a particular bureaucracy, it also

2. See James Q. Wilson, *The Investigators: Managing FBI and Narcotics Agents.*

suggests that they will not be the same groups in each case. If nothing else, those bureaucracies whose professional criteria include a strong ethic of concern for low-income clienteles and those bureaucracies in which street-level personnel deal regularly with such clientele are likely to be more attentive than are other agencies to the concerns of the worse off. The combination of a lack of strong central direction and variation in the politics of the bureaucracies themselves suggests that the overall public agenda in this domain will evidence no systematic bias.

The inequalities associated with the impact of bureaucratic routines and with the content of the public agenda are unlikely, then, to cumulate. This being so, it is also unlikely that the politics of service delivery in the city will cause the same groups of people to see themselves at risk from the general pattern of service politics. Although there will be plenty of adaptive behavior by low-income residents aimed at avoiding what is thought to be the regular manner in which police behave, for example, these sorts of adaptations probably do not occur across the board.

Studies of the distribution of municipal services also support the conclusion that there is no systematic bias in service delivery. To date, there have been major investigations of the distribution of city services across major population groupings in Oakland, San Antonio, Detroit, Houston, and Chicago. They all come to essentially the same conclusion: in the words of one of the leading students of the subject, "distributional decision making is routinized and largely devoid of explicit political content." [3] It is, instead, the impact of past decisions, population shifts, technological changes, rational technical criteria, and professional values that is largely at work. In short, the givens of the situation in which the bureaucracy operates and its character as a particular kind of bureaucracy are largely crucial. None of this adds up to systematic bias. Perhaps the best way to characterize service delivery in the city is to say that it is a matter of unpatterned inequalities: those who come out on the short end in one case do not do so in all cases. And a little reflection suggests that it would be odd if it were otherwise. Bureaucracies are, after all, defined by their efforts to operate according to rules. Systematic bias is unlikely to spring from such soil.

City Jobs

The comments on the distribution of city jobs can be brief. The two principal devices for allocating them are the civil service system

3. Kenneth Mladenka, "The Urban Bureaucracy and the Chicago Political Machine: Who Gets What and the Limits of Political Control," *American Political Science Review* 74, no. 4 (December 1980): 996.

and the politics of coalition building in the city, with the mix between them varying by the type of city political economy. Both, however, point in the same direction: new entrants into the city political arena will find it difficult to gain a share of city jobs that corresponds with either their absolute numbers or their voting strength. The reasons are not far to seek. More or less by definition, the civil service system will slow the entry of new groups into the city bureaucracy. As for coalition building, the leaders of politically dominant groups are usually adept at doling out relatively large favors to the leadership of the new groups while at the same time giving little in the way of tangible benefits to the mass of new claimants.[4] The politics of city jobs is not an engine of redistribution from those who have to those who want. The claims of the latter must wait a long time before they become the subject of public discussion and decision.[5]

This having been said, ethnic and racial succession does occur and over a period of time substantial voting strength does convert into the material benefits of jobs. And if we add to this the more obvious point that city jobs have not been the object of burning desire by the better off, the case for the city as an engine of inequality is not easy to sustain. City politics is perhaps not the great equalizer that it is sometimes made out to be, but, at least in the case of city jobs, if new claimants are sufficiently numerous and willing to wait around long enough, they will eventually get their share.

The organization of the public agenda of city politics works, then, against city jobs for newcomers, and in its early stages the bias will be systematic. But eventually members of poorer racial and ethnic groups do get access. This is confirmed by detailed studies of the allocation of city jobs. For example, Browning et al., in their investigation of black and Hispanic political struggles in cities, conclude that from 1966 to 1978 minority employment in city jobs in ten cities increased faster than minority population. This was as true for lower-level jobs as for administrative positions. Particularly suggestive are the differences between black and Hispanic populations: the latter, who are comparative newcomers, lagged behind the former in the speed with which they entered the city employment force.[6]

4. See Stephen L. Elkin, "Political Structure, Political Organization and Race," *Politics and Society* 8, no. 2 (1978): 225–51.

5. See the discussions in Steven P. Erie, "Rainbow's End: From the Old to the New Urban Ethnic Politics," in Joan W. Moore and Lionel A. Maldonado (eds.), *Urban Ethnicity: A New Era;* and Raymond Wolfinger, *The Politics of Progress,* esp. chap. 3.

6. Rufus P. Browning et al., *Protest Is Not Enough: The Struggle of Blacks and Hispanics for Equality in Urban Politics,* chap. 5.

Land-Use Control

The situation with land use is different. Here systematic bias is strongly and persistently evident, and thus there is a substantial failure of popular control. The extent of the failure is that much greater because land-use patterns are not just like the other "outputs" of city governments. They are more important to the shape of people's lives than variations in the quality of the services provided by the city. Spatial location means, among other things, access to jobs, friends, facilities, entertainment—in short to a whole environment. The importance of this access might be captured by saying that land-use patterns are not like commodities that are incidental to a life; they are, at a minimum, important contexts in which a life develops. More expansively considered, land-use patterns are integral to a person's conception of himself, to how he wishes to carry on his life: his life is *defined* by access to certain kinds of persons and activities. As such, access cannot be easily substituted for, as can a commodity. The loss of the environment in which the self has taken shape is likely to be an especially painful experience. Since in most cities city politics is now and for some time has been a matter of rearranging land use, the shape of the public agenda is a fundamental matter to the citizens of the city. Which powers and resources are to be brought to bear to influence land-use patterns matters in a way that few other public choices do.

The implication of the last three chapters is that the land-use agenda is, in fact, heavily tilted toward the land interests of the city. It is to their views that public officials are most attentive, and even when land interests are poorly organized, officials will have strong reasons to think about rearranging land use to promote city growth. As the Dallas case makes clear in a particularly vivid way, officials themselves happily will focus on city growth and, as circumstances demand, on rearranging land use. The concerns of those who can be expected to bear the principal burden of such changes are given less attention as are those who wish to argue that the growth of the city might be pursued in other ways or through other sorts of land-use projects.

Land use in the city is at the convergence of three streams of forces, and the public agenda represents the balance between them. Land is capital for those who own it or manage it, a context for the day-to-day lives of the citizens who live in the city, and a source of political benefits and revenues for the officials who govern the city. Once the mutuality of interest between those for whom land is capital and those for whom it is a benefit and revenue stream is noted, it is no great mystery that the city as community receives so little attention. Those for whom the city is a setting for their lives can of course make their concerns known to officials in their role as voters and members of interest groups, but in this they are competing not only with those for whom the city is capital but with officials who also are not focused on the city as community.

It only needs to be added that the bias of the land-use agenda also follows from what is considered to be a technical and legal matter not subject to public decision at all. If it were necessary to argue at every turn that a principal task of city government is to promote economic growth and to induce new investment, then the land-use agenda would undoubtedly look different. But the very jobs of many officials are defined in terms of responsibility for saying just these things. The principal reason why their jobs are defined this way resides in the division of labor between state and market and in the concomitant ability of capital to relocate relatively easily across regions. Said less abstractly, there would be fewer officials whose jobs are defined in terms of concern with investment and revenue—and thus fewer routine actions such as city promotional campaigns and studies of tax rebates—if the city did not need to compete for resources in the fashion that it does. The land-use agenda of the city is, at least in part, simply a question of public officials following their job specifications.

Not surprisingly, the record of the results of land-use projects parallels this characterization of the land-use agenda. There are several studies of the effects of land-use changes across the full range of cities, but their focus has been largely confined to the impact of the urban renewal program.[7] To get a sense of the full scale of land-use changes undertaken and the size of the effects on city residents, it will be more helpful to look briefly at two cities—San Francisco and Atlanta—that have been intensively studied. First, consider San Francisco.[8] As in many other older cities, one key to rearranging the land-use patterns in San Francisco was the effort to expand the central business district into the surrounding areas of lower-intensity use that typically housed the small businesses and the poorer residents of the

7. See, among others, Martin Anderson, *The Federal Bulldozer: A Critical Analysis of Urban Renewal, 1949–1962;* Scott A. Greer, *Urban Renewal and American Cities;* Heywood Sanders, "The Politics of City Redevelopment," Ph.D. diss., Harvard, 1977; and James Q. Wilson, ed., *Urban Renewal: The Record and the Controversy.*

8. For background on San Francisco politics and land-use trends, see Frederick M. Wirt, *Power in the City: Decision Making in San Francisco;* and Susan S. Fainstein et al., *Restructuring the City: The Political Economy of Urban Redevelopment.* The following discussion is based on Chester H. Hartman's, *The Transformation of San Francisco.*

city. Expansion to the west was impossible since this was the location of major hotels, and, in any case, the topography was difficult. To the north, lay the politically well-organized area of Chinatown, in addition to other difficulties, and to the east lay the Bay and wholesale-produce market. The latter proved easy to move. But the difficult and important part of the exercise was the move south into what became known as the Yerba Buena Center. At its core was to be a convention center and sports facility surrounded by office blocks. The convention center has, in fact, been built, along with some office buildings and housing for the elderly. The project, still not completed, has resulted in the displacement of some 4,000 people, the vast majority of whom were low- or modest-income residents, and some 700 businesses.

The other key to promoting the growth of the city was to rework some of the residential land-use patterns at the edge of the downtown.[9] The Western Addition (A-2) project was on land near the downtown, west of the city hall and within walking distance. The urban renewal plan called for clearing 103 of 276 acres of the project area, including two-thirds of the acres then in residential use. By 1970, some 2,000 housing units had been demolished and some 7,000 people, a substantial number of whom were low-income blacks, had been displaced. The A-2 project followed on the A-1 Western Addition project and displaced some 4,000 (mostly low-income) households and built some 1,800 new housing units, 65 percent of which were rented or sold at market rates and the rest of which were subsidized for middle-income people.[10]

The scale of these projects is suggested by the fact that they demolished 10,000 low-income housing units[11] in a city whose total population is now just over 700,000. Most of the units were either replaced by those at higher rents or not replaced at all. The answer to the question of whether the displaced residents might have gained from enhanced employment generated by the new office development is suggested by the fact that from 1965 to 1980 office growth in San Francisco created 16,000 new jobs but the number of employed residents of the city dropped by 18,000. This suggests that most of the jobs went to those who lived out of the city. So, unless taxes went down or services went up as a result of the land-

9. The discussion here is based on John H. Mollenkopf, *The Contested City*, chaps. 4, 5.

10. Susan S. Fainstein, Norman I. Fainstein, and P. Jefferson Armistead, "San Francisco: Urban Transformation and the Local 'State' " in Fainstein et al., *Restructuring the City*, 218.

11. Hartman, *The Transformation of San Francisco*, 231.

use changes, the displaced residents gained little if anything. It is difficult to say much about the impact of the changes on city services, but we do know that the central business district's share of property taxes for the period 1965 to 1980 *fell* from 21.3 percent to 13.3 percent of the total. The question of compensation is not so easily disposed of and will be picked up again in a moment, but it is worth emphasizing that these figures are hardly comforting to those who wish to argue that significant changes in land use generate benefits for virtually all residents of the city.

The outline of Atlanta's alteration of its land-use patterns is not markedly different from that of San Francisco's; the same themes of expanding the central business district and eliminating low-income residences from the core of the city appear. In the case of Atlanta, however, there is an estimate available of the impact of all major public projects, not just of several large ones, as in San Francisco. It is estimated that from 1956 to 1966 21,000 families were displaced by governmental action in the city. This is on the order of one-fifth of the population of the city during that period.[12] This is simply an extraordinary figure—and any discussion of the supposed benefits of city-growth strategies built around land-use change must come to terms with it.

Those not yet convinced that both the land-use agenda and its results evidence systematic bias might also wish to contemplate that New York City has recently awarded $500 million in tax abatements to encourage businesses to remain in the city.[13] What is taken away with one hand—residences—is also taken away with the other, namely, potential tax revenues to support city services.

The effects of land-use changes are not confined to those that are a direct consequence of the exercise of governmental authority. Although large numbers of residents of the city will not be directly affected by land-use changes (though many more will be than typically is supposed), they will not be equally well placed to adapt to these changes. So, while one's home and job may remain intact, shops may be moved or their nature changed. For those with resources, reasonable and not markedly more expensive substitutes are available, whereas for whose with limited resources, this is unlikely to be the case.

The question of compensation for the various sorts of burdens discussed up to this point must now be faced. After all, land-use

12. Clarence N. Stone, *Economic Growth and Neighborhood Discontent: System Bias in the Urban Renewal Program of Atlanta*, 237.
13. *New York Times*, May 4, 1983. The Industrial and Commercial Investment Board, which awards the abatements, began operating in 1977.

changes are not advertised as being for the benefit of a selected few. They are presented in the language of the common good, and those who are inclined to believe—or, indeed, to make— such claims cannot be dismissed out of hand as being either deeply cynical or hopelessly naive. Might it not be true that one gives up one's home in the service of some future benefit—perhaps for a better job or for more city taxes, which will come back in the form of a safer neighborhood? Thus, the argument might go, however important land-use patterns are to the lives of city residents and however much the land-use agenda reflects projects that are to the taste of land interests, it is either wrong or incomplete to conclude that this is a case of systematic bias. Some of these considerations have been addressed above, but there are some general remarks that can be made about the nature of such arguments.

It seems reasonable to assume that people do not wish to move house or change jobs except as they choose to do so. So the question of whether someone can be said to approve of being displaced because he looks to future benefits (which is the form that the argument most often takes) depends on the understanding of "choice" in this context. The easiest way to make the point is to say that compensation for what one loses may assuage one's pain at a loss but is not the same thing as choosing to undergo the pain in order to get the prospective benefit. Of course, a person may in fact weigh up what he is losing and his prospective gain and in a meaningful sense choose to undergo the present loss for the future gain. The crucial point is simply that we cannot infer that he has made such a choice from the fact that he has in fact received a gain great enough to bring him out ahead (which, in the present context, is doubtful in any case). People who accept post-facto compensation for automobile accidents that make them rich cannot be said to have chosen to undergo the accident. In much the same way, rational individuals who are thinking about the promised gain of relinquishing their homes will be aware that the gain is in the long run. And even if they have not heard of Keynes, they will no doubt reflect, with him, that in the long run we are all dead. In this they will be more realistic than those who argue that in the end benefits will be widely distributed.

The bias in the land-use agenda persists even if major land-use projects have come to a halt, as they probably have in many cities. Bias consists of the difficulty of substituting some other conception of how the powers and resources of the city shall be used in shaping land-use patterns—some conception that less closely follows the preferences of land interests and their allies among city officials.

The flaw in the workings of popular control is that even if the land-use alliance is not for the moment in a position to engineer major land-use changes, it is still in a position to prevent the emergence of any other conception of the use of city powers. The new cannot be born even if the old is, for the moment, less ambitious than it has been.

PROBLEM SOLVING

The success or failure of popular control is not confined to matters of systematic bias, since the benefits of government are not confined to parceling out goods and services to particular persons and groups. City residents face collective problems, difficulties that, if not dealt with, will reduce the well-being of all. The distinction made by economists between private and public goods captures what is at issue.

What is the connection between effective problem solving and popular control? The simplest answer is that popular control is itself an organized way of solving social problems. Popular control is a mode of coordination, the way in which some collectivity is organized to consider the alternatives before it and decide on them. Of course, it may not do either of these in a conscious way, constructing a decision-making process designed to array the alternatives and choose among them. The point is simpler: coordination can take place without a central, directing mind, and thus problem solving is a generic aspect of all sorts of interactions. What from one viewpoint are relations of political control are, from another viewpoint, efforts at coordination as a means of coping with social problems.[14] Politics here meets problem solving.

An important implication of the coincidence of control and co-ordination is that, if the operation of popular control is systematically biased, problem solving is also likely to be ineffective, simply because some desirable alternatives will go unexplored. This is, of course, what is happening in cities: one version of how to make cities grow dominates and others—which might either spread the costs differently or involve something different than rearranging land use with an eye particularly to downtown development—are given little or no consideration.[15]

14. The premier statement in this regard is by Charles E. Lindblom. See *The Intelligence of Democracy* and *Politics and Markets*.

15. For some other possibilities and comments on the shortcomings of presently employed strategies, see Jane Jacobs, *Cities and the Wealth of Na-*

Any of the cities heretofore mentioned could provide an example of the domination of one solution to the problem of how to make cities grow economically, since a principal point of the preceding discussion has been that this is fundamental to what cities have in common. But a little detail, in the form of a brief description of Detroit, will prove useful here. First, consider that Detroit has been experiencing a significant decline in employment, from 630,000 in 1968 to 421,000 in 1977, a fall of 33 percent.[16] This correlates with an increase in both permanent unemployment and the welfare case load. Additionally, there has been a major fiscal crunch, with capital leaving the city, budget shortfalls, and property evaluations falling behind revenue needs.[17] Here, then, is a city with more than the usual need to promote city growth, and one in which doing so will have large collective benefits. Not doing anything will make virtually everyone worse off, not least by making the city an increasingly unpleasant place to be as a consequence of the resulting concentration of misery and anger.

In common with other cities, Detroit has adopted what might be termed a corporate-center strategy.[18] The underlying conception is to transform an aging industrial city into a modern headquarters city with the latter's attendant service sector, young professionals, and luxury consumption. This is, in short, the sort of city that corporate elites would like to work in, that they possibly might want to live in, and that they assume that their managers will also prefer. In other cities, the energy for promoting this conception is less likely to come from corporate leaders and more likely to come from the variety of other land interests, but the results are much the same. The centrality of the automobile industry to the Detroit economy explains the difference.[19]

Two comments are worth making about the strategy adopted. First, even if the overall conception of how to promote economic growth is granted, the mix of projects chosen is not exactly self-evident. The emphasis on the Renaissance Center, a development of hotels, shops and offices, betrays more a taste for making busi-

---

tions; Katharine L. Bradbury et al., *Urban Decline and the Future of American Cities;* and Todd Swanstrom, *The Crisis of Growth Politics.* See also the discussion in chap. 9 below.

16. Richard Child Hill, "Crisis in the Motor City," in Fainstein et al., *Restructuring the City.*

17. See the account of some of the roots of Detroit's fiscal dilemma in *Business Week,* June 29, 1981.

18. Robert Fitch, "Planning New York," in Roger A. Alcaly and David Mermelstein (eds.), *The Fiscal Crisis of American Cities.*

19. On Detroit politics, in addition to Hill, see Thomas J. Anton, *Federal Aid to Detroit;* and Bryan Jones and Lynn Bachelor, *The Sustaining Hand.*

ness decisions in pleasant surroundings than a serious concern for generating jobs. Beyond the short-lived construction jobs, it is hard to see how a local economy with a skilled industrial work force is going to gain very much.[20]

More telling, perhaps, is that the strategy itself is so oriented to restructuring land use. The model is one of building infrastructure and providing attractive parcels of land, along with attendent incentives to build on them. There is, of course, some connection between such construction and city economic activity, but it is not as obvious as the actions taken would suggest. At a minimum, there is some evidence—and certainly much belief—that fostering educational and entrepreneurial skills might do a good deal more to promote growth. But such nonphysical approaches receive little attention. Like some other cities, Detroit is like nothing so much as a third-world country that equates wealth with physical structures. This is, to say the least, strange in an economy whose managers (at some level) certainly know better. Popular control as it operates in cities does not allow such knowledge to shape the agenda of problem solving. Not surprisingly, it does not work much better in Detroit than in Africa.

As Lisa Peattie and her colleagues comment, development planning is difficult to do and far from generally supported. There are, they comment, a number of competing conceptions of what city planning should be about, but "development planning—i.e., planning for business—consistently remains the central concern of city government."[21] Increasingly, even in newer cities such as Dallas— where perhaps it once might have been argued that the strategies adopted for promoting growth made a good deal of sense—the signs are now apparent that they are starting on or are already well into the bricks-and-mortar version of city politics. The workings of popular control strongly dispose cities to such limited conceptions of the economic vitality of the city.

CONCLUSION

The promise of popular control of political authority is that it will make the benefits of collective life widely available and will draw on

20. Two extensive reviews of the financial difficulties of the Center can be found in the *New York Times* for July 4, 1983, and September 1, 1986. The Center has had difficulty holding major retailers, and its owners have twice defaulted on mortgages.

21. Lisa Peattie et al., "Development Planning as the Only Game in Town," *Journal of Planning, Education and Research* 5, no. 1 (Autumn 1985): 17.

the intelligence of a wide range of citizens. Focusing particularly on
the use of land—which is so central both to the politics of cities and
to the lives of its citizens—cities evidence serious failings of popular
control because they do not honor these promises. Of paramount
importance are the common roots of these failings of city political
institutions: both systematic bias and limited social intelligence stem
from the historically constructed political-economic arrangements
that strongly shape how city politics is carried on. Thus the failings
are, in large part, systemic and can be traced to, among other things,
that definition of property rights that provides significant incentives
for public officials to join in alliance with city businessmen. The
question of property rights will occupy our attention again below.
Here I want to emphasize that efforts to improve political equality
in the city will be doubly rewarded. Because of the common roots
just noted, the result will be not only that the benefits and burdens
of collective life will not be systematically skewed but also that there
will be an increased chance for canvassing a wider range of views
regarding how to make the city vital economically and in other ways.
In the same vein, leaving the political institutions of the city as they
are is to incur two losses. To talk, then, of a trade-off between equality and efficiency is to employ a misleading abstraction. When the
actual political arrangements by which equality and efficiency are
generated are entered into the equation, it is apparent that we are
dealing neither with distinct processes nor distinct results. Not surprisingly, at least in this regard, political life is all of a piece. Benefits
cumulate as do failures.

The reasons for systematic bias and limited social intelligence are
not to be found in a kind of economic determinism in which cities
are assumed to respond to the economic facts of life in the only
way that makes sense. The argument here is more complex: things
look as they do because of a complex of inherited structural factors,
important among which is how officials get and stay elected. Officials pursue the policies that they do because the structural features within which they work dispose them to certain interpretations.
The facts of economic life for the city offer choices regarding how
to respond, but some kinds of choices—particularly a bricks-and-
mortar strategy—have the inside track. A belief in the supposedly
inexorable march of economic reality is the basis for arguments
that, to get equality, some efficiency must be sacrificed. One must,
that is, do something other than what the facts of economic life
supposedly dictate. The discussion of the last several chapters points
in a different direction—not to the reign of necessity, but to that
of interpretation. The roots of the city's failures are not in the

necessity of earning its keep but in how that impulse gets translated into action.

The political life of the city has, then, its own very important weight. Moreover, this conclusion, and the reasoning on which it rests, have a significance beyond the present discussion. The same worries about economic determinism and trade-offs will emerge in the later analysis of the city and citizenship. There too it will become apparent that, in the pursuit of a secure material foundation for the city, we need not trade off some measure of concern for the kind of citizenship necessary for a commercial republic to flourish. The sad thing in all this is that it is thought to be necessary to exchange the coin of political equality (and of appropriate citizenship) for that of effective problem solving. It is doubly sad because the supposed gains are mostly chimerical.[22]

Others have reached more benign conclusions about city politics. It would be tedious to inquire at length into why this is so. At the core of such views, however, are probably two beliefs. The first belief is that, since businessmen play so important a role in the politics of the city—and, indeed, are crucial to deciding on and carrying out a wide range of the most important policy choices, in short because they are much like public officials—they should be similarly understood. That is, it is appropriate to see them as actors whose concerns are citywide rather than parochial. That many businessmen have such large concerns is true. And indeed, at their best, they may act, as the Dallas case shows, in ways that are not overwhelmingly tainted by naked self-interest. But there is as much reason to inquire into such claims as there is to inquire into the claims of clubhouse political hacks that they speak for the commonweal even while they put in their bids for more patronage.

The second belief is that, since the benefits of at least some land-use schemes are immediate and large and the costs difficult to see, an inference can be made about the full run of development projects. Notions about compensation and long-run benefits smooth the way. In much the same way, since it seems that officials and businessmen are so naturally drawn to each other, the slide between what is natural and what is acceptable is easily made. The preceding discussion has offered at least some reasons why such convenient transitions need to be treated skeptically. More generally, it has offered reasons why skepticism is the appropriate response to ar-

22. See Todd Swanstrom, "Semi-Sovereign Cities: The Political Logic of Urban Development"; and Marie Howland, "Property Taxes and the Birth and Intraregional Location of New Firms."

guments that cities must devote themselves to growth strategies
while other levels of government handle whatever problems of
inequality are to be found in the city. The difficulty is simply that
the two cannot be so neatly separated. There is good reason to
believe that growth strategies themselves contribute to inequality.

Resistance to these arguments about the shortcomings of popular
control in cities might also come from those who would point to
the efforts in some cities to alter systematic bias and to advance
more effective strategies for promoting city growth. They might
point to recent efforts in Boston to link downtown development to
aid for the city's poor[23] or to innovative planning efforts in Hartford
and other cities, where those calling themselves progressives have
attempted to reorganize the way in which city politics is practiced.[24]
There is nothing in such efforts that is inconsistent with the analysis
offered here. Electoral coalitions that have at their heart something
other than rearranging land use to favor downtown interests are
certainly possible. Politicians in cities *are* independent, not in the
employ of land interests, and if there is sufficient public interest
they can and will attempt to join their fate to that of other forces.

The problem is not whether aspiring politicians can run for office
on some other platform and get elected. It is not easy, but they
can. The problem, instead, is to sustain such efforts over any period
of time. The difficulty is that eventually even officials otherwise
committed will be drawn to large land-use schemes. This will be
not so much because of the influence that land interests can wield
and the campaign contributions they can offer, although these will
help. But there are other forces at work as well: the exigencies of
coalition building make large land-use projects attractive; and land
interests and their schemes will look like an appealing way to keep
mobile investors in the city and to attract new ones. Officials thus
are likely to find their attention wandering down the paths suggested by land interests.

The battlefield of city politics is not flat but is tilted toward an
alliance of public officials and land interests. Those who want it

23. Which, it must be noted, has recently been overturned by the Mas-
sachusetts Superior Court. The decision was, however, overturned on appeal (*Bonan et al. v. City of Boston et al.* 398 Mass. 315, 496 N.E. ad. 640
[1986]), but the substantive merits of the linkage concept were not adju-
dicated. The Supreme Judicial Court suggested that the City of Boston
seek authorization from the state legislature, where the matter now rests.
In San Francisco similar efforts have been made to tie downtown development to neighborhood investment. Some cities have also started to impose exactions for purposes in addition to housing.

24. See Pierre Clavel, *The Progressive City.*

any other way must push uphill, whereas such an alliance only has to sit still and wait until the task of pushing the rock up the incline grows too burdensome. This alliance is the status quo. Others who seek new political arrangements are thereby considered to be radical. And, in addition, they must sustain their efforts and win at most if not at every turn. They must also build electoral coalitions, maintain them, and make them do some work. The natural order of things in city politics, therefore, is for the alliance between public officials and land interests to be in business.

The shortcomings of popular control in cities contribute to failings in the national political economy, and this is perhaps the saddest comment of all. It is in cities that the relative concentration of the have-nots might be expected to count politically, for numbers are, after all, their prime resource, as theorists from Aristotle to Dahl have pointed out. But the structural factors that make city politics what it is strongly militate against a politics that is attentive to those with limited resources. Thus, to the systematic bias characteristic of national politics must be added that of cities. In much the same way, the limits on intelligent social problem solving in cities are especially unsettling, since city governments provide the services that, in a day-to-day way, most affect the lives of the citizenry. A high order of social problem solving by city officials and citizens is, then, particularly important. But what one notices instead is a dreary sameness: cities do much the same things for much the same reasons. Again, structural factors are at work.

6
City and Regime

The works of Tocqueville and Mill suggest that understanding the connection between popular control in cities and liberal democracy is not exhausted by a discussion of systematic bias and intelligent problem solving. Each points to a connection between the way in which popular control is organized in cities and the kind of citizenry that is needed for popular government to flourish. To the degree that the political institutions[1] of the city do not contribute to the fostering of such a citizenry, another shortcoming of popular control in cities comes into view, a shortcoming that is likely to be particularly significant since it suggests that any failure will directly affect the entire political order.

The arguments of these theorists can be interpreted as saying that city political institutions must be considered in light of a possible contribution that they can make to the larger political whole. City political institutions have a *specific* role to play and therefore an intrinsic significance. What might this specific contribution be, and how is it connected to the question of citizenship?

The analysis presented to this point is not well equipped to answer this question. Its premises do not easily allow discussion of the particularities of political institutions, of the specific contribution that they might make to the larger political order. There is, in fact, a strong homogenizing tendency at work in the analysis. On its basis, it cannot be said whether, if popular control was strengthened outside of cities so that systematic bias and ineffectiveness were alleviated, anything of consequence would be lost. The analysis points away from consideration of cities as such toward the question of whether popular control is adequate overall. It thus does not rule out the extreme conclusion that cities might appropriately be administrative

1. By "political institutions" I mean the regular patterns that make up the exercise of authority in the city. These institutional arrangements define not only the municipal corporation but other governments that exercise authority within its boundaries.

102

units of a central authority. More generally, the underlying point of view has been that political institutions are to be judged by their problem-solving capabilities and by whether their workings are systematically biased. The implication is that, in the pursuit of better problem solving or political equality, one institution can be substituted for another.

This all becomes clear when the issue of reform is squarely posed. The implication is that the task is to balance a variety of considerations. For example, it may be easier to reduce systematic bias outside of cities than inside them, and this needs to be balanced against the loss of local knowledge if decisions are made by other than city authorities. In addition, scale needs to be balanced against the diversity of constituencies. What is lost by having decisions made by people far from the scene might be compensated by a greater chance to find, in the enlarged sphere, allies for those who have lost out locally.[2] Overall, the balance might point to the choice of expanding the reach of larger governmental units into cities and strengthening the apparatus of popular control in these units so that the decisions that they make for cities will evidence less systematic bias than is presently the case. As it happens, this has been the tendency during the postwar period, when the effort has been made to strengthen popular control nationally to compensate for the bias that characterizes city politics.[3] An analysis of problem solving would look much the same way: forms of popular control would be treated as essentially interchangeable devices whose merits are to be judged by comparisons with the alternatives available and in light of the circumstances that impede or enhance problem solving for each of them.

Not surprisingly, then, what has proved useful in answering one set of questions is not helpful for another. As long as the focus has been *within the city*, the homogenizing tendency has actually been helpful, since it points to how all aspects of institutions contribute to a single outcome. Comparisons are thus facilitated. But once the discussion turns to the intrinsic significance of city political institutions— that is, to particularities—a different frame of reference is required. It will not do to pursue a line of argument that, in effect, precludes any consideration of the intrinsic significance of political institutions.[4]

2. See, e.g., Robert A. Dahl, "The City in the Future of Democracy," *The American Political Science Review* 61, no. 4 (December 1967): 953–70, on the advantages of small scale and Grant McConnell, *Private Power and American Democracy*, on the advantages of large constituencies.
3. There have been limits to this expansion, the sources of which will be considered in the next chapter.
4. The larger argument here concerns the limits of a wholly instrumental

To give content to the intrinsic significance of city political institutions requires a substantive understanding of the larger political order. The discussion of systematic bias and effective problem solving could proceed without reference to the specific character of a popular government, since it is reasonable to assume that *any* popular government should not be characterized by systematic bias and ineffective problem solving. When it comes to cities, these aspects of popular control can thus be discussed as abstracted from the larger political order, in the instrumental terms just noted. But any consideration of the intrinsic significance of city political institutions requires an answer to the question, Significant for what? If the answer is to be compelling, a substantive account of the larger political whole is necessary. There is a second, even more obvious requirement before there can be discussion of the intrinsic significance of city political institutions— namely, a conception of political institutions that suggests in what sense they are not interchangeable devices.

The following formulation meets both requirements: political institutions help to form a political way of life to which we aspire.[5] It suggests the intrinsic significance of political institutions—and thus the sense in which they are not interchangeable—by pointing to what might be called their formative bearing. A substantive conception of the larger political whole is suggested by the idea of aspiration for a political way of life. The two are joined together by the implied question, What political way of life do we wish to form?

The task now is to build on this formulation so that a conception of what city political institutions might contribute can be offered. Once this has been accomplished, the question of the adequacy of the present political institutions of the city can be addressed, as can the more specific question of whether popular control in cities evidences shortcomings over and above the ones already considered. To pursue this task requires that discussion turn away from cities to address what is meant when it is said that political institutions are formative; then, in light of how the larger political economy actually operates, what these institutions are supposed to form and what the implications of these aspirations are must be considered. These topics will occupy the rest

---

analysis of political life. See the arguments of Laurence Tribe, "Technology Assessment and the Fourth Discontinuity: The Limits of Instrumental Rationality," *Southern California Law Review* 46, no. 3 (June 1973): 617–60; Alasdair MacIntyre, *After Virtue;* and Jurgen Habermas, *Knowledge and Human Interests.* See also Stephen L. Elkin, "Economic and Political Rationality," *Polity* 18, no. 2 (Winter 1985): 253–71.

5. As to who "we" are, see the discussion below where the comments of Judith Shklar are quoted.

of this chapter and all of the subsequent one. Then the discussion can turn back to cities.

FORMATIVE INSTITUTIONS

That political institutions are formative has long been recognized. It is central to the thought of such students of republican government as Tocqueville and Montesquieu.[6] Closer to home, the Anti-Federalist Melancton Smith commented that "government operates upon the spirit of the people, as well as the spirit of the people operates upon it."[7] Two modern voices echo the point. In the contemporary idiom of the social scientist, Robert Lane flatly asserts that "the idea that governments could, even if they wanted to, fail to shape personality is vacuous. Every framework of government, every constitution, necessarily embraces and reinforces a theory of personality."[8] And George Kateb, reflecting the concern of contemporary political philosophers with the justification of representative democracy, says, "We may say then that constitutional representative democracy helps to foster certain traits of character and hence certain ways of being in the world that no other form of government does."[9]

Writing about social policy, Richard Titmuss provides a vivid example of the formative bearing of institutions. In this case, the institution is the system of blood giving in the United Kingdom that is based on voluntary donations of blood to unknown others. Titmuss can be interpreted as saying that the institution embodies and fosters an ongoing series of actions—the giving of blood to strangers or a "gift relationship"—that helps to define how the members of the society stand in relation to one another; they stand, that is, not only as consumers and producers but as fellow citizens who have certain obligations to each other. The giving of blood—and thus the institution that defines and embodies it—reinforces, through a kind of symbolic reiteration, a certain sort of relationship, one that we might

6. Alexis de Tocqueville, *Democracy in America*, esp. 2: Books 2–4; and Montesquieu, *The Spirit of the Laws*, particularly Book XIX, "Of Laws in Relation to the Principles Which Form the General Spirit, the Morals, and Customs of a Nation."

7. Quoted in Herbert Storing, *What the Anti-Federalists Were For*, 19. Storing himself comments on p. 21, "More often the Anti-Federalists thought of the whole organization of the polity as having an educative function."

8. Robert E. Lane, "Market and Politics: The Human Product," *British Journal of Political Science* 11, no. 1 (January 1981): 12.

9. George Kateb, "The Moral Distinctiveness of Representative Democracy," *Ethics* 91, no. 3 (April 1981): 363.

call fellowship. Titmuss himself makes the essential point when he comments that "social gifts and actions carrying no explicit or implicit individual right to a return gift or action are creative in the sense that the self is realized with the help of anonymous others." [10]

Lon Fuller's discussion of the internal morality of law is also suggestive in this context. For relations between citizens to be lawful, according to Fuller, they must be characterized by, among other things, publicness in the proclamation of and absence of contradictions in the law. These procedural moralities are necessary if there is to be genuine law—as opposed to mere statements made by those who have the ability to enforce them. Law for Fuller is not the one-way projection of the sovereign's will but a certain sort of relation between citizens and lawgivers. [11] A people governed by law will be a people for whom certain procedural forms characterize relationships. Fuller goes on to imply that these procedural forms will develop over time, as efforts to make law give rise to expectations about such matters as publicness, expectations that spring from the idea of law itself. Citizens and lawgivers learn to organize their affairs according to law by attempting to do so. [12]

From its prominent place in the thought of some of the foremost early theorists of republican government, however, the importance of the formative bearing of political institutions has receded in the minds of most contemporary political scientists. The reasons are not far to seek. The emphases on who gets what and on preference aggregation both treat political institutions as instrumental, as devices that only have the life that is breathed into them by their users or participants. From this perspective, a conception of institutions as having intrinsic significance and being active is difficult to accept. To make matters worse, insofar as the ideas are grasped, they are thought to be frightening. As Robert Lane puts it, "the thought of governmental shaping of character is unattractive," conjuring as it does the possibility of the creation of new socialist or fascist men and of religious communities preoccupied with the state of men's souls. [13]

The comments of these various students of political institutions strike several notes, from Lane's strongly psychological focus to Fuller's more institutional conception. It is possible that these are simply different

10. Richard M. Titmuss, *The Gift Relationship*, 212.

11. Lon L. Fuller, *The Morality of Law;* and "Human Interaction and the Law," in Kenneth I. Winston (ed.), *The Principles of Social Order: Selected Essays of Lon L. Fuller*, esp. 234–35.

12. For a parallel line of argument, see Philip Selznick, *Law, Society, and Industrial Justice*.

13. Lane, "Market and Politics", 12.

ways of talking about the same thing. Certainly we are talking about a family of ideas around the common theme of institutions being not merely the setting of political activity but the direct shapers of the form of political activity and thus of the citizenry acting within them. In any case, it will be useful to distinguish the different themes being struck— especially the psychological and the institutional, since, at first glance, they point to different directions for study.

The most common version of the idea of the formative effect of political institutions is that participation in certain sorts of political decision making, most notably democratic types, has effects on the moral and psychological qualities of those who participate. This is a major theme of many advocates of participatory democracy, who emphasize such results of democratic decision making as an increased feeling of political efficacy. A sense of this psychological version of the formative view is provided in Carole Pateman's remark that, in the view of participatory theorists, "the human results that accrue through the participatory process provide an important justification for a participatory system." [14] By way of contrast, consider the comment of Lon Fuller: "We should not conceive of an institution as a kind of conduit directing human energies toward some single destination. Nor can the figure be rescued by imagining a multipurpose pipeline discharging its diverse contents through different outlets. Instead we have to see an institution as an active thing, projecting itself into a field of interacting forces, reshaping those forces in diverse ways and in varying degrees. A social institution makes of human life itself something that it would not otherwise have been." [15]

In the formulations of theorists such as Lane and those who emphasize the effects of institutions on individual attributes, it is the formation of individual character that is being emphasized, [16] whereas in the case of Fuller it is the character of the collectivity, its formation. The emphasis in the first formulations is intrapsychic, in the second it is collective (that is, on the forms of relation that define the citizenry

14. Carole Pateman, *Participation and Democratic Theory*, 25. See also the discussions in Jane Mansbridge, *Beyond Adversarial Democracy;* and Robert A. Dahl, *A Preface to Economic Democracy,* 94–101.

15. Lon L. Fuller, "Means and Ends," in Winston (ed.), *The Principles of Social Order,* 54.

16. In addition to the paper by Lane cited above, see his "Government and Self-Esteem," *Political Theory* 10, no. 1 (February 1982): 5–31,"Interpersonal Relations and Leadership in a Cold 'Society,' " *Comparative Politics* 10, no. 4 (July 1973): 443–59, "Markets and the Satisfaction of Human Wants," *Journal of Economic Issues* 12, no. 4 (December 1978): 799–827, and "Autonomy, Felicity, Futility: The Effects of the Market Economy on Political Personality," *Journal of Politics* 40, no. 1 (1978): 2–24.

as a certain sort of citizenry). The basic difference is suggested by noting that in the psychological version the formative effects are a by-product of institutional processes whereas in the institutional version it is the nature of the processes themselves that is in focus. The psychological view directs our attention to the processes by which individuals are formed, whereas the institutional view directs us to the conditions necessary for the institutions to operate. In this latter, relational view, once institutions are operating, they are formative simply because they help to define the manner in which the citizenry regard one another.

The two versions of the "formative" theme reflect two meanings of that term. One meaning of "formative" is educational or tutelary; the other is "to make a thing what it is," [17] in other words to give it form. It is this last meaning that is of principal concern here. It points to what may be called a constitutive view of political institutions, a conception that emphasizes that these institutions help to form the citizenry.

In a constitutive view, political institutions such as legislatures are forms of activity through which citizens are brought into relation with one another; they help to define the manner in which members of a collectivity are to take account of one another. Political institutions are like constitutive rules.[18] Such a rule both creates a certain sort of activity and says how it shall be performed if it is to be that kind of activity. A constitutive rule does more, that is, than regulate previously existing activity. In much the same way, political institutions bring into being forms of activity.

From any individual's point of view, the members of a political community are overwhelmingly "unknown others." [19] They are neither friends nor lovers, but strangers. But what sort of strangers? In what relation do they stand? as bargainers engaged in political exchange? as partisans attempting to impose their views? as deliberators in a forum? Political institutions help to provide the answer by defining the forms of relation in which citizens stand.

Each form of relation poses an implicit question. To take two simplified cases, in an exchange relation the question posed to each

17. This is part of the Oxford English Dictionary's definition.
18. See Elkin, "Economic and Political Rationality." For a parallel discussion in philosophy, see John Rawls, "Two Concepts of Rules," *Philosophical Review* 64, no. 1 (January 1955): 3–22; John Searle, *Speech Acts*, 33–42; and Hannah Fenichel Pitkin, *Wittgenstein and Justice*, chap. 2. See also Laurence Tribe, "Technology Assessment and the Fourth Discontinuity," *Southern California Law Review* 46, no. 3 (June 1973): 617–60.
19. Titmuss, *The Gift Relationship*, esp. chap. 13 ("Who Is My Stranger?").

individual is what he or she wants for him or herself—whereas in certain sorts of public forums, the question is what an individual thinks the community ought to have. Concomitantly, the form of relation might emphasize the seeking of quid pro quos or the giving of reasons. Overall, institutions make available certain ways of experiencing others. And for those not directly involved in the interactions, they teach the lesson of what those most visible in the society consider as valuable. It is reasonable to say that we will be a different sort of people if we come to understand what we want as individuals through participating in and observing exchange relations or through participating in and observing deliberative ones.

In much the same way, political institutions ask us to use language in different ways. In deliberative institutions, language is used in an effort to say what something is, to name it. For example, Is it just or efficient? In exchange-based institutions, language is used not to develop collective definitions but as an instrument to identify and pursue the interests of individual actors. Language is essentially manipulative. In bureaucracies, language is used to interpret existing rules. Since from one point of view a community is a network of language, how it is used is essential to defining that community. How we talk to one another is crucial to who we are.

Cicero makes the fundamental point when he comments that "a people is not any collection of human beings brought together in any sort of way." [20] In helping to form a people, political institutions are thus both means and ends. In their formative bearing, they concern the morality of a people—or, perhaps it is best to say, their mores.

The emphasis in a constitutive view of political institutions, I have said, is on the decision processes themselves. The important questions, then, are how political institutions come into being, how they may be created, and of what sorts of actions they are composed. The concern is with ways of carrying on collective life and their creation. The working assumption is that, once an institution is created, its effects carry over outside its specific domain in the form of habits and dispositions. This assumption plainly assumes that a certain psychology is at work and also that no countervailing forces are present to prevent the transfer. In the nature of the case, the latter must be a matter of empirical investigation. The psychological assumption is no more complicated than an assertion that what people come to expect of themselves in one context they will transfer to other contexts and that these expectations will be generalized to include all those involved in the new context.

20. Marcus Tullius Cicero, *The Republic* I, XXV 39. Loeb Classical ed., 65.

POLITICAL ASPIRATIONS

Political institutions help to form what may be called the political way
of life of a people. But we as Americans do not wish for just *any*
political way of life. We aspire to one that is worthy of us.[21] I will call
the desired political way of life the "regime." It encompasses what
exists insofar as it conforms to our aspirations, and thus the term has
both an empirical and a normative dimension.[22]

It is not necessary here to provide a full account of the political
way of life to which we aspire. All that is needed is a characterization
that can provide a basis for answering the question of what specific
contribution, if any, city political institutions can make to the regime.
Therefore, at present it is not important to consider how systematic
bias and social intelligence fit into our aspirations.[23] Restricting the
discussion in this fashion has the additional advantage of increasing
the likelihood that the proffered account of our aspirations will secure
wide agreement.

What political way of life, then, do we believe is worthy of us, and
on what do these aspirations rest? There are a variety of possible
starting points for answering the question, but the most accessible is
the observation that we possess some experience of what we aspire
to be, some concrete understanding that arises out of what we already
have in common. Much of our sense of what we desire to be arises
out of that which is implicit or intimated in present political practice.[24]
We are not simply standing around, with each of us offering up
versions of our aspirations; we already stand in some particular political relationship to each other, and our aspirations are shaped by
this fact. Our reflections start from *these* practices, not from just any
practices. Moreover, if our aspirations are to be worthy of *us*, then

21. Sotirios A. Barber, *On What the Constitution Means;* Joseph Cropsey, "The
United States as Regime," in Robert Horowitz (ed.), *The Moral Foundations of
American Politics;* and Stephen L. Elkin, "Regulation as a Political Question,"
Policy Sciences 18, no. 1 (March 1985): 95–108.

22. Aristotle (*Politics*, 1289a) says that a regime is "the regulation of offices
in a city, with respect to the way in which they are distributed, what is sovereign
in the regime, and what the end of each community is." I will reserve the
term "political economy," as in the phrase "the American political economy,"
for the political economic whole as it actually operates in all its features.

23. In the last chapter, I will discuss some connections between the various
aspects—both instrumental and constitutive—of political institutions and suggest some of the implications for our aspirations.

24. Michael Oakeshott, *Rationalism in Politics, and Other Essays;* and Michael
Walzer, *Spheres of Justice: A Defense of Pluralism and Equality,* chap. 1.

the problem of defining them is not an abstract one, a matter of thinking about a people that is situated nowhere in particular. Instead, we must think in terms of where we are now—that is, in terms of what we can presently accomplish given our political organization, virtues, and vices. In short, as Oakeshott makes clear, we are not able to be importers of political regimes, to be what he calls "rationalists." [25]

We puzzle and struggle, then, over the meaning of our political tradition. As we attempt to resolve our historically given difficulties, we argue about the connection between our political tradition and the larger body of political principles that tie us to political orders like our own. And in this effort, we are not precluded from moving beyond such reflections to a critique of the liberal democratic principles that we share with these other systems.

Our aspirations, while deriving, to be sure, from habits and conventions, are not, therefore, merely a restatement of current practices. They are also a product of reason. So, not just any version of what our present practices imply will serve, since not all of us wish to "exchange reasons" or are in a position "to think clearly," as Sotirios Barber nicely puts it. [26] What matters, as James Boyd White says, "is not the other witnesses who can be brought forward to support your view or mine but whether you can make me your witness or I can make you mine." [27] Being reasonable, we also know that our aspirations should be subject to revision. This tentative quality means that they are subject to further test. They are, after all, only our aspirations as they have been worked out in our history.

Philip Bobbitt's description of the physicist John Wheeler's version of the game Twenty Questions provides a useful summary of how historically given practices and reason intermesh in our efforts to define our aspirations. [28] In Wheeler's version, according to Bobbitt, the players agree that they will not agree in advance on any word at all. Each can respond yes or no as he pleases to inquiries by the questioner, but whatever he replies must be consistent with a word that he has in mind and with all the replies made by others that precede it. Bobbitt likens the game to the process of constitutional decision, to which I would add that it is also illuminating of the political reasoning that informs our aspirations. Such reasoning is collective and constrained by what has gone before in the sense of

25. Oakeshott, *Rationalism in Politics.*
26. Barber, *On What the Constitution Means,* 170.
27. James Boyd White, *When Words Lose Their Meaning,* 102.
28. Philip Bobbitt, *Constitutional Fate,* 238.

commitments made, particularly to the political practices that already shape us. It is a form of *practical* reason, since the question being decided is how we ought to live together given our circumstances.[29]

The brief account offered here concerning the sources of our aspirations parallels the formulations of a variety of theorists who, it is important to note, write from a variety of philosophical perspectives. And so Judith Shklar, who is inclined to approach questions of political theory through commentary on a variety of texts, including literary ones, asks, "Who are the 'we' of whom I seem to talk so confidently?" She answers that we are the people "who are familiar with the political practices of the United States and who show their adherence to them by discussing them critically, indeed relentlessly." She goes on to say that "we can draw on a considerable range of other possibilities to sharpen our political imagination" and that, as a result of our givens and these other possibilities, we can know why we agree or disagree.[30]

Shklar's view is echoed by John Rawls, who, on the basis of his now famous analysis of the "original position" from which our political commitments can be said to spring, might be supposed to be disinclined to emphasize the connection between our present aspirations and past practises. And yet he says, "What justifies a conception of justice is not its being true to an order antecedent to and given to us, but its congruence with our deeper understanding of ourselves and our aspirations, and our realization that, given our history and the traditions embedded in our public life, it is the most reasonable doctrine for us."[31]

If our aspirations can be discovered, in part, by examining our present practices, then the thoughts of those who set the practices in motion—namely, the framers of this republic—can be helpful in establishing their meaning. What we think is worthy is profoundly shaped by the sort of regime that they hoped to create, because both our practices and our reasoning spring, in part, from their efforts;[32] that is, not only are we inheritors of the practices that

29. Aristotle, *Nicomachean Ethics,* esp. Book VI.

30. Judith Shklar, *Ordinary Vices,* 226–27.

31. John Rawls, "Kantian Constructivism in Moral Theory," *Journal of Philosophy* 77, no. 9 (September 1980), p. 519. In a subsequent paper Rawls comments that "justice as fairness is a political conception in part because it starts from within a certain political tradition." "Justice as Fairness: Political Not Metaphysical," *Philosophy and Public Affairs* 14, no 3 (Summer 1985): 225.

32. See the comments on the influence of the Founding Fathers by Forrest McDonald, "The Constitution and Hamiltonian Capitalism," in Robert A. Goldwin and William A. Schambra (eds.), *How Capitalistic is the Constitution?* See also Jennifer Nedelsky "American Constitutionalism and

they set in motion, but the language in which we reflect on these practices bears their stamp. In our efforts to voice our aspirations, we try to give words like "legislative" and "corporation" concrete meaning. In doing so, we inevitably turn, for example, to historical efforts to create workable legislatures, especially to those upon which our own practices have been built. It is natural that we should pay special atttention to the political efforts of Americans who came before us: we speak not only our own language but theirs as well, and we are defined not only by our own institutions but also by theirs.

There is no point in trying to play out to its conclusion the game of what the founders really thought, because, of course, they thought many things and were in serious disagreement about some. Still, if we do not try to make fine distinctions, a core of agreement does emerge. Its manifestations are to be found not only in the most authoritative documents that they produced—the Declaration of Independence and the Constitution—but also in their principal interpretative effort—The Federalist papers—and in the actual practices of the early years of the Republic.[33] As stated by Herbert Storing, if those who supported and were critical of the new Constitution "were divided among themselves, they were, at a deeper level, united with one another. . . . They were . . . men agreed that the purpose of government is the regulation and thereby the protection of individual rights and that the best instrument for this purpose is some form of limited, republican government." [34]

Those founders, especially those who carried the day in shaping the republic that we have inherited —that is, the people whom we have come to call Federalists—thought that this enterprise of limited republican government was to be guided by two principles: a concern for individual rights and the promotion of a commercial society. These principles were shared, although less enthusiastically, by those who have come to be known as Anti-Federalists.[35] Altogether, the founders hoped to perpetuate a

the Paradox of Private Property," paper presented at the Annual Meeting of the Law and Society Association, Toronto, 1982; and Storing, *What the Anti-Federalists Were For.*

33. On the last, see Nedelsky's "American Constitutionalism" and "Private Property and the Formation of the American Constitution," unpublished paper, Princeton University; and McDonald, "The Constitution and Hamiltonian Capitalism."

34. Storing, *What Anti-Federalists Were For*, 5. See also John A. Rohr, *To Run a Constitution*, pt. 1.

35. As Storing makes clear, they were deeply committed to protecting individual rights; and, of course, the existence of the Bill of Rights owes

regime of popular sovereignty that would work to serve these
two principles.

The first principle, a concern for individual rights, is the one
that present-day Americans consider as most characteristic of the
founders' concerns. Or as Montesquieu, one of the founders' teach-
ers in these matters, put it, what was wanted was "political liberty,"
which he understood as "a tranquility of mind arising from the
opinion each has of his safety." [36] A principal intention of the founders was to establish a form of popular government in which individual liberty would be secure. They were committed to individual
liberty as the test of government and looked on popular government as the political order most likely to secure it.[37]

There were many dangers to individual liberty, but in the founders' diagnosis, the tyranny of majority factions was the principal
one. This stemmed, the most sophisticated among them believed,
from the basic working principle of popular government—that is,
from where real power in it lay. As Madison explained to Jefferson,
"Wherever the real power in a Government lies, there is the danger
of oppression. In our Governments, the real power lies in the
majority of the community, and the invasion of private rights is
chiefly to be apprehended, not from acts of Government contrary
to the sense of its constituents, but from acts in which the Government is the mere instrument of the major number of the
Constituents." [38] The problem was to arrange government so that
a majority "united and actuated by some common impulse of pas-
sion, or of interest, adverse to the rights of other citizens, or to the
permanent and aggregate interests of the community" [39] could not
carry the day. To this end, a number of institutional devices were
adopted, including the most famous one of pitting ambition against
ambition by separating power among the various branches of government. The aim in all this was to secure the rights of property
and what we today would call civil liberties. The history of popular
government had shown how difficult this was to do, but virtually

---

much to their insistence. But they were in fact less concerned with majority
tyranny than with official licentiousness. See esp. chaps. 3, 6. Also, as will
be noted below, they were unenthusiastic about a full-blown commercial
society but did, in fact, accept its necessity.

36. Quoted in Martin Diamond, "The Declaration and the Constitution:
Liberty, Democracy, and the Founders," *The Public Interest* 41 (Fall 1975):
53.

37. Diamond, "The Declaration and the Constitution."

38. Quoted in Storing, *What the Anti-Federalists Were For,* 39.

39. *Federalist,* no. 10. This and all subsequent references are to *The
Federalist,* edited by Jacob F. Cooke.

all of the founders, Federalists and Anti-Federalists alike, thought that securing individual liberty was the ultimate test of government.

The founding generation also thought that if republican government of the kind that they preferred was to flourish, it would have to be joined to a commercial society. They wanted, that is, to lay the foundations for a commercial republic.[40] There were a number of reasons for wishing to do so, including severe doubts that any free government could be built principally upon virtue (although many of the founders understood the importance of the latter). Many thought that the pursuit of interest is the most enduring motive and that free government must somehow harness it. Whereas people of similar interests would be inclined to band together and use the powers of government to pursue their purposes in a fashion that threatened the liberties of others, a commercial society would increase the diversity of interests, and thus reduce the possibility of such factions forming—or, if they should form, of dominating. If these diverse interests were properly channeled by the institutions of government, the principal threat to republican government could be avoided.

In addition, a commercial society would likely generate sufficient prosperity to increase the attachment of citizens to the republican form of government. Those who associated their own material well-being with the new form of government would, consulting their

40. Storing, *What the Anti-Federalists Were For* (46), says: "There was some hankering after a simple, subsistence agricultural life, but the Anti-Federalists were irrevocably committed to a commercial order. . . . The Federalists drew out the implications of the commitment." Later, on the same page, Storing comments: "The basic problem of the Anti-Federalists was that they accepted the need and desirability of the modern commercial world, while attempting to resist certain of its tendencies with rather half-hearted appeals to civic virtue." An appreciation of the importance of a vibrant commercial society was as pronounced among those who might be classed as Jeffersonians as among followers of Hamilton. See Joyce Appleby, *Capitalism and a New Social Order: The Republican Vision of the 1790's.* Readers familiar with the historiography of the period will know that the questions of the extent (1) to which any of the founding generation might be classified as classical republicans and (2) of the connection between republicanism and a commercial society are vexed ones. See, most prominently, J. G. A. Pocock, *The Machiavellian Moment: Florentine Political Thought and the Atlantic Republican Tradition;* Bernard Bailyn, *The Ideological Origins of the American Revolution;* Gordon Wood, *The Creation of the American Republic, 1776–1787;* and Storing, *What the Anti-Federalists Were For.* For helpful overviews, see Keith Thomas, "Politics as Language," *New York Review of Books* 33, no. 3 (February 27, 1986); and Issac Kramnick, "Republican Revisionism Revisited," *American Historical Review* 87, no. 3 (June 1982): 629–64.

self-interest, be supporters of it. And, finally, a commercial society would engender habits of thrift, sobriety, and the like and otherwise divert people from a passionate interest in such matters as the purity of other men's souls. The result would be that many of the principal causes of civil strife would be reduced.

Some founders probably hoped that all that would be required from government for this commercial society to flourish was the protection of property rights and the guaranteeing of the security of commercial transactions. But it soon became widely recognized that more was at stake and that a commercial society, especially one that was to promote the desired prosperity, would require something more from government. This somewhat more activist stance was associated with Hamilton—and, as Forrest McDonald makes clear, Hamilton carried the day.[41] The crucial point was that a society that was adept at securing property rights need not be a commercial society, or, to use a modern term, need not be a capitalist one. It is the propensity to turn property into capital—that is, to use wealth as a source of investment—that is fundamental. Without such investment effort, the kind of increase in natural wealth that the founders hoped for, with its attendant increases in "the means of gratification,"[42] multiplication of interests, and fostering of sober habits, would not occur.

In short, the task became one not just of securing property but of *promoting* a commercial society. This constituted the second important principle of popular republican government: a fundamental component of the public interest should be the promotion of a commercial society. As Publius put it, "The prosperity of commerce is now perceived and acknowledged, by all enlightened statesmen, to be the most useful as well as the most productive source of national wealth; and has accordingly become a primary object of their political cares."[43] Or, as Forrest McDonald puts it after surveying debates over economic affairs in the formative period of the republic, "The United States would be built under a government-channeled, government-encouraged, and sometimes government-subsidized system of private enterprise for personal profit."[44]

41. McDonald, "The Constitution and Hamiltonian Capitalism." See also the same author's *Novus Ordo Seculorum*, chap. 4; and Martin Diamond, "Democracy and *The Federalist*: A Reconsideration of the Framers' Intent," *American Political Science Review* 53, no. 1 (March 1959), esp. 63.
42. *Federalist*, no. 12.
43. *Federalist*, no. 12.
44. McDonald, "The Constitution and Hamiltonian Capitalism," 71.

In their concern to create a commercial republic and in their sense that this was the most secure road to free government, the founders were greatly influenced by the emerging "science of politics." [45] Its principal proponents were the great figures of the Scottish Enlightenment, particularly Hume and Smith, who were forceful in praising the beneficial political effects of commerce. One of their arguments, most forcefully presented by Smith, was that the promotion of a commercial society should not be under the guidance of businessmen. As Smith phrased it, "The interest of the dealers . . . in any particular branch of trade or manufactures, is always in some respects different from, or even opposite to, that of the public." [46] To want a commercial republic did not mean that public officials were to take their direction from commercial men. Such businessmen would at a minimum be inclined to strangle competition, be inattentive to the safety of the nation, and be uninterested in finding ways to mitigate the bad effects of commercial expansion. These views were echoed in the thought of people such as Hamilton and Madison, both of whom, while appreciative of the value of government forbearance in economic matters, were well aware that a commercial society must be the subject of governmental action. [47] Because the primary value of a commercial society was *political*, the founders might be interpreted as saying that the central burden of defining how best to promote it and what its specific features should be should fall not on the shoulders of owners and controllers of productive assets but on those of officials attentive to the concerns of citizens. Businessmen, no doubt, would have many useful things to say about these matters, but their concerns were inevitably partial and were not to be allowed to dominate.

The founders might be understood, then, as saying that the running of a commercial republic would require attention to the commercial public interest. To an important degree, this was to be a matter of public decision, not just one of leaving private parties to arrive at whatever marketplace arrangements that they found mutually advantageous. Public officials, therefore, would need to be guided by their best understanding of what this commercial

45. Albert O. Hirschman, *The Passions and the Interests: Political Arguments for Capitalism;* Stephen Miller, "The Constitution and the Spirit of Commerce," in Goldwin and Schambra (eds.), *How Capitalistic is the Constitution?*, and Garry Wills, *Explaining America: The Federalist.*

46. Quoted in Miller, "The Constitution and the Spirit of Commerce," 155. For a modern statement of this view, see George T. Stigler, *Citizen and the State: Essays on Regulation.*

47. See Miller, "The Constitution and the Spirit of Commerce," esp. 161.

public interest entailed. At a minimum, they would need to resist
the temptation to see the promotion of economic prosperity as its
own justification. Increases in material well-being were finally to
be justified for political reasons. And the arguments concerning
the connection between a commercial economy and majority factions pointed to a complex range of considerations to be taken into
account, not just to the relatively easy assertion that national wealth
is associated with political stability. Similarly, officials should not
assume that impact on economic growth is the primary criterion
in judging policy initiatives that affect the distribution of property
and wealth in the society. The founders believed that a commercial
republic required a wide dispersal of property for essentially political reasons and that a great increase in the concentration of
property, even if it were associated with greater national wealth,
might well undermine one of the foundations of this kind of political order.[48]

A crucial point in serving the commercial public interest was that
businessmen could not be supposed to have some privileged understanding of what was entailed. On the contrary, the founders,
as already noted, thought that businessmen's views were likely to
be narrow and self-interested when it came to fundamental questions such as how and to what extent economic growth should be
promoted and what was an acceptable distribution of wealth and
property in the society.[49] Public matters were to be in the hands of
public officials who would need to take account of a wide range of
(mostly political) considerations in their struggle to give some content to the commercial public interest. Undue attentiveness on the
part of officials to the views of businessmen would be a clear sign
that the commercial public interest was not being well served.

This concern for a commercial republic and for the commercial
public interest is part of a more general effort by the founders not
to allow public authority to be dominated by private interest. With
this more general formulation in mind, we can follow James Q.
Wilson in saying that "finding arrangements that would permit a

48. See Robert A. Dahl, *A Preface to Economic Democracy*, 69–70. Dahl
comments (70): "Both sides (in the early debates about property) agreed,
then, that in order to ensure the wide diffusion of property an American
republic would require, some regulation would be needed." Note also the
discussion, in *Federalist* no. 10, of factional conflicts between rich and poor.

49. The most sophisticated modern students of republican government
have shared the founders' views about businessmen. See, in particular,
Joseph A. Schumpeter, *Capitalism, Socialism, and Democracy*, chaps. 6–8;
Theodore Lowi, *The End of Liberalism*, chap. 10; and Charles E. Lindblom,
Politics and Markets, chaps. 12–15.

democratic republic to avoid rule by either impassioned majorities that were heedless of the barriers between public and private life or by self-seeking factions that ignored the distinctions between private and public power was the central problem confronting the Founders."[50] This formulation neatly captures the twin principles that were to guide popular government: (1) to secure private rights against public depredations, especially as these grew from impassioned majorities, and (2) to secure public authority from powerful private interests, among the most important of which were those who owned or otherwise controlled productive assets.

The aspirations of contemporary Americans may not employ the founders' language at every turn, but our formulations echo theirs.[51] We hope for a political order of popular rule in which a private sphere of autonomous choice is widely available and in which the commercial public interest is to be central to public debate and political decision making.[52] If a single label is appropriate, these principles define the core of a liberal democratic regime—that is, a regime built around popular sovereignty, individual rights including property rights, and commerce. What remains is to draw out some of the implications of our principal aspirations. This will be especially important to do in the case of the promotion of a commercial society and the commercial public interest, since they will play the crucial role in succeeding chapters.

I want to emphasize that the implications to be considered are present in our holding of the aspirations, even if these implications are not always understood. By saying this I do not mean to imply any stretching of the meaning of the aspirations, for the implications are present in the core of the aspirations' meanings. A useful first step will be to emphasize the distinction between the promotion of a commercial society and rights, particularly property rights. The former is a matter of "policy"—and policy and rights exist in some tension, not least because government activity aimed, for example, at promoting economic development is unlikely to be able

50. James Q. Wilson (ed.), "Introduction," in *The Politics of Regulation,* viii.

51. For an argument that this way of talking does not imply a personification of the community, see Ronald Dworkin, *Law's Empire,* chap. 6.

52. Are these really our aspirations—or the ideas of those who are powerful enough to enforce such views? Michael Walzer comments: "The common understanding of particular goods incorporates principles, procedures, conceptions of agency, that the rulers would not choose if they were choosing *right now*—and so provides the terms of social criticism." *Spheres of Justice,* 9.

to uniformly respect property rights. To put the matter somewhat differently, the meaning of the public interest of a commercial society is not exhausted by the protection of property rights.

Let us now consider further the meaning of this commercial public interest. Several points merit emphasis. First, the purposes of a commercial society are not confined to promoting economic performance and whatever is required to achieve it. Such concerns are certainly included, but by saying that the founders thought that the reasons to have a commercial society were political I mean to convey that, for us and for them, the organization of economic life is to be guided by its contribution to a constitutional popular government: it is a commercial *republic* that we want.[53] Differently stated, the public interest is not exhausted by facilitating the performance of business enterprises—and may, in some circumstances, be hurt by it. Promoting a commercial society is an exercise in neither free-market economics, profit maximization, nor economic growth but rather in political theory. The idea of the commercial public interest, which is at the core of that political theory, has at its center the need to judge major economic policies by their contributions toward solving the central problems of republican government. Economic policies of this sort are simply "political" policy in different guise.

The second point requiring emphasis is a corollary of the first. In the discussion over how to provide for and nourish a commercial society and in the narrower concern of how to facilitate satisfactory economic performance, businessmen's voices are important but should not dominate. We wish for a regime in which public authority is in the service of public interests, not directed by private or particular interest. Public authority is not a franchise for private advancement, and its exercise should be an effort to rise above private interest.

In short, the commercial public interest is not what businessmen say it is. And when public officials take their cues from businessmen or from what they believe will serve business interests, it is evident that the fundamental political dimension of the commercial public interest is being lost to sight. What the commercial public interest in

53. For striking evidence of just how devoted Americans are to a commercial republic—and especially to enterprise-based markets as the fairest means of coordinating social decisions—see Robert E. Lane, "Market Justice, Political Justice" *American Political Science Review* 80, no. 2 (June 1986): 383–402; and Herbert McClosky and John Zaller, *The American Ethos: Public Attitudes toward Capitalism and Democracy.* McClosky and Zaller report, among other data, that 80 percent of the general public think that "the free enterprise system [is] necessary for free government to survive" (133) and that 78 percent (87 percent in another survey) believe that "private ownership of property is as important to a good society as freedom" (140).

fact is will be the subject of dispute, but the struggle should be about the interests of the public, not some particular sector of it. Public officials will have to argue and contend; it is not a matter of some conception being readily available. But their efforts are not without guidance: their arguments should be informed by how fostering a vital commercial economy will serve the cause of republican government. Thus, as inheritors of the founders' design, we hold some substantive conception of the public good, but its particulars must be filled in. In the continuing effort to do this, pride of place goes to public officials and citizens. We no more wish those who conduct the public debate to be beholden to churches or families than to owners and controllers of productive assets.[54] These are public questions both because they are questions about the public good and because the principal burden of answering them is to fall on those acting in public ways—namely, on officeholders and citizens.

Third, it should be clear that, in talking about the promotion of a commercial society, we are not, properly speaking, considering the desirable scope of government, although the two in fact do become conflated. Virtually all of us, even the most devout worshippers at the free-market shrine, would agree, however, that government has a role. Free-market proponents thus concede that economic markets cannot stand on their own and must be the subject of government action. There is, then, a public interest to be served—namely, that of promoting a commercial society—and a role for public officials in defining it.

An elegant way of summarizing our aspirations is suggested by Michael Walzer when he comments that, in a liberal regime, what he terms the "art of separation" should "work against both state capitalism and the capitalist state." [55] The first subverts individual liberty and the second subverts the integrity of public decision. The continuity in thought between this, a version of our aspirations, and the concerns of the founders is not hidden by the changes in vocabulary.

CONCLUSION

The regime principles discussed here do not exhaust our aspirations.[56] The two that I have considered are, however, central to the political way of life whose realization we hope to facilitate. Once the

54. Michael Walzer, "Liberalism and the Art of Separation," *Political Theory* 12, no. 3 (August 1984): 322.
55. Walzer, "Liberalism and the Art of Separation," 322.
56. See chap. 10 below and the analysis in Barber, *On What the Constitution Means,* for an extensive discussion.

full range of our aspirations is set out, there may well be among the principles additional tensions that parallel those that I have touched on briefly above.[57] One primary source of tension is likely to be encountered in the attempt to reconcile our aspiration to be a regime of popular sovereignty with our other aspirations. A regime devoted to the realization of popular control will not find it easy to contain within itself various kinds of devices to tutor and limit citizen opinion. There is no serious substitute for a regime of popular sovereignty if the aim is mass well-being understood materially and morally. But to devise ways in which citizens can govern themselves intelligently is plainly no easy matter, requiring as it almost certainly does the need to inculcate a capacity for reflection regarding the purposes to which popular sovereignty is to be put. In any case, the presumption should be that our aspirations are complex, as befits any serious commitment to a decent political way of life.

It is also worth emphasizing that our aspirations should be understood as real claims about justice, not as mere assertions of class interest and attempts to balance social forces. Our aspirations are not for a capitalist economy with an admixture of popular control as a concession to popular power. Otherwise stated, although political life is surely about power and domination, its concerns do not end there. Political life is also an attempt to reduce the exploitation inherent in much of social existence. Politics is not merely the extension by other means of the attempts of some to dominate others. It is also an effort to ameliorate such exploitative arrangements by creating some things in common and by resting justificatory principles on these commonalities. This does not mean that the exploitative side of political life simply disappears. The tension between its two sides is always present. But except where the subject is the most obviously vicious forms of political life—labor gangs, robber dens, and gulags all writ large—interpretations of political orders must make room for efforts to be just as well as for efforts to gain advantage and to exploit. It is, however, only fair to add that those who seek to create commonalities—and to build just political principles around them—are .too often insufficiently interested in political schemes consistent with those principles.

This understanding of politics is consistent with recent efforts to defend liberal democracy as, if not an entirely adequate guide, then at least a valuable one.[58] These discussions, my own included, are

57. I will pick up this theme again in chap. 9, where I will argue that property rights must be loosened if we wish to maintain our commitment to a commercial regime.
58. William Galston, "Defending Liberalism," *American Political Science*

not attempts to establish that liberal democratic regimes are the best regimes. This seems an unlikely project in any event, since circumstances and a people's aptitude for politics vary. Rather, the aim is to defend such regimes against the claim that their principles are either, at worst, merely the rhetorical facade for the claims of the powerful (the scheme of constitutionally based representation then being essentially a sham) or, at best, a compromise among major social forces.

Our aspirations can perhaps best be summarized in the form of a question: Can a regime dedicated to popular control work so as to respect individual liberties, promote a commercial society, and give it concrete meaning in the course of defining the commercial public interest? This is the core question of American political life for which the actual operations of our politics provide the effective answer. Having posed this question, I am now obliged to attempt an answer by saying something about these actual operations. I will do so in a manner that takes us back to the opening question of how the political institutions of the city should help form the citizenry.

Review 76, no. 3 (September 1982): 621–29; and Walzer, "Liberalism and the Art of Separation".

7

A Commercial
Republic?

Are we the commercial republic that our aspirations direct us toward?
Do our governmental processes facilitate struggle and debate directed
at defining the commercial public interest? The answer that I propose
to these questions is that we have not done very well in serving these
aspirations.

This answer is likely to occasion vigorous dissent, at least from those
who think of the United States as the quintessential business society.
They will point to the important and well-regarded place that businessmen play in our national life and so will likely be puzzled by my
statement. Others will likely be puzzled for a different reason. They
too will say that this is a business society but will argue that this is at
the cost of our commitment to democracy. Some will go even further
and say that the very design of our (and perhaps any) popular regime
fosters great attentiveness to business interests.

Of course, those who contend that we are the quintessential business
society most often mean this approvingly—the business of America
is business—whereas those who advance these other views mean to
be critical of representative democracy, capitalism, or (usually) both.
All of these advocates however, typically give little attention to the
distinction between governmental attentiveness to business interests
on the one hand and to the promotion of a commercial society and
the effort to define its public interest on the other. Those who think
that the business of America is business need to entertain the idea
that there is a commercial public interest from whose vantage point
any identification of businessmen's satisfaction and the public good
can be disputed. In just the same way, those inclined to be critical of
capitalism need to consider that American public officials and citizens
have available to them a way to argue against any undue solicitousness
of businessmen's views. Citizens and officials have a place within the
American regime by which to judge the workings of its political economy. This distinction between governmental attentiveness to business
interests and the commercial public interest is, I believe, crucial to

understanding both the workings and the relative success or failure of our political life.

The difficulties do not end here, however, for there are students of American political life who realize that our aspirations in this context are not exhausted by a fondness for businessmen and their interests. But the tension between aspiration and reality—which, in my view, is more nearly a yawning gap—is virtually absent in their analyses. The tendency is to talk as if the regular meeting of corporate figures and public officials over what will serve business interests is simply a necessary part of our attachment to a commercial society.

My own view, developed in this and the preceding chapter, is that we are engaged in an attempt to carry out a thoughtful assessment of how a popular regime might reasonably operate. The attempt may well prove misguided, and our actions to date provide little enough in the way of comfort. Certainly, our performance has fallen far short of our own assessment of what is best in us. It has also failed to measure up to what appears to be possible. But not to take our aspirations seriously is to misunderstand the significance of what is occurring. By contrast, those who take their political lessons from Marx typically find it hard to believe that anything more is at work than an ideological subterfuge.[1] And, in a kind of quaint mirror image, those who take their political lessons from what they believe James Madison meant find it difficult to grasp that the easy access of the large-scale business corporation to our policy processes is not a sign that the founders' intentions have been honored.[2]

In the pages that follow, I will emphasize the distinction between our aspirations to be a commercial republic and the reality of our governmental processes. The actual workings of the latter give great weight to what will induce business performance, and the definitions of what will do so are heavily influenced by businessmen's conceptions. In the workings of our public discussion and policy making, the political heart of the commercial public interest typically has been lost from sight. It is our failure to be a commercial republic—that is, a popular regime that aims at the commercial public interest—that should direct our attention to the reform of the political institutions

1. Among others, see James R. O'Connor, *The Fiscal Crisis of the State;* Ralph Miliband, *The State in Capitalist Society;* and Fred L. Block, "The Ruling-Class Does Not Rule—Notes on the Marxist Theory of the State," *Socialist Revolution* 7, no. 33 (1977): 6–28. For general discussions, see Martin Carnoy, *The State and Political Theory;* and Claus Offe, *Contradictions of the Welfare State.*

2. See Michael Novak, *The Spirit of Democratic Capitalism;* and Marc F. Plattner, "American Democracy and the Acquisitive Spirit," in Robert A. Goldwin and William Schambra (eds.), *How Capitalistic Is the Constitution?*

of the city. Properly constructed, the political institutions of the city can help to create a citizenry capable of rejecting any easy equation between inducing business performance and serving the public interest of a commercial society.

INDIVIDUAL RIGHTS

Before turning to our aspirations to be a commercial republic, a brief comment needs to be made about individual rights. By and large, our aspiration to be a popular regime in which a sphere of individual autonomy flourishes has been well served. If we refer for the moment to the founders' version of what is necessary to secure such a sphere, it is reasonably plain that, except for the historically crucial fact of slavery, no illiberal majorities have succeeded over long periods in using the governmental apparatus to quash civil liberties. The basic freedoms, such as those of speech, assembly and religion, have not succumbed to a majority determined to use governmental power to impose their version of the truth of things. Similarly, the propertyless have not succeeded in dislodging the propertied from their grip on the means of production. Whatever the momentary panics of the well endowed, they have remained relatively secure in the comfort of beds provided by the fruits of property ownership.

To be sure, the sphere of individual rights has proved to be less secure in the face of a national security apparatus and those who claim to speak for our safety in an ideologically divided world. There is ample evidence that those who direct and operate the security apparatus find individual rights at least a nuisance and are inclined, when they think that it is necessary and possible, to make substantial inroads.[3] Our aspirations indeed seem to be compromised here, but how compromised is not easy to say—if for no other reason than that these very words are being openly written.

Our relative success in these matters should come as no surprise. As many commentators have pointed out, the founders devoted a good deal of effort to contriving a government and political economy that would work in this fashion. This was, indeed, their dominant aim, as I have already commented.[4] They separated powers, wrote a

3. See, e.g., Morton Halperin, *Lawless State: The Crimes of the U.S. Intelligence Agencies.*
4. See also Jennifer Nedelsky, "American Constitutionalism and the Paradox of Private Property," paper presented at the annual meeting of the Law and Society Association, Toronto, 1982; Herbert J. Storing, "American Statesmenship: Old and New," in Robert A. Goldwin (ed.), *Bureaucrats, Policy An-*

Bill of Rights, and evolved the process of judicial review, for example. Whether for these or for other reasons, political elites have, for the most part, remained sufficiently attached to individual rights to resist temptations to abrogate or reduce them.[5] Contemporary social science evidence suggests that the mass of citizens are perhaps more hesitant in their support of these rights,[6] but a plausible hypothesis is that the governmental arrangements contrived by the founders have reduced the temptations, inherent in the situation, for political leaders to exploit the less pleasant inclinations of the mass of citizens.

In short, we have been relatively successful in defining a usable distinction between public and private when the direction is public to private and the question one of the public sphere not supplanting the private. Here we can draw on a long history, an elaborate vocabulary, and knowledge of a variety of helpful devices. Here we also have centuries of citizen and leadership education on the relevant public-private distinctions. This is the domain in which liberalism excels—the domain of rights, of limited government, and of constitutionalism generally, in all its glory. It is no wonder that we have been relatively successful.

We have been less successful when the direction runs the other way—from private to public—and the question is one of preventing public authority from being the tool of private interest. The typical American response has been to construe problems under this rubric of the private use of public authority as if they were really matters of individual rights—that is, of public authority invading the private sphere. This is perhaps most visible in the recent Supreme Court ruling on whether businesses can be restricted by the state governments in how much they may spend on attempting to influence the outcome of referenda votes. The Court has said that this is a matter of free speech, not of corruption of the political process by private interest.[7]

---

alysts, Statesmen: Who Leads?; Marc F. Plattner, "American Democracy and the Acquisitive Spirit," in Goldwin and Schambra (eds.), How Capitalistic is the Constitution?; and Martin Diamond, "Democracy and The Federalist: A Reconsideration of the Founders' Intent," American Political Science Review 53, no. 1 (March 1959): 52–68.

5. See Robert A. Dahl, Who Governs?, chaps. 27, 28; V. O. Key, Public Opinion and American Democracy, chap. 21; and Herbert McClosky and Alida Brill, Dimensions of Tolerance: What Americans Believe About Civil Liberties.

6. See James W. Prothro and Charles M. Grigg, "Fundamental Principles of Democracy; Basis of Agreement and Disagreement," Journal of Politics 22, no. 2 (1960): 270–94; Dahl, Who Governs?; and McClosky and Brill, Dimensions of Tolerance.

7. First National Bank v. Bellotti, 435 U.S. 765 (1978).

THE PUBLIC INTEREST OF A COMMERCIAL SOCIETY

When we turn from individual rights to promoting a commercial republic, the situation is different. We are a popular regime that falls far short of our aspiration to be a commercial republic. Inducing business performance dominates much of the effort to define the commercial public interest, and little attention is given by public officials and citizens to its political content. The connections between promoting a vital commercial economy and the foundations of republican government are neglected. The dominance of the concern to induce business performance has deep roots in the structure of the political economy. It is not the case that organized businessmen need to prompt this attention and that they have the power necessary to do so; on the contrary, public officials are strongly disposed to worry about inducing business performance. But it is also the case that they are very solicitous of businessmen's views in the matter. The prominent place of businessmen in the discussion of how to induce business performance is a clear indication (as is the very focus on the inducement of business) that the commercial public interest is being lost to sight.

I will start my discussion of the commercial public interest by considering those domains of governmental activity where economic performance is more or less obviously at stake. This does not exhaust what is at issue in promoting a commercial republic, but it is central to it. Here is where the focus on business inducement is strong and the voice of businessmen weighty. A useful place to start is with the electorate.

There is a good deal of evidence that voting behavior is strongly shaped by the electorate's assessment of how well public officials[8] have done in promoting prosperity. Although a concern for material well-being is far from the only thing that occupies the minds of citizens (as I shall further discuss below), it is one of the most important. This characterization of the views of the citizenry is at the core of studies of what has come to be known as retrospective voting, in which assessments of past governmental performance—especially, but not only, in economic matters—are said to guide present voting choice.[9] It also is the foundation for studies of the political business cycle. These studies argue that, because of electoral incentives, officials are driven to manipulate

8. Here and elsewhere in this chapter, by "officials" I mean those who are subject to popular approval, either directly (through elections) or indirectly (through appointment by those elected).

9. See Morris Fiorina, *Retrospective Voting in American National Elections;* Key, *Public Opinion and American Democracy;* and James E. Alt and K. Alec Chrystal, *Political Economics.*

the business cycle to shore up or to bolster their political fortunes.[10] There are a variety of problems with these analyses,[11] but, taken together, they strongly support the compound proposition that citizen's votes are shaped by their assessment of economic performance and that officials know this, and are stimulated to do something about it.

How do officials, in fact, respond? The studies of the political business cycle imply that their principal response is to manipulate the economy for short-term political advantage. Without denying that this sometimes occurs, it is open to grave objection as in fact being the principal response to citizen concern with prosperity. Most obviously, it is more difficult for officials to manipulate the economy than is often allowed.[12] Although some tools are available to do so, they are unreliable and few in number. Moreover, they are not always in the hands of those who can be trusted to perform the right ministrations. In addition, many of the officials involved in the potential manipulations are not likely to have the short-term horizons implied in the analysis. On the contrary, they will be looking past the next election, not least because they plan to run for office or seek appointments over a considerable time period. Thus, it will matter whether they—and, more particularly, the party to which they belong—is broadly associated with prosperity. All this suggests that officials generally, regardless of party, will be strongly disposed to respond to the continuing concern of citizens with prosperity not only or even importantly by short-term manipulation but by looking to steady ways to ensure satisfactory economic performance.

Where will such a concern lead them? Officials are free to respond in a variety of ways, but they will start by worrying about inducing business performance. The question is whether this is where they will also finish.

10. M. Kalecki, "Political Aspects of Full Employment," *Political Quarterly* 14, no. 4 (1943): 322–31; Gerald H. Kramer, "Short-Term Fluctuations in U.S. Voting Behavior, 1896–1964," *American Political Science Review* 65, no. 1 (March 1971): 131–43; W. D. Nordhaus, "The Political Business Cycle," *Review of Economic Studies* 42, no. 2 (April 1975): 169–90; C. Duncan MacRae, "A Political Model of the Business Cycle," *Journal of Political Economy* 85, no. 2 (April 1977): 239–63; and Edward R. Tufte, *Political Control of the Economy.*

11. Henry W. Chappell, Jr., and William R. Keech, "A New View of Political Accountability for Economic Performance," *American Political Science Review* 79, no. 1 (March 1985): 10–27; and Alt and Chrystal, *Political Economics,* chaps. 5–7.

12. See Kristen R. Monroe, "Political Manipulation of the Economy: A Closer Look at the Political Business Cycle," *Presidential Studies* 13, no. 1 (Winter 1983): 37–49.

Why will officials start with such inducement? The answer parallels the analysis already presented for cities. It turns, that is, on the division of labor between state and market that is the defining feature of the American political economy. A highly compressed sketch of this division begins with the observation that, on their own, businessmen will not produce a level of economic activity sufficient to meet the electoral concerns of officials. They will clearly make some investments, take some risks, and employ some labor even in difficult times, but the great productive apparatus that is required to employ a growing population, generate future investment capital, and provide for present consumption will not arise unaided. At the heart of the matter is likely to be the large scale of investment required and the high degree of uncertainty, necessitating some fragile combination of the following: daring entrepreneurial vision—or at least "animal spirits"— and the promise that risks can be controlled, rewards will be high, and compensation for failure possible.[13] John Kenneth Galbraith, for example, argues that firms, especially those contemplating large-scale investments, will not do so unless they can "plan." They need to reduce the principal sources of uncertainty in order to make such investment a rational proposition.[14]

Ownership of productive assets is largely placed in private hands in the American political economy, and major social decisions, including the pattern of work organization, industrial location, compensation for labor, and choice of industrial technology, are made through private exchange relations in which owners and managers are afforded a good deal of discretion.[15] Social well-being thus depends significantly on market transactions even as state action has been directed at shaping the terms of these transactions. Public officials share responsibility for the level of citizen well-being with private controllers of assets, but they cannot command economic performance. Commanding businessmen to perform will not be sufficient, precisely to the degree that they are guaranteed disposition of productive assets. As Charles E. Lindblom puts it, owners and managers must be *induced* to perform.[16]

13. See Joseph A. Schumpeter, *Capitalism, Socialism, and Democracy*, chaps. 6–8, for a discussion of entrepreneurs and the problem of risk and reward. See also John R. Commons, *Legal Foundations of Capitalism*.

14. John Kenneth Galbraith, *The New Industrial State*, esp. chaps. 1–10.

15. See Charles E. Lindblom, *Politics and Markets*, esp. pts. II, IV, V. The specific formulation here freely draws on my "Pluralism in its Place: State and Regime in the American Republic," in Roger Benjamin and Stephen L. Elkin (eds.), *The Democratic State*.

16. Lindblom, *Politics and Markets*, chap. 13.

In the most general way, inducements are directed at facilitating large-scale investment, with the control of risk, the ample size of rewards for succeeding, and compensation for failure being central to the process. Public officials really have two tasks.[17] On the negative side, they must try to avoid reducing the confidence of businessmen. Low confidence means low investment. Erratic management of the currency or talk about nationalization will distress businessmen and make them less inclined to take risks. On the positive side, actual inducements must be offered. These may range from tax incentives and state provision of research money and research findings to facilitating the granting of various permits. The latter may involve punishing rapacious officials and replacing them with those who will perform in nonarbitrary ways. Not only are the alternatives manifold; they can be organized in a variety of ways.

The division of labor and the election of public officials more or less guarantee some interest on the part of officials in inducing business performance; however, relatively recent changes in both the business corporation and the state have substantially strengthened this disposition. Two changes are of particular importance: (1) the elimination of many of the barriers to the sort of inducements that public officials may offer and (2) the increased degree of business concentration.[18] As for the first of these, the biggest change is probably that officials are now able to offer elaborate insurance against risk and other forms of risk reduction. It is now plausible, for example, for businessmen to ask for various kinds of loan guarantees, because legal and political barriers to doing so have fallen. Indeed the process has gone so far as to cause one commentator to christen the present American political economy as the "state of permanent receivership."[19] But loan guarantees are only the tip of the iceberg of a large array of subsidies, favorable regulations and grants of self-regulation that are presently available.[20] Both corporate statesmen and public officials have grasped that the connection between business and the state has become more intimate (even if there is much current public rhetoric that it ought not to be so).

17. Block, "The Ruling-Class Does Not Rule," 6–28.
18. See Michael Useem, *The Inner Circle: Large Corporations and the Rise of Business Political Activity in the United States and United Kingdom;* Martin S. Feldstein (ed.), *The American Economy in Transition;* Edward S. Herman, *Corporate Control, Corporate Power;* and Betty Bock et al. (eds.), *The Impact of the Modern Corporation.*
19. See Theodore J. Lowi, *The End of Liberalism: The Second Republic of the United States,* chap. 10. See also Robert B. Reich and John D. Donahue, *New Deals: The Chrysler Revival and the American System.*
20. On the array, see Lowi, *The End of Liberalism,* esp. chap. 10.

As for the increase in business concentration, the larger size of corporate entities invites officials to think in terms of direct inducements. The impact of any inducements will likely be visible, direct, and large, and, in addition, the relatively few entities involved presumably makes it easier to tailor the incentives for maximum effect.

How do officials arrive at a definition of what inducements to offer? The easiest thing for public officials to do would be to take their cues from businessmen. Businessmen could happily be left to sort out among themselves what was necessary for their performance and to convey through various means the results of their deliberation. The recent increase both in contact between businessmen and public officials and of broad-based business organization makes this an altogether attractive and plausible alternative.

Businessmen have become more organized in recent years. To an important degree they have overcome past fragmentation and formed a variety of classwide organizations that can speak for business concerns generally.[21] They include such multiple-purpose organizations as the Business Roundtable, as well as those devoted to narrower tasks, such as PACs.[22] These broadly based organizations are in a position to argue for a variety of general inducements for business performance and have sufficient resources—including access, money, and expertise—to make a powerful case. Moreover, businessmen are sufficiently anxious about the burden of government regulation, criticism of business corporations, and foreign competition to make pressing the state for a variety of aids, inducements, and advantages a compelling task. Also, as noted above, the state is in a position to deliver. Whatever businessmen can imagine in terms of help can, in principal, be delivered; from tax advantages to wage controls, from research dollars to tariffs, all are possible. Finally, there has been a secular trend over the course of the present century toward more business contact with government and more elaborate business organization.[23] It is also likely that business attempts to influence government are now at a high point.[24] Cer-

21. See Useem, *The Inner Circle.*
22. See Amitai Etzioni, *Capital Corruption: The New Attack on American Democracy.*
23. One survey reveals that two-thirds of business executives interviewed visited Washington at least once every two weeks (Useem, *The Inner Circle,* 92). In addition, in 1970 only a handful of large corporations had a public-affairs office. Ten years later, 80 percent of the 500 largest manufacturing firms had one (Useem, *The Inner Circle,* 150).
24. See Useem, *The Inner Circle;* and David Vogel, "How Business Responds to Opposition: Corporate Political Strategies During the 1970's," paper presented to the American Political Science Association, Washington, D.C., 1979.

tainly business influence is a good deal more visible—and apparently more successful—than it was in the mid-1960s.

Two additional factors are pertinent. First, businessmen are more divided among themselves than the discussion has so far allowed.[25] As a consequence, public officials must themselves sometimes supply a definition of what will facilitate economic performance. In any case, public officials have their *own* views of what will promote performance. This is the second factor. Precisely because they take citizen worries about prosperity seriously, they will be unwilling to be guided completely by businessmen.[26] In the end, however, because promoting satisfactory performance requires at least the tacit cooperation of controllers of productive assets (since they will not do what is necessary on their own), their definition of what is required to gain the desired result will weigh heavily in the choices made by officials. The increasing ability of businessmen to arrive at such definitions—and the regular contact with corporate statesmen who offer them—mean that officials can lean heavily on businessmen's definitions.

An interest in inducing business performance will be central, then, to the concerns of public officials, and the voice of businessmen will be listened to with great care. But will other considerations and other voices enter in?

There are two kinds of dissent at issue. There are those who believe that the public interest of a commercial society is not exhausted by policies to induce business performance; moreover, they may doubt that the amounts and kinds of inducements being offered are necessary to maintain reasonable levels of prosperity. Much of the criticism here may not be directly expressed, since the issues themselves are complex. But arguments over the proper division of the social product among investment, consumption, and various forms of governmental benefits touch on these issues, as does the debate over what has come to be known as industrial policy. Most dissent, however, is more limited and springs from resistance to the workings of the inducement process itself. It does not touch the larger question of the relation between inducement of business performance and the public interest of a commercial society.

25. "Corporate America has been waging a civil war, industry against industry, over the final shape of President Reagan's tax code revisions and heavy industry is coming out the loser." Steven Greenhouse, "New Threat to Smokestack America," *The New York Times,* May 26, 1985.

26. " 'Business is split in our favor,' insists one senior Administration official. 'And when those opposed stand up to fight us, they'll look like special interests.' " Quoted in *Business Week,* June 10, 1985, 44.

The extent to which citizens make known their views and press them with vigor will vary, but the potential for this is always present. However, the expression of dissent does not often imperil the inducement process.[27] Consider, first, that the effect of citizen views on officials diminishes the farther we move from the electoral arena, that by the time we get to decisions made by executive agencies it is clearly weak and indirect. Yet, the administrative arena can and does serve as a forum for negotiating over businessmen's concerns, particularly what is necessary for inducing economic performance. In addition, even if the methods of maintaining business confidence and facilitating performance appear on the public agenda, owners and managers have fundamental advantages in the discussion. As is already apparent, they need not press for access to public officials; the most visible of them may even be solicited. Moreover, the very fact of owning productive assets provides controllers of these assets with the solution to a problem with which other interests must struggle (and indeed may not master). Opinion without benefit of organization and other resources is weak. Business enterprises, especially larger ones, are, however, already organizations with a complement of human and financial resources that may be employed to pursue other than business ends.

One implication of these built-in advantages must be emphasized: they operate with a kind of historical carryover. As any set of citizens at a given moment attempts to offer an assessment of the distribution of the social product, for example, they are attempting to do so in the context of a set of institutional arrangements. These arrangements are themselves at least partly the results of historical disputes in which the built-in advantages have operated. In short, the built-in advantages cumulate. This has the simple but profound consequence that the ordinary flow of public action works to screen out challenges; for example, those citizens who think that the operation of banking laws is unnecessarily weighted in favor of promoting business performance not only must object to particular actions but must undo the institutional arrangements that have created agencies to take such actions.

However, even though there are certain features of the political economy that work to limit expression of dissent about the inducement process, citizens will still offer assessments. Expressions of citizen's opinions are constrained rather than quashed, not least because there will always be available some public officials who derive advantage from mobilizing citizens to challenge the present form of in-

---

27. In this and immediately following paragraphs, I draw freely on my "Pluralism in its Place."

ducement of business performance. But there will be limits to the number of public officials so inclined and to the distance that they will be willing to travel.[28] This is, after all, a dangerous road, since a citizenry in full cry may come to look askance at the present institutional arrangements that the existing—as well as the aspiring— officials wish to help manage. In addition, even combative, disaffected politicians are likely to be leery of inducing deep dismay in businessmen, since eventually they either will have to operate a political economy in which businessmen are central or will have to deal with the consequences of poor performance that may well attend any major transformation. In their turn, however, businessmen are likely to recognize that officials must be seen to be responsive to strong expressions of citizen opinion, quite apart from any preference that the officials themselves may have in the matter.

In contrast to those who dissent and who face barriers to making their dissent felt, some number of citizens actively equate inducing business performance with promoting the public interest of a commercial society. It is easy enough to see why businessmen themselves may be so inclined, but it is less obvious why ordinary citizens should lean toward equating the well-being of General Motors with that of everyone else. Here we encounter difficult questions of business propaganda and social class indoctrination. There is probably also at work a natural tendency to approve of those who flourish under the existing rules. In any case, John Gaventa, among others, has made the powerful argument that the origins of such an equation must be sought in complex historical processes.[29] Regardless, public officials and businessmen have a reservoir of goodwill on which to draw as they attempt to arrive at an accommodation regarding the scope and character of inducement.[30]

Public officials do not have to be told to worry about economic performance or to facilitate it; they understand that, if they are to do their job as public officials, stay in office, and pursue their ambitions, then owners and managers of productive assets must

28. Publius comments that "these ties which bind the representative to his constituents are strengthened by motives of a more selfish nature. His pride and vanity attach him to a form of government which favors his pretensions, and gives him a share in its honors and distinctions." *Federalist*, no. 57.

29. See John Gaventa, *Power and Powerlessness: Quiescence and Rebellion in an Appalachian Valley.*

30. Consider here the data reported by Herbert McClosky and John Zaller: 77 percent of the general public and 89 percent of influentials agreed that "on the whole, our economic system is just and wise." *The American Ethos: Public Attitudes toward Capitalism and Democracy,* 133.

do *their* job.[31] Differently stated, officials do negotiate with particular business interests—and power struggles may well result. But their real interest lies in the level of economic performance more generally, and that is not a matter of particular businessmen coordinating their efforts,[32] deciding to invest or not, and bargaining with or attempting to coerce government; instead, it is a matter of large numbers of businessmen responding as individuals to market incentives.[33] Officials, then, are concerned with the workings of a social process—namely, the market.

The division between market and state is a two-way street. Businessmen are not unschooled in the workings of the political economy. They know that if they demand too much—and/or do it in a clumsy, overweening fashion—their position may become precarious. For their part, public officials see the performance of owners and managers as a central question because the latter have a *choice*. For example, they may consume substantial portions of their capital in ways that do little to foster future productivity, or they may export it. But the choice is theirs, because property rights are extensively enforced; if owners and managers do not exercise discretion, they may find the basis for their choice eroded. To this consideration we may add that the division between market and state means that those who control productive assets also require various state authorizations; this, too, is understood. To be sure, the disposition of businessmen to restrain their desires is probably less powerful than that of public officials to see that economic performance is substantial—since the consequences for public officials are more proximate and tangible. But as public officials pursue their concerns about economic performance, they are likely to find businessmen exercising some restraint.

Within the terms of the analysis presented here, it is possible simultaneously to say that the state is devoted to facilitating business performance and that public officials may in fact get it all so wrong

31. Cf. Block, "The Ruling-Class Does Not Rule." Witness John Kennedy's statement in 1961: "This country cannot prosper unless business prospers. The country cannot meet its obligations and tax obligations and all the rest unless business is doing well. Business will not do well and we have full employment unless there is a chance to make a profit. So there is no long-run hostility between business and government. *There cannot be. We cannot succeed unless they succeed.* (Emphasis supplied.) Quoted in Alan Wolfe, *America's Impasse: The Rise and Fall of the Politics of Growth* (New York: Pantheon, 1981), p. 67.

32. As it would be with workers. This, as well the degree of choice that each has, helps distinguish labor from capital.

33. Block, "The Ruling-Class Does Not Rule," makes a parallel argument.

that performance declines. Thus, businessmen's assertions that state action does not help economic performance can be correct even as it is also true that officials aim to do so. Public officials are, at various junctures, likely to arrive at independent judgments about what is necessary for satisfactory performance—and, for a considerable time, may insist to businessmen that it is *they* who have it wrong. As a consequence, businessmen may lose struggles concerning the creation of new perquisites or the protection of existing ones, and (since they believe that such perquisites are necessary for economic performance) therefore conclude that public officials do not share their concern for the economy.

More generally, two common and seemingly diametrically opposed observations about the present character of business-state relations can now be reconciled. Some observers contend that the state is promoting capital, whereas others argue that businessmen feel constrained and overwhelmed by an expansive state. We can now say that there is some truth in both observations. The state can come to assert a conception of facilitating business performance that businessmen find disagreeable. And assert and attempt to act on such a conception it will—if public officials feel compelled to do so by electoral and related concerns. Businessmen are neither a ruling class dominating the state nor merely a particularly powerful interest group. But then, neither are public officials neutral with regard to the well-being of business. Business-state relations cannot be captured in any of these simplifications.

The result of the pattern of politics that I have been describing is a focus on what businessmen contend is necessary if they are to perform. The crucial point is that discussions of economic performance broadly understood are typically discussions about inducing business performance. Such discussion precludes and otherwise displaces other definitions of what is at stake. Public officials engage in negotiation (often indirectly) with businessmen and conduct an elaborate minuet that involves being attentive to likely citizen responses to the variety of business inducements under consideration. The consequence is that the distinction between the public interest of a commercial society and the mutual accommodation between officials and businessmen over how to get the latter to perform is not honored.

Other Domains

So far the discussion has only dealt with domains where economic performance broadly understood is plausibly at stake. To be sure, questions touching on this matter are a crucial part of any concern with shaping the public interest of a commercial society. But they do not exhaust the subject; several points concerning other domains are particularly important in the context of a discussion of the commercial public interest.

Although there is a good deal of variation in the pattern of politics in these other domains, they have one important thing in common: those who actively participate do not display much interest in struggling over the content of the public interest of a commercial society. This is as much true, for example, of the entrepreneurial politics of social regulation[34] as it is of the more tightly organized politics of, say, agriculture.[35] Whether it is a politics in which formally organized groups are important or a politics that revolves around broad movements of public opinion matters little in this regard.[36] Nor is this terribly surprising, since there are substantial benefits in focusing one's attention elsewhere—for example, on securing policies that confer substantial group advantages. This is not, it should be emphasized, a matter of actively dismissing any concern with the commercial public interest but a matter of the existence of ample rewards elsewhere.

That the politically active have been successful in reaping substantial gains can be seen from a brief examination of two important policy domains: social welfare and regulation. The striking fact in both cases is the extent to which these programs confer major benefits on the nonpoor and produce little in the way of equalization of incomes across income classes. The social insurance component of social security for the most part provides money to people who were not poor when they made their contributions, and so smooths out their lifetime earnings. Since it is not means tested, it of course also provides income to those who presently are well to do. Social security is more nearly a kind of forced savings plan for individuals than it is a means by which some subsidize others. The latter does occur, but the former is the more powerful effect. Given the substantial evidence that the most politically active are the better off,[37] a reasonable conclusion is that the shape of the program

34. See James Q. Wilson (ed.), *The Politics of Regulation*, 370.
35. See Grant McConnell, *Private Power and American Democracy.*
36. Useful discussions of the various political patterns at work can be found in Morris Fiorina, *Congress, Keystone of the Washington Establishment;* David R. Mayhew, *Congress: The Electoral Connection;* Michael Malbin, *Unelected Representatives: Congressional Staff and the Future of Representational Government;* and Wilson (ed.), *The Politics of Regulation.*
37. See any study of political participation, e.g., Sidney Verba et al., *Participation and Political Equality: A Seven Nation Comparison.* Compare here

reflects officials' attentiveness to those who can most easily punish and reward them. As for medicare, the program not only secures middle- and upper-income people against economic disaster stemming from illness but has conferred—and will continue to confer—enormous benefits on middle- and upper-income *children*. They need not empty their pockets to pay for their aged parents' illnesses (or let them die or go to charity wards). The expansion of middle-class status, at least among middle-aged and younger persons, owes much to the existence of medicare. This is widely understood by politicians and by citizens, who act accordingly in order to protect the gains.

The distributive effects of regulatory activity are much harder to estimate. Some regulations probably protect producers, and some, such as the minimum wage, are at least intended to improve the lot of the poor. However, environmental controls (and perhaps consumer safety measures) probably most benefit middle- and upper-income citizens.[38] The consistently strong voting support that environmental regulation enjoys in the Congress suggests that politicians are acting on this information.[39]

Now, unless the politically active are successful in securing substantial benefits, they might turn their political energies in other directions, most notably toward the politics of inducement. The problem here is not one of hostility, since it is by no means impossible that some number of politically active citizens would find satisfactory the accommodations being reached between officials and businessmen. An increase in the number of participants would, however, considerably complicate the process of agreement between businessmen and officials. Moreover, because the politics of these other policy domains are free from the disproportionately weighty voices of businessmen and operate so that politically active citizens can reap substantial benefits, the politics of business in-

retirement benefits and AFDC payments:

Mean Monthly Payment (in 1980 dollars)				
	1950	1960	1965	1970	1980
Retired workers . . .	138	184	195	228	341
AFDC family of four . . .	NA	396	388	435	350

(The data are reported in Christopher Jencks, "How Poor Are the Poor," *New York Review of Books*, May 9, 1985, 43.)

38. See Benjamin Page, *Who Gets What From Government.*

39. Witness the June, 1985, 94—0 vote on extension of the Clean Water Act. See *The Congressional Quarterly*, June 15, 1985, 1147.

ducement itself can flourish. It is the relative independence of these
various domains from the question of business inducement that is
crucial. The many different political patterns at work outside the
domain of economic performance have in common the provision
of sufficient rewards for the politically active. This enables the
politics of inducement to flourish, thereby effectively displacing
any broad consideration of the commercial public interest.

What happens when the autonomy of the various domains break
down—when, for example, a strong connection is asserted between
the size of the welfare state or the extent of regulatory endeavors
and the problem of inducing business performance? Here again,
officials must conduct an intricate minuet, this time trying to mesh
the concerns both of businessmen and of those active in the policy
domain at issue. The important feature of such minuets is that
inducing business performance sets the terms of the struggle. The
question posed is, for example, How much social welfare or economic regulation can be afforded if *we are to continue to get business
performance?* Sometimes the question is posed just this explicitly, as
when very conservative administrations face it. But it also can be
discerned in disguised forms, such as in discussions about tight-
ening up social welfare disbursement provisions. The point here
is not that business-inducement considerations always triumph and
certainly not that businessmen's versions of what they need always
carry the day. It is simply that it is a concern for inducement that
guides the discussion. This is consistent with the analysis above—
that businessmen do not get everything that they want even in the
politics of inducement.

In summary, the domains other than those concerned with economic performance add little or nothing to the struggle over the
appropriate content of the commercial public interest. Beyond that,
they facilitate the focus on business inducement as the effective
definition of the commercial public interest.

The Discretion of Officials

Up to this point I have been proceeding as if public officials are
sharply constrained by electoral considerations; whether it is officials worried about promoting prosperity or entrepreneurial politicians catering to citizen desires for governmental benefactions,
the electoral connection has been treated as very strong. But representatives do not act only on what they take to be the instructions
of constituents. Electoral controls are loose enough to afford ample
discretion. Where does this discretion lead? The short answer is

that, like electorally oriented politics, it, too, either leads to a focus on inducing business performance or does not interfere with this focus.

Consider, first, that some officials will be drawn to inducing business performance for other than electoral reasons. State activities require revenues, the production of which is not in the hands of state officials. Economic performance to produce revenue is required for a variety of reasons, ranging from officials paying for their perquisites to financing policies that are central to their careers and their conception of larger national purposes—including national security. The performance of owners and managers of productive assets is of even more concern to the state to the degree that a substantial portion of national revenues originate through foreign trade. If the nation is highly integrated into the world economy, owners and managers in effect become public officials helping to earn the nation's keep. Many of these officials, both elected and appointed, are best understood as state managers, who see it as their task to strengthen the ability of the American state to project its power and economically compete in an unforgiving and often hostile world.[40] Such efforts, of course, cannot be separated from these officials' preferences for particular policy proposals or from the pleasures of office; overlapping motives are at work that converge in a continuing attentiveness to what businessmen say that they need if they are to perform.

To this consideration should be added the realization that the more seriously these officials see themselves as custodians of state interests, the more likely they are to offer their own versions of what is necessary for business performance.[41] Those particularly concerned with international affairs are probably most likely to do so. Other sorts of officials undoubtedly find being attentive to businessmen's worries a convenient way to explain the purposes of their careers to themselves and to others. At their worst they become the kind of capitalist lackeys much beloved by authors of the cruder Marxist literature. Such officials sometimes display the same touching faith as the ordinary citizens mentioned above who believe that businessmen's versions of the public interest are particularly worthy of consideration. Or these officials may simply be cynical. Nor should

40. The logic of such a view is suggested in Samuel Huntington's "The Democratic Distemper," *The Public Interest* 41 (Fall 1975): 9–38.

41. See Stephen D. Krasner, *Defending the National Interest: Raw Materials Investment and U.S. Foreign Policy;* and Franz Schurmann, *The Logic of World Power.*

we rule out the possibility that they are merely corrupt, their personal and professional budgets showing the presence of unwholesome amounts of corporate cash.[42]

Other officials use their discretion—and thus pursue their ambitions—in other ways. They neither reach as far as state managers nor fall as low as the convenient cynicism or corruption of the businessman's helpmate. Perhaps the most common paths are devoting oneself to becoming an expert and expending one's energies in servicing the needs of constituents.[43] Here we have the activities characteristic of so much of contemporary American politics: the politics of issue networks and the elaborate maneuvers of "home style."[44] Officials in the first category happily spend their days consorting with academic and other experts, being instructed by the staffs of what have come to be known as public interest groups, and chairing subcommittee hearings.[45] Of course, they are not above making as much of this as they can for home consumption, but the politics of issue networks are often too arcane to be of much use in this regard. It is a closed politics, and its principal rewards are those of conviviality among the skilled and mastery of difficult subject matter. Officials devoted to home-style are, by definition, members of Congress, and their days are devoted to such tasks as acting as ombudsmen, overseeing the assiduous use of the franking privilege to send out reminders of their devoted services, and taking credit for the promotion of legislation dear to their constituents.[46]

Both issue experts and devotees of home-style have found outlets for their ambitions that make the politics of inducement of little interest. It takes place outside their purview, and, as a result, they do little to direct the attention of citizens to any broader conception of the commercial public interest. The result, again, is to facilitate the accommodation between officials and businessmen.

42. See the fine discussion by Robert Caro in *The Years of Lyndon Johnson* on the relationship between Lyndon Johnson and Brown and Root and on the political uses of oil money. See also Etzioni's *Capital Corruption* on PACs.

43. It should be clear that nothing prevents officials from using their discretion in multiple ways.

44. Richard Fenno, in *Home Style: House Members in Their Districts*, reserves it for campaign-related activities. It seems appropriate to extend it to legislative activity contrived for home consumption.

45. Hugh Heclo, "Issue Networks and the Executive Establishment," in Anthony King (ed.), *The New American Political System*.

46. See David R. Mayhew, *Congress: The Electoral Connection;* and Peter Aranson and Peter Ordershook, "Public Interest, Private Interest, and the Democratic Polity," in Benjamin and Elkin (eds.), *The Democratic State*.

The discretion accorded public officials is not invariably used to focus on or otherwise facilitate business performance. It would be surprising if there were not some officials who understand and see the sense of the principles of the regime. They may simply see further into the problems of free government or have a sensitivity borne of experience—or both. It seems appropriate to call them statesmen, and it may generally be the lot of such men and women to be lonely voices. In any case, that is certainly the implication of the argument here. The workings of political economy mean that, as these officials[47] attempt to broaden struggle and debate beyond business inducement, they typically find few allies among other officials. In a real sense, statesmen exist because of the gap between our aspirations and the actual workings of our political economy. If there were no gap, we would all be statesmen.

Forums

One last point remains. In order for the commercial public interest to be given content, forums that encourage struggle and debate must be readily available. As many students of American politics have pointed out, however, the drift has been away from institutions that put a premium on public debate toward those that operate in a managerial mode; notable in this regard is the decline of Congress and the rise of the administrative state. But there is a corollary that has also gained wide recognition. The principal deliberative institution, the Congress, has itself increasingly come to operate as if public debate were a by-product of the legislative process. The rise of highly specialized subcommittees and staffs has turned much congressional activity into an adjunct of the administrative process. Those (such as the officials whom I have termed statesmen) who seek to mount a discussion about something other than inducing business performance find few formal opportunities to do so. This is not a matter of excluding dissenting opinion, but a change in the overall character of governmental institutions.

George Reedy captures a piece of what I am suggesting here when he boldly says: "The president, for all practical purposes, is the United States. He affords the only means through which we can act as a nation and the only consciously creative governmental force."[48] The presidency is, above all, not a deliberative body. The president may be said to represent, but he is not a representative

47. They may also be private citizens, but that is another matter.
48. George Reedy, "Discovering the Presidency," *The New York Times Book Review,* January 20, 1985, 23.

in the sense that members of Congress are. His decisions, although they may be wise, are not the product of public deliberation. Neither, increasingly, are those of the Congress.

CONCLUSION

The commercial public interest must include economic prosperity—and therefore, given the basic division of labor between state and market—must include some attention to inducing business performance. But these considerations do not exhaust its content. Promoting a commercial republic—and thus attending to the commercial public interest—requires that inducing business performance be seen in the larger context of securing republican government. It is not, then, just a question of what ways can be found to secure business investment, with success being measured by how much is forthcoming; rather, the alternative ways to do this must be judged, for example, against their impact on the potential for factional strife. Promoting a commercial society is, I have argued, an exercise in political theory.

We have, in fact, largely failed to maintain the distinction between the essentially political reasons for a commercial society and how to contrive a happy environment for businessmen. The confusion of the two is a characteristic form of corruption in liberal regimes. At its crudest, such corruption involves the identification of business profit with the public interest. The United States has not come that far, since our aspirations are still real. But our political life is not now organized so that our aspirations take precedence over political convenience.

At the heart of our failing, is not the dominating power of business, however. To be sure, businessmen are prominent in policy discussion, and their views are treated with undeniable attentiveness (more so, indeed, than are those of other participants). But the real source of our failure is that officials lack strong incentives to think beyond business inducement. The incentives that they do have largely point toward taking such inducement as the defining feature of the commercial public interest. Those who hold some other conception must work against the grain. It is not important—or even fully accurate—to say that officials seek to serve business interests. They do when businessmen have a clear view of what their interests are and when officials are not compelled to take other considerations into account. But the deepest concern of public officials is inducing business performance, not serving business interests. The two need not—and sometimes do not—coincide. At that point, officials will typically prefer their own views. Even then, however, they are not necessarily seeking to give content to the commercial public interest. To reliably do that, they must have incentives to take a larger, more political view. As I have said, these incentives are largely absent. This, not any tendentious argument about business dominance, is the crucial point.

The failing that I have described is also not one of business corporations short-circuiting democracy. As a regime we are not in the business of grafting democracy onto capitalism. In the view of those who emphasize the incompatibility of capitalism and democracy, the implicit (and sometimes explicit) conception of democracy is one in which all interests should have equal say in policy making, either directly or through representatives. It has been argued that, since businessmen are given greater attention (and since this bias seems to be built in), democracy must fail.[49] My own view is closer in spirit to Madison's. It is thus a critique from within our political tradition, not the application of categories drawn from the experience of others and imposed with little or no modification. For Madison, popular government and capitalism are not necessarily at loggerheads—and, indeed, if properly designed, can serve one another. That is what has gone wrong for us—the design is faulty. We have thus fallen far short of our aspiration to be a regime of popular sovereignty attentive to the political reasons for economic prosperity.

49. See, e.g., Joshua Cohen and Joel Rogers, *On Democracy.*

8
The Commercial
Public Interest and the
Urban Citizenry

To remedy the failure of the national political economy to serve the commercial public interest would require a large-scale reform effort. To bring into being this essential feature of a commercial republic, it would be necessary, among other things, to do the following: (1) lower the barriers to dissent, (2) reduce the tenacity with which businessmen pursue official inducements by, for example, reducing business concentration, (3) reduce the advantages that organized businessmen have in the collection and dispersal of political money, (4) curb the tendency of officials to use whatever discretion they have to facilitate business inducement, and (5) improve officials' grasp of the considerations that should guide their efforts to give content to the commercial public interest, particularly those considerations having to do with the connection between a commercial society and republican government.

In addition, the audience to which officials play will need a different character. If, in going about their political rounds, officials confront a citizenry that has a lively sense that inducing business performance does not exhaust the meaning of the commercial public interest, then they likely will find it rewarding to broaden their considerations. The tendency to take their bearings from businessmen might be reduced, and more vigorous debate and struggle over the implications of policy choice for the public interest of a commercial society might be stimulated. Public officials, in short, need incentives to engage in such struggle and debate. As it is, the incentives point to narrowing the problem or avoiding it altogether. The point is both obvious and powerful: public officials will be induced to struggle and debate in the manner described if they have an audience that rewards such undertakings. Without such reasons, businessmen's definitions will carry undue weight, business inducement will be the focus of policy making, and the political heart of the commercial public interest will drop from sight. Equally important, those statesmen who *do* understand that the public interest of a commercial society is not coterminous either with what businessmen contend to be necessary to induce economic performance or with inducing performance generally will receive little help.

The reform problem involves, then, intertwining elements: no single reform, on its own, will be sufficient. Reform touching on all of the principal weaknesses of the political economy also probably must be undertaken. At a minimum, it seems likely that, without a citizenry able to grasp that the commercial public interest is not exhausted by inducing business performance, no other reforms will work, at least if those reforms are not to be worse than the disease. Officials might find it attractive to debate and struggle over the commercial public interest if businessmen were not allowed to organize at all, but the net gain from such a situation is not obvious. But anything less draconian will allow too much room for evasion unless there is present a citizenry that has the requisite understanding. To restrain political ambition requires multiple checks. Attention to the character of the citizenry is a necessary line of reform even if it is not a sufficient one. Therefore, no matter how difficult the subject may be, it must be addressed if our regime aspirations are to be served.

Beyond any other considerations, however, it is simply appropriate, in remedying the failings of a popular regime, to concentrate first on the citizenry itself. James Madison states the case as well as anyone:

> But I go on this great republican principle, that the people will have virtue and intelligence to select men of virtue and wisdom. Is there no virtue among us? If there be not, we are in a wretched situation. No theoretical checks, no form of government, can render us secure. To suppose any form of government will secure liberty or happiness without any virtue in the people, is a chimerical idea. If there be sufficient virtue and intelligence in the community, it will be exercised in the selection of these men, so that we do not depend on their virtue, or put confidence in our rulers, but in the people who are to choose them.[1]

We may have to rely on political leaders to carry on much of our public affairs, Madison suggests, but they will not do so in ways consistent with our aspirations without the prompting of a certain sort of citizenry.

1. James Madison, June 20, 1788, as quoted by Ann Stuart Diamond, "Decent, Even Though Democratic," in Robert A. Goldwin and William A. Schambra (eds.), *How Democratic is the Constitution?*, 38.

The question, then, becomes, How is the citizenry to develop the sense that there is something more to a commercial society than promoting business performance? What is wanted is a habit of mind, a collective disposition to ask, What is the public interest of a commercial society? If this is a continuing vital presence, officials will be less inclined to focus strongly on business performance because citizens will have a lively sense that it does not exhaust the matter.

We can, in principle, learn the necessary habit of mind from the experience of regarding one another as fellow participants in the struggle and debate to define the commercial public interest. In short, political institutions of the proper sort can help to form a citizenry in which the disposition to focus on the definition of the commercial public interest is a strong element. The argument thus has come full circle, back to the formative bearing of institutions and their role in fostering the political way of life to which we aspire. The question now is, What is the possible contribution of *city* political institutions to the regime. In particular, what role might city political institutions potentially play in helping to realize our aspirations? What must these institutions look like if they are to help form a citizenry with the necessary habits of mind? How do the present political institutions of the city compare to what is wanted? And, finally, what are the consequences if the appropriate sort of institutions are not created?

A substantial gap between the kind of city political institutions that are wanted and those presently in operation means another shortcoming in the working of popular control in the city, a shortcoming of the kind that would probably have concerned Tocqueville and his theoretical successors. It is also one of great potential seriousness, since it calls into question the whole political way of life to which we aspire.

REASON GIVING AND INSTITUTIONS

Struggle over the content of the commercial public interest is an effort to determine the framework of law and policy within which the self-interested behavior that is characteristic of markets and political bargaining can occur. A republic in which self-interest can flourish needs the regular attention of citizens and leaders who are capable of thinking in other terms.[2] What sort of character will a citizenry that expects

---

2. Compare Fred Hirsch's remark that "Keynes assumed that the managers of the system would be motivated by higher goals than maximization of their private interests." *Social Limits to Growth*, 124.

political leaders to struggle over and debate the content of the commercial public interest have? Its central feature must be a disposition to think of political choice as involving the giving of reasons. When possible—and where the stakes are not trivial—public choices should elicit arguments about what is beneficial to us as a political community. Political choice is to be public-spirited and to involve justification, not just the aggregation of wants and interests.[3]

Now, the disposition to think of political choice as requiring deliberation is always present in popular regimes. They are quintessentially political regimes because they recognize that politics is a public affair, not an affair of the closet or bedchamber.[4] And because it is public in the sense that others have to be convinced, justification is essential. I must, that is, move beyond assertions of what is beneficial to me. This constant effort to thus formulate my claims helps to form my conception of the essential nature of democratic politics. This point is beautifully captured by Hannah Pitkin, who therefore deserves to be quoted at length.

> Drawn into public life by personal need, fear, ambition or interest, we are there forced to acknowledge the power of others and appeal to their standards, even as we try to get them to acknowledge our power and standards. We are forced to find or create a common language of purposes and aspirations, not merely to clothe our private outlook in public disguise, but to become aware ourselves of its public meaning. We are forced, as Joseph Tussman has put it, to transform "I want" into "I am entitled to," a claim that becomes negotiable by public standards. In the process, we learn to think about the standards themselves, about our stake in the existence of standards, of justice, of our community, even of our opponents and enemies in the community; so that afterwards we are changed. Economic man becomes a citizen.[5]

The task is to strengthen this disposition so that it is central to citizens' conception of political life; and when it has become central, citizens will expect of their leaders what they expect of themselves. If I think politics must revolve around reason giving, then I will expect those

---

3. Jon Elster says "that the central concern of politics should be the *transformation of preferences* rather than their aggregation." *Sour Grapes*, 35.

4. See Hanna Fenichel Pitkin, *Wittgenstein and Justice*, esp. 204.

5. Hanna Fenichel Pitkin, "Justice: On Relating Private and Public," *Political Theory* 9, no. 3 (August 1981): 347. The reference is to a book by Joseph Tussman, *Obligation and the Body Politic*. See also Benjamin R. Barber, *Strong Democracy: Participatory Politics for a New Age*. For the classic statement, see Rousseau, *The Social Contract*.

who politically represent me or otherwise claim to speak for me to
act in the same way.

There is no implication here of an inclination to offer or expect
heroic feats of discernment in which each person presents a fully
developed conception of the public interest. To state it is to dem-
onstrate its implausibility. Rather, the disposition to think of politics
as broadly deliberative—for that is what reason giving means—implies
a conception of politics as involving constant reformulation. Arguments are to be tested, reworked, and withdrawn, not asserted as if
their blinding rationality compels assent. Bargaining and compromise
will be in order because the warrant of reason runs out at some point.
And splitting the difference and trading will be acceptable as long as
the substance of what is split or traded are claims about what will
benefit the community. Politics as reason giving is political argument,
not geometry. Politics educates judgment.

It is also important to distinguish the conception that political institutions can help to form a citizenry that has a concern for the public
interest from other views that emphasize the formative impact of
political life. The oldest such view is the classical Greek conception,
in which political and moral (as moderns would say) life are inex-
tricably bound together and the broad purpose of politics is thought
to be the promotion of virtue.[6] But the conception of the citizenry
being presented in this chapter is not premised on such transpolitical
or transregime virtues—and, to the degree that such virtues are central to Greek thought, there is a sharp difference in emphasis. The
focus here is on dispositions that are necessary if a certain kind of
popular regime is to flourish.

A modern version of the formative idea is to be found in the civic
republican tradition. It is closer in spirit to the view presented here
than is the classical conception. Its central concern is the primary role
that civic virtue must play in the workings of free government. Civic
virtue might be understood, in the words of one of its most trenchant
critics, Carter Braxton, as "a disinterested attachment to the public
good, exclusive and independent of all private and selfish interest."[7]
There is in this concept a strong overtone of an organic public interest

6. See Stephen Salkever, "Virtue, Obligation and Politics," *American Political
Science Review* 68, no. 1 (March 1974): 78–92; and Alasdair MacIntyre, *After
Virtue.* The Greek conception certainly has room for the virtues appropriate
to particular regimes, and my argument in this respect parallels the classical
conception.
7. *An Address to the Convention of . . . Virginia: On the Subject of Government
. . . (Williamsburg 1776),* as quoted in Gordon Wood, *The Creation of the Amer-*

and a sense that the principal political motivation should be the reward of attempting to achieve the good of the community. Self-interest is denigrated as a source of political motivation and as the basis for principles of political justice. Political life is to be dominated by disinterested deliberation on the public good and by citizens appropriately disposed.

Nothing so demanding is required here.[8] There is no presumption of a single public good, only commitment to the idea that a portion of the public good involves the promotion of a commercial society. The public interest will emerge from argument borne of diverse starting points. It is not necessary that citizens be either similarly situated, as the civic republican idea implies, or motivated in so strict a fashion, as we shall see. Citizens only have to be disposed to believe that there is something more to public choice than combining private interests and that those who participate in the making of those choices (who may be themselves) must be held to a standard of advocacy that requires that they talk in larger terms.

A remark by Martin Diamond is especially helpful in clarifying what is at issue. He comments that "the American Founders followed Montesquieu in their reliance on institutions, and not the ancients regarding the necessity of character formation."[9] If by character here is meant the inculcation of virtue as the Greeks understood it, then the discussion presented here parallels Diamond's emphasis on institutions. The view here is that of John Adams, who said "that all projects of government founded in the supposition or expectation of extraordinary degrees of virtue are evidently chimerical."[10]

---

ican Republic, 1776–1789, 96. For a modern definition, see Robert A. Dahl, *Dilemmas of Pluralist Democracy: Autonomy versus Control.* Dahl says: "Civic virtue may be said to exist among some aggregate of persons if each person involved in making collective decisions (hence in a democratic system, all citizens) acts steadily on the conscious intention of achieving the good of all the persons in the aggregate" (142).

8. Nor is it readily available to us if the discussion in chap. 7 is correct. As John P. Diggins comments, "it may be tempting to see in classical political ideals an answer to the problems of American liberalism." John P. Diggins, *The Lost Soul of American Politics,* 14. See also the discussion by Amy Gutman, "Communitarian Critics of Liberalism," *Philosophy and Public Affairs* 14, no. 3 (Summer 1985): 308–22.

9. Martin Diamond, "The Declaration and the Constitution: Liberty, Democracy, and the Founders," *The Public Interest* 41 (Fall 1975): 51.

10. John Adams to Sam Adams, October 18, 1790, as quoted in Diggins, *The Lost Soul of American Politics,* 71. Adams starts out by saying that he is "not often satisfied with the opinions of Hume, but in this he seems well founded."

How, then, is this disposition to be encouraged, so that it is a central feature of the political understanding of the citizenry? To start, it will help to restate a central point of chapter 6: the form of relation between citizens poses a question. One way to understand the formative impact of institutions is that it occurs through the effort of answering such questions. The political institution(s) at issue here must, then, pose the question, What is the content of the public interest, as against my interest? in such a fashion that it will become central to the understanding of politics of a large part of the citizenry, a portion large enough to induce political leaders to act accordingly. Political institutions must place citizens in relation to each other as deliberators or reason givers, not, for example, as bargainers engaged in exchange.

It follows that the necessary political institution(s) will emphasize publicness and participation. They must be public because the arguments must be so and participatory because each must be a potential deliberator. Not everybody need be in the same room—the people literally assembled—but each must have the possibility of speaking and be within reach of others. None of this need happen simultaneously. The argument may go on over time and space. A deliberatively based politics need not aspire to defy elementary laws of nature.

Perhaps the most concise way to define the institutional form in question is to say that it will be legislative. To understand what this entails, the authority of Rousseau, the premier student of the subject, can be invoked. Rousseau distinguishes between the legislative and the executive power. The hallmark of the executive power is that its decisions concern particular persons or actions and thus have as their object the advancement of particular interests. Legislative decisions are general: they "both come from all and apply to all," [11] the implication being that they are not directed at somehow summating the particular interests of those concerned. [12]

The antithesis of legislative institutions are those that elicit privately developed claims and simply total these up by means of whatever decision rule is at work. A computer will do this admirably, and for optimum results each citizen (assuming the label is still appropriate) should be wired to the machine so that the moment that a want is consciously felt it can, without benefit of public espousal, be registered and added to the total. A further refinement would be to have the registering of wants occur before they reach consciousness—the registering of raw desire.

11. Rousseau, *The Social Contract*, 29.
12. See, generally, Rousseau, *Social Contract*, esp. Book II, chaps. 4, 6; Book III, chap. 1; and Book IV, chap. 2.

It is one thing to describe the appropriate form of relation between citizens. It is a different matter to understand what will breathe life into the institutions, that is, turn them into more than formalities. Understanding the difference will help in the effort to see why city political institutions are crucial to the realization of our aspirations and what these institutions should look like.

So far, the discussion has implicitly conceived of political institutions as bits of machinery that will commence operation once the operating rules are spelled out and the button is pushed. But institutions work because of the actions of the individuals who compose them. The viability of the rules—or, more broadly, the form of relation that is the institution—depends on these individuals acting in the appropriate ways. Why will they do so? What will turn an empty formalism into an ongoing form of relation? The legislative-like institutions must depend on the harnessing of powerful motives.[13]

Two motives are particularly deserving of consideration in this regard. First, struggle and debate over the public interest must be connected to the day-to-day vital interests of citizens. This will be in contrast to much contemporary political struggle, in which, when the question of the content of the public interest is raised, it is done in such a way that allows only vague and abstract answers. Naturally enough, those involved will emphasize what they understand, the implications of choices whose dimensions can be grasped. Political argument about the public interest must be tied, then, to specific policy choices, and those choices must be of such a kind that at least the major dimensions are comprehensible to those involved; in the case of ordinary citizens, this means choices that involve such things as neighborhood matters, schools, the land-use patterns of their localities, and a variety of features of their work lives. The question of the public interest will only be pursued if it is the centerpiece of struggle and debate over such matters as what sort of investment should be encouraged in a neighborhood or what, beyond a minimum curriculum, secondary schools should offer.

The second motive to be harnessed is the deep interest that each of us has in enjoying the esteem of others.[14] Tocqueville provides a powerful formulation of the point.

13. It will also be useful to see the following remarks in the context of the discussion in chap. 9 on the possibility of the appropriate institutional arrangements being realized.

14. See Rom Harré's discussion in *Social Being: A Theory for Social Psychology* of a "moral career," which he draws from the work of Erving Goffman.

When the public is supreme, there is no man who does not feel the value of public good-will, or who does not endeavor to court it by drawing to himself the esteem and affection of those amongst whom he is to live. Many of the passions which congeal and keep asunder human hearts, are then obliged to retire, and hide below the surface. Pride must be dissembled; disdain does not break out; selfishness is afraid of itself. Under a free government, as most public offices are elective, the men whose elevated minds or aspiring hopes are too closely circumscribed in private life, constantly feel that they cannot do without the population which surrounds them. Men learn at such times to think of their fellow-men from ambitious motives, and they frequently find it, in a manner, their interest to be forgetful of the self.[15]

Tocqueville teaches that, in democratic societies, it is the opinion of others that dominates our motives,[16] in contrast to those societies in which honor, salvation, or virtue may be the dominant forces. In one sense, societies *are* democratic because opinion is so dominant. So, if political institutions are to act as I have been describing, if they are to be more than formalisms, they must turn the desire for the esteem of others into a disposition to act politically by the giving of reasons.[17]

In one sense, the point here is a variation of the earlier observation that politics, being public and not private, has justification at its core. No one, if he or she can help it, wishes to make naked assertions of self-interest when the acquiescence (and, possibly, active cooperation) of others is at stake. But here the emphasis is not on the nature of the appeal to others but on what will gain their good opinion.

Two other points deserve emphasis. First, it must be assumed that most people will actually accord esteem to those who make the sort of public-oriented arguments being discussed. If they, in fact, will only willingly accord it to those who engage in conspicuous displays of getting and spending, then it will be impossible for political institutions to help form a public-spirited citizenry. If esteem is not granted at all for efforts to argue about the public

15. Quoted in Diggins, *The Lost Soul of American Politics,* 245–46.

16. "Opinion is more than ever mistress of the world." Alexis de Tocqueville, *Democracy in America,* vol. 2, p. 11.

17. Concomitantly, Tocqueville says: "No power on earth can prevent increasing equality from turning men's minds to look for the useful or disposing each citizen to get wrapped up in himself. One must therefore expect that private interest will more than ever become the chief if not the only driving force behind all behavior. But we have yet to see how each man will interpret his private interest." *Democracy in America,* 527 (Mayer edition).

interest, then the problem of free government is on a totally different footing from anything implied here; it seems doubtful that a popular regime devoted to individual freedom can survive if its citizens accord no respect to those who make an effort to do more than say "I want." A corollary observation—and the second point deserving emphasis—is that this whole discussion assumes that a genuine desire to reason is widely dispersed. If dissimulation is a major art form, then, once again, the problem of free government is other than that presented here.

The Centrality of the City

What is the connection between the present discussion of reason giving and the importance of city political institutions for our aspirations? The preceding discussion regarding harnessing the two motives of a concern for day-to-day matters and a desire for the esteem of others provides the link. The effort to harness the desire for the good opinion of others favors smaller-scale institutions, in which its effects are likely to be more powerful. At the same time, since there is no presumption here of a single correct definition of the commercial public interest, small numbers ought not to bring in their train homogeneity of social characteristics. The danger, of course, is that the desire for esteem will mean the tyranny of a dominant opinion. The search for the commercial public interest is quintessentially a political act, and politics requires a plurality of diverse persons—that is, persons that are not joined by some bond of communion, pity, or love. Scale and heterogeneity both point to local government institutions as being most appropriate in helping to form the citizenry. But these considerations do not specifically favor cities and, if anything, given their larger scale, point away from them.

The effort to harness the concern for vital day-to-day interests also points to local governments. This is where issues of neighborhood, schools, and at least some aspects of work—that is, the sorts of issues whose definition in terms of the public interest is least likely to be fraught with empty abstractions—are decided. Again, cities have no particularly favored position, since any suitably arranged multipurpose local government will serve.

The key to understanding the potentially unique position of cities is to recall that the focus here is on the *commercial* public interest. The discussion of the public interest generally has led to local government; its commercial dimension takes us to cities.

The crucial point is apparent from the discussion in chapters 2 and 3. Unless cities are to become wards of the federal government, a prospect not now in evidence, they must be concerned with economic performance. The central concern of city politics is to ensure the economic wherewithal to provide public services and generally support the public life of the city. As these earlier chapters also suggest, a key to economic vitality is the arrangement of the land-use patterns of the city. Moreover, as these same chapters argue, cities conspicuously present the temptation to allow the commercial public interest to be defined as the facilitating of the activities of businessmen concerned with land use—and this definition often substantially reflects what these businessmen say is needed. This is the natural alliance between public officials and land interests. All that needs to be added is to emphasize that there are, at a minimum, alternative ways to promote economic performance aside from providing the inducements requested by the relevant businessmen. There are also alternative formulations of the connections between economic vitality, the means by which to achieve it, and the broader life of the community.[18] The various formulations are all consistent with a commitment to promote a commercial society, the definitions offered by businessmen not being the only obviously correct ones.

Any discussion of the public interest in the contemporary city must focus, then, on economic performance and, more to the point, concern itself with land-use patterns. And land use is at the core of the vital concerns of citizens. It affects neighborhood quality, jobs, crime, and schools. Cities provide the meeting ground for a consideration of the commercial public interest that both can connect its discussion to the vital concerns of citizens and can do so in a context in which harnessing the motive of gaining the esteem of others may occur. Cities are thus potentially crucial for creating the kind of citizenry that will reward leaders who struggle and debate over the commercial public interest.

There is, however, a difficulty to face here. Cities now contain only somewhat more than one-quarter of the total population, and

18. See the discussions in chaps. 5 and 9 for why these alternatives are available. It is not necessary to indicate here what they are, since the only points at issue are whether the bricks-and-mortar strategy analyzed in chaps. 2–5 is the only one that can promote economic vitality for the city and whether alternatives are politically feasible. Political feasibility must be contemplated in the context of those altered institutional arrangements and powers of the city that are discussed below. In addition to what has already been said in earlier chapters about alternative economic strategies, see Jane Jacobs, *Cities and the Wealth of Nations,* for a strong argument that present strategies of economic development are poorly conceived.

if the goal is a citizenry generally having the requisite character, are not the numbers inadequate? Several points suggest a different conclusion: 1. One-quarter of the population is not, in any case, a negligible number. Assuming that this figure translates into a roughly equivalent number of voting-age citizens, if these latter were strongly disposed to judge political leaders in the manner described here, the results would not pass unnoticed (to which might be added that, if cities are thought to be intractable in the present context, one-quarter of the population is a substantial barrier to the success of other reform proposals). 2. Cities stand at the center of the national communication network. The national media are housed there and pay more attention to the affairs of cities than to those of other local governments. It seems plausible, then, that whatever city political institutions teach will be transmitted across the nation, thus having an impact beyond what occurs among the citizens of the cities themselves. 3. Perhaps most important, the combination of factors that make city political institutions potentially so crucial may also be apparent in other local governments. To the degree that a wide range of local governments now face the question of actively shaping their economic destiny, they too will confront citizens with the problem of the relation between what businesses say will facilitate economic performance and the commercial public interest. In this case, the argument being made here can be extended to a broad range of local governments. But there is no doubt that, historically, the tendency to define the commercial public interest in terms of facilitating business performance has been strongest in cities, and it is still the case that the question is most forcefully posed there. The future, however, may be different—and, if it is, then the emphasis here on cities will have to be adjusted.

It should be emphasized that the meaning of the preceding discussion is that city political institutions can act as a kind of surrogate. The question of the commercial public interest gets posed *locally*. The disposition to struggle and debate over the commercial public interest is directed at the commercial public interest of the city. Citizens then will extend their expectations to national political leaders. In their struggle to give content to the public interest of the city, citizens will face the question of how to achieve reasonable prosperity—and also the questions of whether any sort of economic performance and any way of achieving it are appropriate. But even with such a broad focus to their deliberations, the citizens of the city are unlikely to be so far-ranging as to linger over the connection between a commercial society and the success of republican government. At best, the experience of struggling locally over com-

parable matters will make a citizenry more supportive of national
leaders who wish to resist a focus on business inducement and who
argue for policies that pay heed to the political content of the
commercial public interest.

It would be better, of course, if the citizenry were to struggle
and debate over the commercial public interest of the national
political community. But the demands of information make this
unlikely. To be sure, much present empirical and theoretical discussion in political science takes its bearings from what citizens now
know and neglects to notice the limited incentives, given the present
political arrangement, for them to learn more. Still, it does not
seem useful to assume that most citizens will freely wish to master
what is necessary. Of course, citizens will have views on national
economic matters, and will push for them, but it is doubtful whether
anything other than institutions in which the commercial public
interest is clearly and directly tied to day-to-day concerns will serve.
Since the policy choices facing the national community will often
appear remote and their implications cloudy and diffuse, if the
idea of public interest is not nourished from some other source, it
will likely weaken or even fade away. Unless the idea of a public
interest—that is, of a conception of the common good that grows
out of the clash of reasoned argument—is connected to the experience of arguing about it—and unless the public interest is connected in the minds of the citizenry to concrete choices that have
consequences for important features of their lives—it will be a
(probably) harmless abstraction. As a consequence, in judging the
actions of leaders, citizens will not seek to hold these officials to a
public-interest standard because they cannot imagine that this is
an important part of political life.

What the sort of city political institutions contemplated here might
sacrifice in directness, then, they will likely compensate with a
stronger sense that the struggle over the commercial public interest
is not an abstraction but is connected to the concrete details of
trying to make a city work. Being concrete, it will be vital. Being
vital, it will be more easily extended to the judging of the actions
of leaders.

There remains a serious difficulty with the surrogate argument:
it is one thing for citizens to take seriously the idea that there *is* a
commercial public interest, but it is quite another idea for them to
know when political leaders are pursuing it. Lacking any developed
conceptions of the public interest of the larger community, why
won't citizens be fooled by the rhetorical flourishes of leaders, especially since these leaders have strong incentives to dress up un-

pleasant private schemes in appealing public garments. There is no easy solution here. As a regime, we plainly would be better off if the citizenry did have developed conceptions of the commercial public interest of the national community. But, as has been suggested, scale, complexity, and the cost of information all suggest that we should not hope for too much. We are left, then, with looking for surrogates. These may indeed present grave difficulties, but there is no reason to expect that the nourishment of regime principles will prove to be an easy task, especially when we are concerned with commercial matters in a regime that is supposed to reap the benefits of self-interested behavior.[19]

CONTEMPORARY CITIES

From a constitutive viewpoint, city political institutions potentially provide what cannot easily be gotten elsewhere. Potential, however, is one thing, reality another. How do the present political institutions of the city help to form the citizenry? The essential point is easily stated: the present political institutions of the city help to form the citizenry in a direction that ill serves our aspirations. Modern city political institutions are executive centered, and it is a central feature of such institutions that reason giving on the part of citizens is not elicited. The citizenry is not being formed in such a way that it is disposed to make an effort to define the commercial public interest.

To see how the political institutions of the city help to form us as citizens, it is only necessary to see chapters 2–4 in a new light. It is not additional evidence that is required but different lenses.

The fundamental form of relation defined by contemporary city political institutions places citizens in relation to each other as bargainers who are bearers of interests. The mode of interaction elicits from those involved conceptions of their private and group interest; and the conception of political life as being primarily about the aggregation of interests is thereby strengthened. Citizens expect to have to define and advance their own interests and are thus inclined

---

19. Is a strong socialist party a substitute for the kind of citizenry being discussed here? This is, by and large, the route that European liberal democracies have taken—with mixed results. It is not apparent that substantial departures have been made from businessmen's definition of the public interest. Additionally, there remains the question of what happens when leftist parties are out of power.

to think that the task of political leaders is somehow to combine these claims.

Some of the eliciting of interest occurs in relatively direct citizen-leader interactions of the kind often described by students of urban politics. Here are the transactions—between neighborhood ethnic leaders and/or ward bosses, on the one hand, and citizens, on the other—in which are arranged exchanges of support in return for promised favors. In their most visible form, the transactions involve reasonably clear statements about the sort of benefactions to be expected in return for specific levels of support. The classic description, noted for its explicitness and wit, is by George Washington Plunkitt, who explained in great detail how he built a political following. The sense conveyed is of a business transaction—and of those involved understanding it in just that way.[20] But it is likely that contemporary transactions are somewhat less explicit than the late-nineteenth-century type described by Plunkitt.

Those who are instrumental in arranging such exchanges are in effect deputized as local leaders who will enter into negotiations with the rest of the political leadership of the city and seek to strike the best bargain. Those managing to become leaders in this context are skilled at such negotiations and at the transactions with citizens. And those citizens who flourish are people adept at conveying their interests and promises of support in such a fashion that advocates will be attracted to their cause. At all levels, the premium is on knowing what one wants and being skilled at making promises of support that do not bind too tightly; it is skilled calculators and bargainers who succeed.

Much of the interaction between political leaders of the city, however, is not prompted by local neighborhood and group leaders seeking favors for constituents. After all, downtowns are renewed, hospitals are built and schools are run, and the negotiations and struggle over such matters are unlikely to be dominated by the sorts of leaders just described. The principal actors here—such as mayors, agency heads, party leaders, and heads of civic associations—will be guided by a number of considerations, but high among them will be the maintenance of the large-scale organizations over which they preside; they will advance some proposals and resist others in order, for example, to increase the flow of resources into the organization or to secure their position within it.[21] But it is not

20. See William L. Riordan, *Plunkitt of Tammany Hall.* See also the description by James C. Scott, *Comparative Political Corruption.*
21. See Edward C. Banfield, *Political Influence,* chaps. 8–10.

always possible to bring negotiations among such leaders to fruition, and the eliciting of interest-group claims again comes to the fore. Leaders will then make appeals for support of their proposals in interest-group terms,[22] and neighborhood and group leaders will see opportunities to strengthen their position as advocates for their groups.

In general, then, the political institutions of the city link citizens as articulators of private interest, and are forums that focus the various negotiations. Given political institutions such as these, the principal role of neighborhoods is as claimants in a competition for city largesse, rather than as potential assemblies of citizens. Those active in neighborhood politics learn that conferral of benefits arises from offers of political support. They are skilled in external relations, representing the neighborhood in larger political struggles. The focus of neighborhood politics is outward, toward an external statement of claims rather than inward, to a definition of common well-being.[23]

Some of the most acute students of contemporary urban politics have offered analyses parallel to the one presented here. Although they have generally not been explicitly concerned with the formative impact of institutions and the place of cities in the regime, they have seen that the political institutions of the city help to define citizens as bearers of interests. Consider, for example, Edward C. Banfield's description of "political heads" in Chicago—that is, the leaders (particularly the mayor) of its large public organizations. The political head, he comments, "waits for the community to agree upon a project. When agreement is reached, or when the process of controversy has gone as far as it can, he ratifies the agreement and carries it into effect." [24] Continuing the analysis, Banfield comments on the conception of the public interest at work. Since his remarks capture the point being made here with some precision, it is worth quoting him at length:

> The political head's reluctance to reach a decision is only in part a function of the situation in which he is placed. It is also a function of the conception he and his constituents share of the nature of the public interest and of the role of elected representatives. According to the Chicago view, a policy ought to be framed

22. See the description in Robert A. Dahl, *Who Governs*, books III, IV; and, in a different context, by E. E. Schattschneider, *The Semisovereign People*.

23. See Matthew A. Crenson, *Neighborhood Politics*, esp. chap. 6; and Milton Kotler, *Neighborhood Government: The Local Foundation of Political Life*.

24. Banfield, *Political Influence*, 253.

by the interests affected, not by the political head or his agents. In this view, the affected interests should work out for themselves the "best" solution of the matter (usually a compromise). The political head should see that all principally affected interests are represented, that residual interests (i.e., "the general public") are not entirely disregarded, and that no interest suffers unduly in the outcome.[25]

Matthew A. Crenson suggests that citizens themselves are aware of how city political institutions help to form them. It would be hard to find a more powerful statement of the formative impact of city political institutions than the following comment made by a resident of Baltimore quoted in Crenson's book: "Politicians don't do anything to teach people how to be citizens. They teach them how to be consumers. You want something, you go to the organization. . . . But you're not a citizen. You don't know how to do it yourself." [26]

The transformation of urban black politics provides additional support for this characterization of the manner in which the political institutions of the city help to form the citizenry into bearers of interests. To summarize an extremely complex process, the more intense their involvement with the major political institutions of the city became, the more black citizens came to see race as an interest-group category. Rather than racial discrimination being a denial of equal citizenship in the city, it came to be understood as a denial of benefits. In many cases this process built on the already existing involvement of blacks in an interest-driven politics; black submachines were, for example, mainstays of the kinds of politics described here. A principal result of this development of black politics was an expansion in the number of blacks who came to understand city politics as a matter of interest articulation and aggregation. None of these remarks is meant as a dismissal of the contention that benefits were unequally distributed; they are offered only to emphasize that city political institutions help to shape the black citizenry of the city in the image of its white counterpart.[27]

A useful way to summarize the formative impact of city political institutions is to say that they help to form citizens in much the same way that the market system does; there is the same emphasis on accurate definition of self-interest and on exchange. City politics

25. Banfield, *Political Influence*, 270–71. See also Wallace S. Sayre and Herbert Kaufman, *Governing New York City.*

26. Crenson, *Neighborhood Politics*, 258.

27. Among others, see James Q. Wilson, *Negro Politics: The Search for Leadership*, for a discussion of black submachines; and, for the latter period, see Rufus Browning et al., *Protest Is Not Enough.* A parallel argument is made by Theodore J. Lowi, *The End of Liberalism*, chaps. 7–9.

is, then, an extension of the market relationship rather than a part of the foundation from which such self-interested behavior is directed toward serving our aspirations.

Although citizens as bearers of interests is probably the dominant form of relation, the picture so far given of how city political institutions help to constitute the citizenry is far from complete. Citizens also stand in relation to each other as clients mediated by bureaucratic experts. The question implicitly posed by this form of relation is something like: In what category are you? The citizen approaching the bureaucracy is asked or required to define himself or herself or is defined along some set of attributes so that the appropriate decision or service may be delivered. The interaction need not be a willing one for this to occur. By extension, citizens then stand in relation to one another as members of bureaucratically created categories that define what claims they have on public authority and resources. If this were to be the dominant form of relation, citizens would presumably conceive of political life as an exercise in consulting rule books rather than as struggle over the content of common purposes.

This institutional form has become increasingly important, and, for some citizens of the city, being bureaucratic clients defines their urban citizenship. It is not impossible that this will become true for many more. For present purposes, the balance between citizens as bearers of interest and citizens as bureaucratic clients is of little moment, since both point in the same direction. Neither helps to form citizens as reason givers. Nor is there any reason to present any details of a bureaucratic form of relation, beyond commenting that its essential core is hierarchical. By definition, bureaucracies do not revolve around legislative processes.

It only remains to make the observation that the contemporary political institutions of the city, of course, allow for some debate over the content of the public interest, in its commercial aspect or otherwise. As I have argued, this disposition is always present in popular regimes, because justification to others is one of their essential features. But this disposition requires strengthening through appropriate forms of relation if it is to be a significant feature of political life. As it exists in the contemporary city, such reasoning is intermittent, half-hearted, and too often accompanied by a self-conscious shrug or laugh, as if the reasoner is afraid of being thought a rube among the sophisticates of an interest-driven politics.

There should be nothing very surprising about this description of how the political institutions of the city help to constitute the citizenry. As chapters 2 and 3 have described, something very much like this was intended by the principal urban-reform efforts. Present political institutions reflect, among other things, the influence of two major and ongoing reform efforts. One emphasizes the city as a service-delivery system and focuses on administrative reform; the other emphasizes the city as the locus for a congeries of interests and aims at improving the access of each, especially those that are weak. The citizen as bureaucratic client and bearer of interests is the natural corollary of these conceptions. And, in a deeper sense, such a conception of cities and citizenship is advanced by two of the most powerful currents of contemporary political thought: administrative theory and pluralism.

As chapter 3 also describes, these reform efforts were laid over (and partly contributed to) a city politics that embodied forms of relation that were similar to those being advanced by reformers. Even though the intent of reformers was, in part, to advantage groups other than those favored by existing institutional arrangements (consider, for example, the war on poverty and efforts to aid the minority poor), the relations in which citizens were to stand paralleled those of the executive-centered, interest-driven politics that emerged during the early twentieth century. In no case were the institutions that emerged of the kind to have citizens stand in relation to others as reason givers.

It is important to emphasize that how city political institutions presently help to constitute the citizenry is not "wrong," if by "wrong" is meant that such a politics, built around self-interest and bargaining, is a reprehensible form of political life. Quite the contrary: a principal argument of the earlier chapters has been that the American regime is, among other things, devoted to fostering the political expression of self-defined interests. The concern for the public interest of a commercial society is not a substitute for such an interest-driven politics but a foundation for it. Citizens skilled in seeking out mutually advantageous trades and in calculating their own and other interests are as central a part of a flourishing American regime as a concern for the commercial public interest. What we aspire to be, after all, is a liberal regime.

It would be best to say that the political institutions of the city are inappropriate. The point is contextual. If our aspirations were otherwise, how city political institutions now help to constitute us might be appropriate. Their present inappropriateness, however, is substantial. Because the institutions in effect ask for assertions of interest and magnify the voices of land interests, the question of the content of the commercial public interest is not raised. This is a significant failure of popular control, to be added to that of systematic bias and ineffective problem solving.

Some Future Paths

Just how significant a failure by political institutions it is can be seen by looking at some likely paths that the political economy will take if no effort is made to repair the regime.[28] At present, American political life is animated by a tension between regime and political economy. Our aspirations are real and have the power to move us—and talk of failures in the political economy thus has meaning because reality is tested against what we hope to become.

The political life most likely to emerge in the aftermath of deferring or failing to undertake reform of the kind contemplated here is a kind of corrupted liberalism. It represents the smallest departure from the present situation, in which regime and political economy are counterposed and political life is animated by the contrast. In a corrupt liberalism, the tension will be weak as aspirations wither, victims of the failure to create democratized city political institutions and generally to reduce the undue solicitousness of officials for businessmen's views.

Of the kinds of corrupted liberalism possible, the most likely might be termed "corporate liberalism."[29] It represents a kind of Mexican standoff between the principal contemporary currents of political activity: those devoted to the defense of the business corporation and those devoted to some version of an expanded state in the service of social welfare. One of its principal features will be a continuation of the vigorous politics of business inducement already described. Political participation, especially among middle-class citizens, may remain widespread but, as before, will not much affect the terms that such inducement takes. The principal difference from the present situation is that, in a corrupt liberalism, what is now not much talked about among the neighbors—that is, the cohabitation of public officials and businessmen—will be publicly celebrated and the announcement made that the consummation of the marriage is of general benefit. The commercial public interest will also be proclaimed as meaning the inducing of business performance. Here is the corporate part of corporate liberalism.

28. There is no presumption here that there was once a golden age of the American regime from which we have sadly declined; rather, the presumption is that different eras of the political economy have presented different sorts of problems for our aspirations. The focus of the present discussion is the difficulties and remedies of the contemporary era. The reform of local political institutions might previously have been of limited importance.

29. For the term—but not the particular argument—presented here, see Jeffrey R. Lustig, *Corporate Liberalism: The Origins of Modern Political Theory: 1890–1920.*

The liberal part of this corrupted liberalism is less familiar and the nature of the corruption less obvious. The easiest way to characterize it is to say that it is a rights-based liberalism that has succeeded all too well. It will subject a very large governmental domain to judicial procedures in the hope of making it secure against the vagaries of politics and the calculus of the market. These now "judicialized" activities will have the label "rights" attached to them to signify that neither the exercise of power nor calculations of national wealth ought to intrude. The "new property" will have exfoliated and will become neither new nor property.[30]

The point here is not to excoriate the attempt of what might be called "expansionary liberals"[31] to secure the expansion of state guarantees in spheres where private efforts and more traditional judicial remedies have failed. This is an effort that, at least in principle, is driven by a theory that suggests why a wide range of activities should be treated in terms of rights. Such an effort, should it succeed, need not be a corruption of our liberal aspirations, and a reasonable argument might be mounted that it is, in fact, a fulfillment. What is at issue here is the possibility that such an impulse could be taken to an extreme, driven very likely by the despair of containing the pas de deux of corporation and public officials. If political action cannot prevent the damage that could be done by this unseemly embrace, those in despair might say that what we must do is use the language of rights to secure a domain in which politics and wealth cannot easily enter. If they succeed, then a kind of liberal corruption will indeed have arrived. Rights language will then become a rhetorical cover, directed not at justifying a sphere in which individual autonomy can flourish but aimed instead at providing a new principle of social decision in which businessmen will have no advantage, regardless of whether this is in the service of individual autonomy or not. From an argument about individual choice or even individual self-development, the language of rights becomes an argument for social decision rules that will severely restrict business inducement.

Both justifications of the corporate-public embrace and the hyperextended practice of rights will mean that our aspirations have become a rhetorical cover for other purposes. The surface of the political economy will not look very different, and, indeed, many of the features of our present politics will probably continue, in-

30. For the term, see Charles A. Reich, "The New Property," *Yale Law Journal* 73, no. 5 (April 1964): 733–87.
31. See Stephen L. Elkin, "Between Liberalism and Capitalism," in Roger Benjamin and Stephen L. Elkin (eds.), *The Democratic State.*

cluding the vigorous interest politics characteristic of those domains in which questions of economic performance are not seen to be central. But the connection between language and underlying aspiration will have been broken—and thus the ability of our public language to direct reform in appropriate ways will have been severely weakened.

Other political economies are possible outcomes. They may evolve directly from our present political economy or indirectly through a transformation of corporate liberalism. The most likely of these is some version of a class politics, as the incentive of officials to resist businessmen's version of the roots of economic performance wanes and suspicion of governmental purpose correspondingly expands. In such a class-driven political economy, whatever hold liberal aspirations have is gone and any resemblance between the organization of the political economy and a liberal regime is a matter of power and convenience. Differently stated, such a class-driven political economy is characterized by political institutions that essentially reflect the balance of social forces. In the corrupt liberalism just discussed, the damage has not proceeded this far.

A crucial aspect of the liberal regime that we aspire to is that the political institutions that compose it work in such a way that they do not merely reflect the existing balance of social forces. This is implicit in the very idea of a regime. It is an attempt to organize political life so that it is more than a convenience or an accommodation to that existing balance of social forces that is necessary to have a political life at all. The regime is an effort to create something new, something worthy of us—namely, a political way of life that, among other things, serves individual rights and defines and serves the commercial public interest.

In this regard, consider first class politics and the question of rights. Whether it is a politics in which there is a plainly dominant class that staffs the state apparatus for its own purposes or otherwise controls it or whether it is a politics characterized by class struggle and uneasy compromise, something resembling individual rights may still be protected. But such rights will spring from one or some combination of the following: (1) their utility (in the eyes of the dominant class) in diverting attention away from class dominance and in preventing collective action,[32] (2) the fear of some sectors of the dominant class that rights must be protected because one can never tell who will be in power next, or (3) the need to make

32. Consider here Nicos Poulantzas' argument in *Political Power and Social Classes* about how the judicial apparatus of the capitalist state already serves these ends.

concessions to a restless working class that demands, among other things, the protection of individual liberties as the price of civil peace. In short, the rights will be the product of class calculations.

In general, political institutions are understood by all sides in a class politics to be instruments for achieving class interests. The guiding hand is that of Marx rather than that of Madison, and the thought that political institutions can do more than further class interests is absent. In the largest sense, democratic government itself simply becomes one more concession made by the powerful, either to forestall difficulties or in response to them. What is lost in a class politics is the belief central to a liberal politics—that political life can be the focus of aspirations for something more than seems possible in the simple clash of societal interests. A liberal regime, then, is not simply an argument for grafting popular control onto capitalism because it is in some way useful to do so; it is a claim that a certain sort of popular regime can bring us more than the social peace that is the most that even an artfully arranged class politics can provide.

Much the same sort of loss as has just been sketched is probable in a politics completely dominated by interest groups as against classes. Here again, civil liberties could be a kind of mutual insurance policy against one's own coalition losing out. As with a class politics, political institutions will only register and combine the efforts of existing social forces. In the end, there is not much difference between political institutions as a battleground for many interests or only two—except that in the former the losers are unlikely to lose as badly. This is no small matter, and on it rests the case for a pluralist society; but a clash of interests does not itself provide any purposes to which that clash is directed.

None of the possible political economies described represents a crisis, no more than our present situation is one. All might be stable, and none is likely to be especially violent, rapacious, or given to massive disregard of civil liberties or toleration of massive poverty. Still, none is especially appetizing and each represents a more or less significant failure of our aspirations to be a liberal regime. To echo Hamilton, the result would be a "general misfortune for mankind," a weakening of the belief that "societies of men" are able to establish "good government from reflection and choice." [33] The equation appears to be one of balancing the prospect of a politics that at best offers no more than civil peace and avoids a parade of political horribles against uncertain reform in the service of not

33. *Federalist*, no. 1.

only what is best in us but what is instructive for others. It would not be superfluous to add that the choice requires a kind of wisdom not readily available, a matter to which I will return.

CONCLUSION

The political institutions of the city need to put citizens in a form of relation that strengthens the disposition to engage in public-regarding debate and struggle. Such institutional arrangements and the disposition that they help form are necessary if a commercial republic is to flourish. The definition of the commercial public interest that emerges from such political activities need not be an airy abstraction. It can emerge from the harnessing of reliable and powerful motives, largely of a self-regarding kind, rather than from the uncertain diffuse desire to consider the well-being of generalized others.[34] Key to translating these motives into a concern with larger matters are political institutions. In the course of their struggles, citizens will not be attempting to approximate some externally defined conception of the public interest. "Public interest" here stands for no more than that which is consistent with or necessary to serving our aspirations.

Serving our aspirations to be a liberal regime depends on harnessing liberal motives. A liberal society will be characterized by people who think it appropriate to be deeply concerned both with the particulars of their day-to-day lives and with the good opinion of others. The task, then, is to use these motives to create a concern for the commercial public interest, without which such a regime is impossible. The goal is to make citizens more intelligent about public life, not more moral. Here, then, is a powerful shortcoming in the political institutions of the city—the failure to help form a citizenry capable of governing itself in conformance with its liberal aspirations.

34. Cf. Tocqueville: "In this predicament to retreat is impossible, for a people cannot recover the sentiments of their youth. . . . They must go forward and accelerate the union of private with public interests, since the period of disinterested patriotism is gone by forever." *Democracy in America*, vol. 1, p. 252. Also note Robert Livingston's comment: "We must have trade. It is prudent not to put virtue to too serious a test." Quoted in Gordon S. Wood, *The Creation of the American Republic*, 93.

9
The Probable and
the Desirable

The sorts of political institutions that can strengthen a public-regarding disposition are broadly democratic ones, and the principal reason for democratization is to foster a liberal regime. By contrast, those who might be styled "strong democrats" [1] argue that greater democratization is itself a benefit, that the more democratic the regime, the better it is. In this idea that greater democratization is intrinsically valuable, they join hands with civic republicans. [2] Whereas democrats look for guidance principally to the basis of authority in the continuing political activity of the people, civic republicans look, in addition, to whether such participation results in the public good. In effect, both call for new regimes, and neither is interested in the further democratization of an essentially liberal regime. My concern here, by comparison, is for a marriage of liberalism and democracy, with the latter in the service of the former.

Although the absence of democratized city political institutions may imperil the mixed regime of liberal democracy, is it probable that the political forces currently at work will usher in the appropriate reforms? Or, alternatively, are the consequences sketched in the previous chapter a real prospect? Concomitantly, if the reforms are improbable, ought those devoted to the purposes of the regime seek to promote them? Once the implications of such a reform effort for our aspirations are understood, ought friends of the regime devote their talents to urban reform? [3]

---

1. See, as the most prominent example, Benjamin R. Barber, *Strong Democracy*. See also Gerald Frug, "The City as a Legal Concept," *Harvard Law Review* 93, no. 6 (April 1980): 1057–154. See, in general, Amy Gutman, "Communitarian Critics of Liberalism," *Philosophy and Public Affairs* 14, no. 3 (Summer 1985): 308–22; and Hannah Arendt, *On Revolution*.

2. See, e.g., William Sullivan, *Reconstructing Public Philosophy*.

3. Friends of the regime would, of course, be willing to "exchange reasons" and "think clearly" (see chap. 5) and may be said to have an internal point of view.

With appropriate modifications, these questions are equally pertinent to the discussion of systematic bias and unintelligent problem solving. For these failures of popular control, however, both their consequences and the desirability of pursuing certain remedies are better understood, since they have been staple items in political science discussions. Therefore, these matters need not detain us here. That is not the case with the absence of institutions needed to help constitute us in ways appropriate to our aspirations. To help answer the questions about probability and desirability, it first will be necessary to provide more institutional details for the sort of city political institutions that seem necessary to the realization of our aspirations. The suggestions discussed are meant only to set out some widely canvassed proposals that seek to make city political institutions more deliberative and participative and that aim to decrease the prerogatives of those who control assets in the city. These are the crucial first steps in creating political institutions that can help to form the urban citizenry in appropriate ways, but whether the particular institutional arrangements considered are wholly adequate is doubtful. The point is not to design the necessary institutions—no one person can—but to emphasize that certain kinds of institutional features are desirable.

City Political Institutions Revisited

I have argued that the institutional arrangements must be participatory, legislative in form, and public in argument; that is, they must involve a substantial number of citizens standing in relation to each other as reason givers if our aspirations are to be served. This suggests the three following institutional arrangements: (1) neighborhood assemblies with significant powers, (2) citywide referenda, and (3) city legislatures, also with significant powers.[4] Each is an attempt either to place citizens in a deliberative relationship or to contrive a reasonable approximation of one. None reaches for an unattainable assembly of all relevant citizens, and none, therefore, is prone to the danger that may arise from such large-scale assemblies.

Neighborhood assemblies are the most directly participatory and public of the three institutional arrangements. In them, sections of the urban citizenry will be assembled and citizens will be directly

4. For helpful general discussions, see Barber, *Strong Democracy,* esp. chap. 10; Milton Kotler, *Neighborhood Government;* Arthur Maass, *Congress and the Common Good;* and Rousseau, *The Social Contract.*

accessible to one another.[5] These assemblies should not be solidaristic institutions, expressing sentiments of brotherhood in some common substantive enterprise or feelings of personal warmth. The assemblies cannot be solidaristic or homogeneous if they are to be deliberative *political* institutions. For there to be politics, there must be a plurality of views and distance between persons. Otherwise, to take two possibilities, there is management or love.

An important difficulty to be overcome in the design of assemblies is that time constraints and differences in inclination to speak may break down the sense of each standing toward others in a deliberative fashion. Some may come to think of themselves as spectators.[6] Two observations can be made. First, no premium should be placed on each citizen's speaking at each assembly. If this were required, such assemblies would be either impossible or impossibly tedious. If differences in inclination mean that some speak more than others but many speak occasionally, then the formative effects of the institution may still work. Second, and more important, a great deal depends on whether the arguments made by those who do speak are strongly inclusive. That, to some degree, they will be directed at convincing others has already been suggested. But if the appeals are strongly of the sort that treat listeners as deeply involved in the matter at hand and capable of reasoned argument, then listening itself without speaking can be educative. A deliberative relationship is, after all, two sided, and expectations flow as much from listeners to speakers as in the opposite direction.

At first glance, referenda seem an unappealing institutional form for anyone interested in deliberative relationships, since the traditional objection has been that they allow little in the way of public exchange of reasons; by framing the question in a yes/no fashion, they elicit a statement of wants and provide no means by which

5. The idea of neighborhood assemblies may strike some as an incautious proposal after the New York experience with school decentralization. The lessons to be drawn from intense conflict associated with places such as Ocean Hill–Brownsville are, however, more complex than is often allowed. Two points seem especially important for advocates of neighborhood government: (1) unless it is associated with an inability to come to any conclusions, conflict within the neighborhood is not a sign of failure but of success; and (2) it would be better to judge institutions not at the time of their creation but after they are well underway. Why should decentralized school boards start out any more smoothly than other difficult political experiments? For some useful comments on one attempt to think about new neighborhood-based institutions, see Kenneth H. Miller, "Community Development Corporations and the Community Self-Determination Act," *Harvard Journal on Legislation* 6 (1969) 413–61.

6. See Jane J. Mansbridge, *Beyond Adversary Democracy,* esp. pt. II.

intensity of opinion can be registered. But these admittedly important difficulties can be mitigated by a multichoice format of the kind described by Benjamin R. Barber.[7] Referenda items can be written so that citizens must pick from among several responses, each of which both lays out a reason for picking that response and denotes intensity of feeling. The important point about the referenda is that citizens are induced to think about the reasons for their votes. The phrasing of the items serves as a substitute for the public exchange of reasons.

Having referenda actually work in the desired fashion means being particularly attentive to harnessing the sorts of motives earlier considered. Although there is no barrier to referenda dealing with vital day-to-day concerns, harnessing the desire for esteem will not be easy. There is nothing to prevent citizens from construing a referendum question as a way to register their private desires. The formative impact of referenda, then, must depend substantially on the framing of the questions in a manner that elicits reasoned answers. This, in turn, depends on outside authority; and ensuring that such authority will be at hand is itself a complex matter. The framing of referendum questions is part of the larger problem of framing agenda items for legislative institutions, and I will return to it below.

Neighborhood assemblies and referenda cannot settle all matters. There will be citywide questions of great complexity whose connections to equally complex matters will require the patient attention of skilled officials. From the standpoint of deliberative institutions, the preference must be for a legislature with significant powers. Such a legislature would be the least participative—and thus (focusing on citizen involvement) the least deliberative—of the three institutions under consideration. However, a strong legislature still would be a significant departure from the executive-centered politics analyzed in earlier chapters. From the standpoint of helping to form the appropriate sort of citizenry, the principle at work would be that the legislature will be seen to operate by the giving of reasons. It will work, then, to confirm citizens' expectations engendered through more direct participation—instead of pointing in a different direction, as is now the case.

In the case of a citywide legislature, the harnessing of motives is an especially complex problem. A key question is whether the legislature is organized through standing subject-matter committees. The stronger such committees are, the weaker is likely to be the inclination to deliberate over the content of the commercial public interest. There will be substantial temptation to organize legislative life around quid

7. Barber, *Strong Democracy*, 286–88.

pro quos in which subject-matter experts grant each other deference.[8] Although esteem can still be granted to those who present reasoned arguments, nonexpert legislators are more likely to simply rely on those with reputations for expertise. In turn, citizens are unlikely to receive from legislators much confirmation in their own efforts to struggle and debate over the commercial public interest.

Remaining to be discussed are many details concerning how to harness the motives of the desire for esteem and a connection to vital day-to-day interests. One item deserves particular emphasis: how legislative agenda items are framed. If, for example, the questions to be decided on are framed with an eye to their particularities (for example, whether this street should go here or there), they will tend to elicit particularistic responses and decisions will tend to turn on trades among self-interested parties. If the issue is framed very generally (for example, How shall roads be designed?), the danger is that the knowledge, experience, and interest necessary for intelligent deliberation will be missing.[9] The framing of agenda items confronts the problem that those directly involved are unlikely to expend much effort seeing that this is properly done. There are too many tactical advantages to be gained from its neglect. Either outside authority is required or a special sensitivity on the part of at least some of those involved is necessary if the legislative process is to work properly. Neither is unproblematical.

THE COMMERICAL PUBLIC INTEREST

To encourage political institutions to focus on the *commercial* public interest requires steps beyond defining deliberative processes, harnessing motives, and framing agenda items. As earlier chapters have argued, virtually all issues dealt with by cities are deeply involved with economic development and, more directly, with land use. Citizens and officials can hardly avoid considering the commercial well-being of the city. But there are two problems to overcome, both of which stem

8. See, by contrast, Edwin T. Haefele's discussion of a committee system in which legislation is perfected by its "friends," a suggestion that he draws from Jefferson. "Toward a New Civic Calculus," in Lowdon Wingo and Alan Evans (eds.), *Public Economics and the Quality of Life.*

9. The issue is neatly summed by up Frank I. Michelman, "Political Markets and Community Self-Determination: Competing Judicial Models of Local Government Legitimacy," *Indiana Law Journal* 53, no. 2 (1977–78): 186. See also Arthur Maass, "Benefit-Cost Analysis: Its Revelance to Public Investment Decisions," *The Quarterly Journal of Economics* 80, no. 2 (May 1966): 208–26, and *Congress and the Common Good.*

from the structural factors currently shaping city politics that I have analyzed.

First, the extent to which the municipal corporation can become directly involved in commercial matters is presently restricted. This in turn, restricts the extent to which citizens and officials can struggle over the commercial public interest, thereby inhibiting the formative impact of political institutions. The need is to expand municipal authority, which probably involves altering Dillon's rule and the rulings that parallel it, all of which limit the city's powers.

The constitutional law on these matters, however, is not as clear as it might be. It is also apparently undergoing transition, so it is unclear, in any case, how large a barrier to the expansion of municipal powers previous rulings are. On the one hand, there is the Boulder decision, in which the Supreme Court ruled that even home-rule localities could be sued for antitrust violations if the state had not given them either express authority to set prices or other explicit authority. The court ruled that Boulder, Colorado, was no more immune from suit under the Sherman Antitrust Act than was a private corporation.[10] Under such a ruling, cities will have trouble securing even their present powers to provide garbage collection and transportation and to pass ordinances, much less be able to expand their powers.

On the other hand, the Supreme Court in the Eau Claire, Hawaii land, and Berkeley rent-control cases seems to be pointing in another direction. The Hawaii case invites the conclusion that local governments may use eminent-domain powers for a wide range of public purposes, including the rectification of an inequitable land-tenure system. The right of eminent domain, if so interpreted, would look suspiciously like the inherent grant of power that cities are not supposed to have.[11] In any event, there are now efforts to treat eminent domain expansively, including using it to "condemn" factories and then sell them to a private or public-private entity. The aim is to save local jobs,[12] but other purposes presumably are possible. The holding

10. See *Community Communications, Inc. v. City of Boulder.* See also the discussion in James V. Siena (ed.), *Antitrust and Local Government.* In a February 19, 1985, decision, the Court held, in effect, that the federal government is free to ask state and local governments to do a wide range of things even if they do not wish to do so. There is therefore no constitutional prohibition—and, by implication, the idea of powers being reserved to the states holds only in extreme cases. See *Garcia v. San Antonio Metropolitan Transit Authority.*

11. See *Hawaii Housing Authority v. Midkiff.* It should be noted that the decision applied to a state government, although in Hawaii land-use powers are exercised by the state. See, however, the discussion in n. 12 below.

12. See *The New York Times,* June 5 and June 10, 1984, on such an effort by New Bedford, Mass. In *Poletown Neighborhood Council v. City of Detroit,* the

in the Eau Claire case[13] simply seems to say that municipal corporations are protected by the state-action exemption from antitrust laws as long as their actions are pursuant to a "clearly articulated" state policy, which policy need not be expressly stated in statute or legislative history. In the Berkeley case, the court upheld the city's rent-control ordinance, again suggesting that the Boulder decision ought not to be interpreted expansively.[14]

A corollary granting of powers to shape land use must be made to neighborhood assemblies. They must have the ability to take land for specified public purposes in order to have some effect on the direction of private land use. This, in turn, is necessary if assemblies are to help form the character of the citizenry. As has been argued, unless political institutions touch on the day-to-day concerns of citizens, they will not succeed in placing citizens in a deliberative relation. Citizens will soon lose interest when they perceive that their attempts to improve neighborhood traffic patterns or crime rates, for example, are unlikely to succeed because they cannot affect the land-use patterns that helped to cause the problems.

It may, in fact, be the case that cities, in effect, already have expansive powers. But it would be more accurate to say that, because of the ongoing judicial interpretation, no one really knows. What must occur—and already is occurring in places such as San Francisco, Boston, and Los Angeles—are popular movements that will, for example, push for referenda decisions and city legislation that impose "linkage" on commercial development, tying it to housing investment, and for legislation that defines growth restrictions. Then these decisions and laws must be tested in the courts. A new law of the municipal corporation may then emerge. Such popular initiatives can

---

Michigan Supreme Court in 1981 ruled that the city could, under existing Michigan law, take private property in order to promote the "public use" of jobs and economic development. This went beyond the U.S. Supreme Court's 1954 decision that private land could be taken for the purposes of urban renewal. "Public use" in the Michigan decision has clearly become separated from "public ownership" and is akin to "publicly defined purposes." Should states be able to grant such powers to municipal corporations, cities in effect will have something like an inherent grant of powers. See the discussion of the case in Bryan Jones and Lynn W. Bachelor, *The Sustaining Hand*, chap. 8. For how big a departure the Michigan ruling defines, compare the following comment: "The direct acquisition of industrial sites by eminent domain does not appear to be possible under present law." "From Private Enterprise to Public Entity: The Role of the Community Development Corporation," *The Georgetown Law Journal* 57, no. 5 (May 1969): 972.

13. *Town of Hallie et al. v. City of Eau Claire.*
14. *Fisher et al. v. City of Berkeley, California.*

occur, as I have said in chapter 5, but they are unlikely to be sustained unless they result, in turn, in alteration of city powers.

The second problem to overcome is political. To be able to struggle and debate over the commercial public interest, citizens and legislators must be free to arrive at whatever definition they see fit. Any inclination to accord a privileged hearing to businessmen's definitions will interfere with the deliberative process. As long as city officials are drawn into alliance with land interests, the politics of the city will revolve around quiet negotiation aimed at rearranging land use, and land interests will have a favored role in those negotiations. Deliberative institutions will not work under such circumstances.

An easy way to see what is at issue is to consider the situation of neighborhood assemblies that have the sort of land-use powers discussed above. If, as seems likely, such assemblies will have some responsibility for raising neighborhood revenues, why will they not feel compelled to attract investment into their areas? Land interests would likely prove only too happy to oblige and seek out allies from among neighborhood residents. Being allies, residents will no doubt be provided with monetary and other resources that can be used to dominate their neighborhood assemblies. The consequence will be that any deliberative form of relation between citizens will collapse. The question, in short, is, What will prevent small-scale versions of what presently occurs in city politics? Nor is this all a matter of speculation. Something like it already occurs where neighborhood organizations have some power over land use: development interests quickly find local leaders who are willing to smooth their way.[15]

The problem, then, is to ease the concern of public officials—and of citizens acting in their official roles (in referenda and neighborhood assemblies)—about securing business investment. How is this to be done? Two possibilities may be quickly eliminated. One is to allow city financial deficits to be made good by the federal government, so that cities then need not worry about their revenue bases. A second is simply to eliminate private control of productive assets, allowing city governments to control the local investment process. The first is unpromising because central finance will bring with it more central control than is consistent with the kind of vital deliberative city that is being discussed here. As for the second, eliminating or even substantially reducing private control of invest-

15. See the report in the *New York Times*, December 26, 1984.

ment is not a proposal for reforming a liberal regime, whatever else it may be.

This leaves less drastic proposals. The most promising is probably to build on the proposition that property is not a thing but a "bundle of rights" [16] that may be separately adjusted. This adjustment of rights is, of course, currently being done, as restrictions are placed on how technologies may be used. In principle, then, there is nothing in the concept of private property itself that prevents city governments (including neighborhood assemblies) from exacting repayment for public investments made to attract investment in the first place. If public authorities utilize common resources for public benefit and if the realization of those benefits becomes jeopardized, it would be appropriate to attempt to recover the investment. Such a proposal shares much in common with those whose basis is that the costs of a firm leaving a locality should not be borne only by local citizens. Both proposals have the intent of altering the calculus of location for controllers of assets while still leaving them free to decide.

There would be at least two immediate effects of such a repayment scheme. Businesses attracted by new road facilities or property-tax abatements would probably be more reluctant to relocate than they are at present. And if repayment is made, city coffers need not be drawn down to attract new investment, since a revolving fund of sorts would be established. For both reasons, officials and citizens would probably been less drawn into alliance with land interests.

Increased powers to consider land-use questions and the freeing of those who exercise city authority from the need to seek an alliance with land interests will not, however, free city residents from a need to be concerned with the economic vitality of the city. What they will gain is the ability not to be drawn strongly toward businessmen's definitions of the commercial public interest. This follows from a redrawing of the line between public and private, expanding the reach of the former while reducing the protections of the latter. Citizens will be freer to consider alternative formulations of how to promote economic performance as well as the connection between doing so and other aspects of the life of the city. As they argue about these matters, they can define the concrete interconnections between the need to maintain economic vitality, the various ways of doing this, and the impact of these alternative

16. See any good discussion of property rights, e.g., Bruce Ackerman, *Private Property and the Constitution.*

formulations on such things as neighborhood maintenance and school quality.

Altering the inherited structural features that have shaped city politics will give the deliberative politics set in motion by the new city political institutions a chance to flourish. Expanding city powers will allow citizens and officials to be somewhat less attentive to mobile capital, and increased city powers will likely bring in their trail political organizations that rely less than they presently do on the flow of political benefits from capital investment projects. Structural change, then, is fundamental to a politics that has as its core a concern with the commercial public interest of the city.

In this context, it is important to emphasize that an effort to direct the politics of the city toward deliberative processes need not be at the expense of the city's economic vitality. It might be said that, in spite of my argument that economic vitality will be central to the commercial public interest, this is precisely what will not occur. The price of appropriate citizenship will be inappropriate poverty.

As I have suggested in chapter 5, the basis of such an argument is that cities *must* adopt certain policies to promote economic vitality—and that, being rational, they do. In that chapter I argued against this kind of economic determinism and said that bricks-and-mortar strategies are *interpretations* of how to meet the problem of earning the city's keep, not just technical rational responses. Other interpretations are possible. But more to the point here, changes in structural arrangements make it more likely that such interpretations will, in fact, be offered. And, to again repeat earlier comments, these need not fail. In part, this is due to the structural changes themselves, particularly in the city's powers. A great deal depends on whether exporting is the fundamental process by which cities prosper[17] or whether import replacement is also crucial.[18] Import replacement strongly points to other than a bricks-and-mortar strategy, and even an exclusive reliance on exports is not well served by a concentration on large-scale land-use projects. Cities, then, are not tied to presently employed growth strategies in the manner implied by those who assert that there is a trade-off between political reform and prosperity. It is also worth remarking that, if all local governments are structured the same way, neither

17. Wilbur R. Thompson, *A Preface to Urban Economics,* esp. chap. 1.
18. See Jane Jacobs, *Cities and the Wealth of Nations.* For some additional considerations, see Todd Swanstrom, "Semi-Sovereign Cities: The Political Logic of Urban Development," paper presented to the American Political Science Association, Washington, D.C., 1986.

cities in general nor particular cities will be at a competitive disadvantage.

City politics can be other than it is. Otherwise stated, there need not be any trade-off between democratized city political institutions and effective problem solving. Indeed, why should there be, since *both* involve democratization. As is true of equality and efficiency, benefits cumulate—in this case not least because a democratized citizenry is more likely to be receptive to departures from the "dreary sameness" that I mentioned earlier. And political leaders will have greater incentives to suggest such departures. An even more engaging prospect is that the deliberative city politics contemplated here is less likely than the present interest-aggregation variety to handicap the have-nots of the city. Having to reason about the content of the public interest serves as a modest deterrent against advocacy of at least the most mean-spirited proposals. At the base of these arguments is a simple but easily overlooked point—that democracy is not a good that one must pay for in the coin of efficiency or equality. Properly understood, democratic institutions confer powerful benefits along many dimensions.

Additional institutional detail would be needed to complete the picture of how reformed city political institutions might work. There would have to be discussion of such topics as the division of powers within the city, the definition of neighborhoods, and the connection between organizations that deliver city services and the new legislative-like institutions. But enough has been presented to enable the discussion to move on to questions of probability and desirability.

Is It Probable (and Possible)?

It should be remembered that the institutional arrangements being called for do not require heroic discernment about the content of the commercial public interest on the part of the citizenry. The necessary habits of mind are rather modest ones, consisting of little more than the regular offering of arguments about why one's proposals on matters close to home are of general benefit and expecting others, particularly political leaders, to behave similarly. It is not a different sort of human being that is required—the "new man" of various political theories—but people as they are in circumstances that allow them to employ more regularly the talents that they already have.

Still, it is correct to insist that even such modest displays of reason giving are not altogether common in our politics. But that is a far cry from saying that the more extensive displays called for are impossible to achieve. Nor is it pertinent to point to evidence drawn from the political behavior of people distracted by all kinds of other considerations and who thus, naturally enough, perceive politics as a way of extracting benefits for themselves through gaining advantage over others. There is nothing new in saying all this. It is, after all, the obvious line of argument for anyone who wishes to argue for reform. What you see cannot be what you get. Its obviousness does not make it any less true, especially when what is wanted is already present in some degree.[19]

But even if the requirements of reform are relatively modest, this does not mean that the new institutional arrangements will be happily ushered in by those with the power to do so. One thing is tolerably clear: regardless of their merits, the prospects of such reforms occurring are slim, not least because the very workings of the political economy that serve to prompt the concern for reform will substantially impede it. Businessmen are unlikely to be enthusiastic about the variety of efforts to restrict their prerogatives that are entailed by the new institutions, and the advantages that they possess in their guise as interest groups will make their objections formidable. Equally important, it is doubtful that many public officials will be enthusiastic about upsetting those whose performance is the object of their regular worry and attention. This will be especially true if the reforms mean a decline in the various forms of self-indulgence that now characterize their careers. Debate and struggle over the definition of the commercial public interest is likely to prove a bracing experience for those who spend their days in the heartiness of home style, the coziness of issue networks, or the sampling of the more tangible pleasures of being the businessmen's helpmate.

Even if the necessary reforms are improbable of achievement, it is important to emphasize that there are no real alternatives. I have argued that cities (and perhaps local governments more generally) are uniquely equipped to help form the kind of citizenry necessary for a flourishing liberal regime. It will be useful to indicate further why no other institutional arrangements will do the job as well.

One obvious alternative to city political institutions is the workplace. No other institutional possibility has the combination of smallish scale and connection to both commercial matters and vital day-to-day interests. Workplace democracy might be helpful,

19. Those with a skeptical turn of mind may wish to look at the careful analysis of Mansbridge in *Beyond Adversary Democracy*.

then, in forming citizens much as the proposed political institutions are intended to do. The principal difficulty, however, is the degree to which firms are constrained by market considerations. There is room for choice about technology, work rules, and executive compensation, but, in the end, firms must compete and even monopolists must sell their products. No matter how much cities must be attentive to the external economic environment, they have far more latitude than business firms and many more ways to keep themselves economically viable, including outside subventions, new product lines, and the development of internal markets. The crucial difference is that cities have far more room to debate and struggle over the content of the commercial public interest. Moreover, the commercial public interest is relevant to a much broader range of matters than employment-related issues—and thus opportunities for deliberation are, once again, greater. The difference is between an instrumentality and a government.

Still, workplace democracy could contribute to the forming of the citizenry. This is especially important, since, as has been argued, city political institutions can play only a surrogate role. The more contexts in which the citizenry develops the sense that the content of the commercial public interest is not exhausted by what controllers of assets say is necessary for economic performance—and, prima facie, this is the intended result of workplace democracy—the more likely that political leaders themselves will act in appropriate ways.

It only remains to add that there are additional sources of public-spiritedness—all of which are crucial to serving our aspirations—but that none of them focuses the attention of citizens on the commercial aspect of the public interest. At least as far back as Tocqueville, students of the commercial republic have noted the crucial role of both voluntary associations and religion in this regard. It is also possible that public-interest groups help to form a citizenry disposed to frame its inquiries around the question of what is in the public interest, for as E. E. Schattschneider has pointed out, members of the American League to Abolish Capital Punishment are not themselves worried about the gallows.[20] But since none of these organizations has governing responsibilities, they do not dispose citizens to worry about the interconnections between economy and polity that are at the core of the commercial public interest.

20. See E. E. Schattschneider, *The Semi-Sovereign People*, 26.

Is It Desirable?

Friends of the regime must be concerned that creating the kinds of political institutions contemplated here will require changes that are likely to have a significant effect on the ability to serve our other aspirations. Whether they ought to argue for the democratized city political institutions outlined here depends, then, on an assessment of these other effects in light of the seriousness of the consequences that follow any long-term failure of democratization. To see what is at issue, consider the effect on our aspiration for a political way of life characterized by individual rights.

There are a number of aspects to the rights question, and their scope is suggested by the following consideration. The reorganization of the city raises serious worries about civil liberties: for example, Will rampant majorities dominate minorities in a manner that deeply worried the founders? The problem seems particularly important, given the real possibility that neighborhoods will be more homogeneous than is desirable if the principal concern is individual liberty.[21] The question of civil liberties is part of the larger question of the autonomy of the city. Even though cities will still be part of the broader constitutional system, their increased powers suggest increased dangers.

There is also the question of property rights, which is not only as fundamental as the problem of civil liberties but is an aspect of the rights question that has played a larger role in the present discussion. The connection between property rights and democratization arises in at least three ways.

First, to give reasons requires that there be memory. For citizens to engage each other in argument, they cannot be disembodied reasoners coming from nowhere and without history. If nothing else is true, not everything can be debated in the present, and so memory of what has been tried and has failed and what is likely to be deeply disagreeable is needed. Continuity among citizens is thus required, which, in turn, suggests that present rates of movement both into and out of the city will have to be reduced. By one estimate, some 20 percent of Americans five years or older moved from one political jurisdiction to another between 1970 and 1975.[22]

21. But Matthew A. Crenson, after a careful study, concludes that there is sufficient diversity of opinion in neighborhoods to generate disagreement. Whatever socioeconomic homogeneity there is does not seem to lead to homogeneity of opinion. See *Neighborhood Politics*, esp. 144–54.

22. See Richard Dagger, "Metropolis, Memory, and Citizenship," *Amer-*

Since mobility is closely tied to job change, and since that, in turn, is tied to the present built-in incentives for high rates of capital mobility, the question of restrictions on the prerogatives of property arise.

The second type of connection stems from the importance of equality for democratized political institutions. Dependency and the lack of respect that it breeds—both of which have roots in great inequalities—will make the exchange of reasons among citizens impossible.[23] Citizens of the city will have to be substantially more equal than they presently are if city political institutions are to work in the manner outlined. If there is any doubt on the matter, the following statistic ought to give pause: it is currently estimated that one of five families in cities has an income below $10,000, which is less than the federal government says is needed for a poverty-level existence for a family of four.[24] People living below this threshold—and, possibly, many above—are radically disabled from participating in a deliberative politics.

The question posed by such an income distribution is whether it can be sufficiently altered by means widely understood to be acceptable within liberal democracies: a progressive income tax, social welfare measures, and a full-employment economy. Even if some increase in economic equality is achieved by such means, it remains open to debate whether it will be sufficient for the equality of respect that is at the heart of deliberative institutions. In short, the question of the proper organization of productive assets in the society—and the connection of this question to that of inequality—arises. Again, must the present system of private control of productive assets be modified?

The third (and already discussed) connection is the necessity of moving the line between public and private control of assets so that citizens can debate the full range of matters covered by the commercial public interest without land interests having an unduly large voice. The limits imposed on local public powers have been an important part of the way in which the public-private line has been drawn.

---

ican Journal of Political Science 25, no. 4 (November 1981): 715–31 (the estimate is made on 726).

23. "An equality of property, with a necessity of alienation, constantly operating to destroy combinations of powerful families, is the very *soul of a republic*" (emphasis in the original). Noah Webster, as quoted in John P. Diggins, *The Lost Soul of American Politics*, 171.

24. See *The New York Times*, February 27, 1983, report on initial census calculations taken from the long form that was given to one in five people.

Friends of the regime must hesitate, however, before the implication that property rights are fundamentally a political matter, as they must be if the arguments presented here are correct. The reasons for the proposed changes are public ones, having to do with the fostering of a liberal regime. The character of the citizenry cannot be left only to the care of the marketplace, the church, and the home—not if a liberal regime is to flourish. In their uneasiness, those devoted to the regime can reasonably claim to be following the founders' own inclinations to avoid extensive consideration of whether a commercial republic could flourish without the direct nourishing of public-spiritedness. The founders pinned at least their explicit hopes on institutional arrangements that would allow "ambition . . . to counteract ambition" and on the diversity engendered by a commercial society. More generally, they took as their starting point the premise that government itself is "the greatest of all reflections on human nature" and so looked to the "policy of supplying, by opposite and rival interests the defect of better motives."[25]

Still, the implication of chapter 7 is that ambition countering ambition, auxiliary contrivances generally, and the impact of commerce are not themselves enough to make the regime work, at least in terms of the concern here. The institutional contrivances may be effective in the case of individual rights, but they are not so in the case of the commercial public interest.[26] Moreover, whatever the founders' intentions, property rights have already been significantly altered throughout our history.[27]

Perhaps the decisive comment here, however, is that those devoted to the regime should remind themselves of what the Anti-Federalists argued at the beginning. Montesquieu had taught that republican government requires the "love of laws and of our country" and that such love involved "a constant preference of public to private interest." The Anti-Federalists believed that the Federalists had not adequately dealt with that argument; as one of their number said, " whatever the refinement of modern politics may inculcate, it still is certain that some degree of virtue must exist, or freedom cannot live."[28] Liberal regimes require ways to foster a

25. *Federalist,* no. 51.

26. Cf. Herbert J. Storing's remark that the Federalists "took for granted the republican genius of the people; but that cannot prudently be taken for granted." *What the Anti-Federalists Were For,* 73.

27. See Morton J. Horwitz, *The Transformation of American Law, 1780–1860.*

28. *Federal Republican,* quoted in Storing, *What the Anti-Federalists Were For,* 73. In this paragraph, I closely follow Storing's own argument. It will

public-spirited citizenry, however difficult in practice the creation of these may prove to be.

To be sure, there are limits to how far the alteration of property rights can proceed if our aspirations to be a liberal regime are to have any force. There will inevitably be some constraints on popular control in any regime built around a division of labor between market and state. As long as some portion of collective life is given over to a property-based market system, and as long as the citizenry has any interest in material well-being, public officials will have to give special attention to private controllers of assets. *And* this will be appropriate. A liberal regime is not a regime devoted solely to registering popular opinion through collective decision making; its very essence is to remove substantial portions of collective life from the direct and continuous exercise of popular will.

Property is the Achilles' heel of the American regime. It is simultaneously a powerful symbol of individual rights and the core of our commercial aspirations. The market system that is built upon property rights itself helps to shape the self-reliant character of a citizenry composed of energetic calculators skilled in promoting their own interests through exchange. At the same time, property rights as currently defined stand in the way of the democratization that is necessary to realization of our aspirations. Liberal regimes are tension filled because the concept of property is. It is, at one and the same time, the symbol and guarantor of privacy and a key to creating the public life that is necessary if liberalism is to exist.

To treat property as an economic concept is thus deeply misleading, for it is also profoundly political. This is true not only for the standard reasons that its control confers substantial political influence and that it is the foundation of economic inequality—or even for the less-recognized reason that public officials will be especially attentive to controllers of assets. Most important of all, property is a political matter because the constituting of a citizenry necessary to the flourishing of a liberal regime depends on particular definitions of ownership and control.

We are caught, then, on the horns of a dilemma. To allow that property is a political concept and openly to begin its redefinition as a political act is itself an effort that cuts deeply into the core of a liberal regime. We are in the ironic position of having to alter what is rightly thought of as one of the core principles of a liberal

---

be well to reiterate that by "virtue" the Anti-Federalists were not harking back to republican virtue; as Storing argues, they were liberals, if reluctant ones.

regime—that is, that property is not whatever public authorities say it is but is, instead, a barrier against the arbitrary use of such authority—in order to foster that very regime. There are substantial tensions within our aspirations, tensions that are perhaps best captured by saying that, to be a commercial republic, we must treat property rights as fundamentally a public matter.

This is perhaps the much worried-about contradiction at the heart of a liberal regime.[29] The problem is how to make property rights a public matter without denying their symbolic and real importance for individual liberty. Within the broad division of labor between public decision making and private choice, a variety of arrangements are no doubt possible. Neither a vital commercial society nor a concern for individual rights requires the present form of socialized property found in the large-scale business corporation. A liberal democratic regime will require what might be loosely called personal property, and it cannot be built around state ownership of assets. But between these two poles much is possible, although only the untutored would deny the perplexities in defining a version consistent with our aspirations.

There is, however, much discussion of the possibility of rights expansion that tacitly seems to assume that the problem of redefining property is not as serious a problem as is suggested here. The belief appears to be that many years of public decision making regarding both the alteration of property rights and the creation and expansion of other sorts of rights will bring us closer to being a liberal regime.[30] Against this optimistic expansionary liberalism might be set the argument that the trick cannot be pulled off at all. Once the "private" becomes subject to the regular attention of the "public," it might be said, the central liberal proposition—that is, that some matters lie beyond public competence—will erode. It is surely not easy to decide the issue, since it must be true that governments in liberal regimes must control themselves if they are to be liberal regimes.[31] Little stands in the way if a sufficient number of officials decide that restraining the reach of government no longer serves their purposes. Reiterating that some things are out

29. Cf. Bernard Crick's comment that "the bourgeois state, Marx said, contains 'inner contradictions' (indeed it does, that is what it is all about)." *In Defense of Politics,* 43.

30. See, e.g., Bruce Ackerman, *Reconstructing American Law.*

31. Cf. *Federalist,* no. 51. "In framing a government which is to be administered by men over men, the great difficulty lies in this: you must first enable the government to control the governed, and in the next place oblige it to control itself."

of the proper jurisdiction government will work only if officials, for whatever reasons, either act as if they believe this or in fact do so.

CONCLUSION

It is not easy for friends of the regime to be optimistic in light of the preceding assessment. The most worrisome point of all is that it may be impossible to sustain the public-spiritedness necessary for a liberal regime to flourish. Even if city political institutions were initially arranged in the manner outlined here, the passage of time might still result in their being consumed by the strains in the larger political economy. Still, it is difficult to see how else, except through a public-spirited citizenry, a liberal democratic regime is to cope with its internal tensions. The difficulty is that the principal reason to constitute such a citizenry is also the principal barrier to achieving it.

It may be that the idea of a mixed regime—that is, the democratized liberalism that I have been considering—is, in fact, a siren, beautiful but to be avoided. Even if additional benefits of a public-spirited citizenry—for example, its tendency to appreciate that each of us has obligations as well as rights—are weighed into the balance, the contemplated steps may still lead to shipwreck. If this is the case, then the suggestions made by Tocqueville and the Anti-Federalists regarding how to foster a liberal regime will not be of much help. We will then be in the unfortunate position of suspecting that the "auxiliary precautions" at the heart of the founders' design for an interest-driven commercial republic no longer suffice and that the public-spiritedness of the Anti-Federalists and their successors is too dangerous to pursue.

Friends of the regime are—or at least should be—in a quandary. Drawn to the idea of a commercial republic, they seem destined to carry the burden of defending a political economy in which the large-scale business corporation is a prominent feature. Being good friends of the regime, they cannot, however, rest with things as they are, since the business corporation and the general character of state-market relations work to corrupt the regime to whose standard they rally. It is too easy, perhaps, to conclude that those devoted to a liberal regime must make a radical choice between a business-dominated political economy and a difficult and unsettling departure in our institutional arrangements. It is not too easy, however, to conclude that this is the central question.

10
Some Considerations on Political Judgment

In the preceding chapters, the political institutions of the city have been examined for signs of systematic bias, unintelligent problem solving, and failure to help constitute the citizenry in a manner consistent with our aspirations. On all counts they have been found wanting. City politics has proved to be a poor model of political equality, social intelligence, and citizenship. As many observers have noted, cities have not been one of the great American political success stories, and nothing said here points to a different conclusion.[1]

Each of these shortcomings has appropriate institutional remedies, and the question naturally arises of how they may be brought together in a single effort of reform. How should a concern for appropriately constituting the citizenry, effective problem solving, and political equality be reflected in the design of city political institutions? To answer this question requires consideration of one that logically precedes it: How, in general, are the various dimensions of political institutions related? This question is at the core of political judgment, that reasoning that should guide the speech and actions of those devoted to regime purposes. Those whom I have called friends of the regime must seek to discover the connections among the dimensions of political institutions, and between these dimensions and the political way of life to which we aspire. They will see in the concrete task of institutional reform the problem of how to give substance to the political way of life that is worthy of us. It will be a fitting conclusion to this book to address the subject of political judgment, for it not only takes us beyond the subject of cities but also helps bring together the theoretical elements essential to analysis of them.

POLITICAL JUDGMENT

To this point, the connection between institutions as formative and the political regime has been portrayed as follows: to aspire to be a

1. See the comments of Lord Bryce, *The American Commonwealth*, 2: 281.

regime of popular control devoted to the serving of the commercial public interest requires a citizenry constituted in a certain way—namely, one whose political life is defined, in part, by the posing of public-regarding questions to one another. The connection focuses on the character that the citizenry must have if political leaders are to behave in ways that are consistent with our aspirations.

The connection can be more generally stated. Implicit in the preceding formulation of the connection between institutions as formative and the regime is not only the notion that political institutions must constitute the citizenry in a certain manner but the notion that citizens and leaders are also to stand in particular relation to one another; that is, by posing certain kinds of questions to one another, they are to carry on the process of defining the commercial public interest. In the same vein, consider our aspirations to have a political way of life that respects individual rights. Such rights may also be understood in institutional terms; for example, for a citizenry to have the right of free speech, there must be institutional procedures that define how speakers and listeners shall stand in relation to one another. Rights are as much institutionally defined forms of relations as are deliberative assemblies. A useful formulation, then, is to say that our aspirations simply are, in part, about how we shall be constituted.

It is unlikely that our aspirations are often actually stated in this constitutive language. But this kind of understanding of political institutions is not foreign to the manner in which Americans think about political life. The American Constitution can be understood as laying out (among other things) the constitutive forms of relations that will help to define us as a worthy people.[2] And our reputation as a Constitution-worshipping people suggests that our aspirations very much include the constitutive relations set out there. Put differently, our attention to constitutional forms is likely a recognition that we only share so much in the way of substantive goals, that the projects that we pursue as a nation often are projects that must be argued and struggled over rather than drawn from common ends. As George Kateb puts it in discussing Hannah Arendt's conception of a constitution, "a constitution is not a program or policy. . . . It has no goal; it does not make an object. Rather, it is the creation of a frame of institutions for indefinite future possibilities of political action."[3]

2. See Sotirios A. Barber, *On What the Constitution Means;* and Stephen L. Elkin, "Regulation as a Political Question," *Policy Sciences* 18, no. 1 (Winter 1985): 95–108.
3. George Kateb, *Hannah Arendt: Politics, Conscience, Evil,* 19.

The constitutive aspect of our aspirations captures the widely shared sense that political life fundamentally revolves around talking. Politics is a conversational, rhetorical activity as much as it is anything else. James Boyd White emphasizes the point and neatly connects it to a constitutional emphasis when he says: "This Constitution [of the United States]—like other such instruments—is thus in a literal sense a rhetorical constitution: it constitutes a rhetorical community, working by rhetorical processes that it has established but can no longer control. It establishes a new conversation on a permanent basis." [4]

As I have said earlier, a principal task of this talk is definition, the definition of what things are to be called. And this may be thought of as a moral enterprise, involving not only decisions about how our activities shall be characterized but how we are to go about the process of definition. What is being constituted by political institutions may be thought of as the "procedural morality" of a people.[5] This morality consists of the habits of association that help to define us. Our aspirations include what questions we shall put to one another and when we shall speak in the language of exchange and when in the language of persuasion—in short, what we expect of each other. These aspirations are both procedural and substantive, a procedural morality that joins ends and means in a commitment to be a certain sort of people.

This concern with how we shall be constituted—that is, with procedural morality—differs from political equality and social intelligence as I have portrayed them. In my formulation, the latter two concerns are instrumental and therefore deal with results whereas the former concern deals with the intrinsic qualities of institutions, with what makes them attractive in their own right. An institution viewed constitutively is not directed at a goal separate from it but to a purpose that inheres in it. The purpose stems from an institution being of a certain type, and when the question, What is the institution for? is posed, the constitutive answer is, To be the best of its kind. An institution *expresses* this purpose more or less well, as opposed to being an instrument used to achieve it. Institutions are thus purposive in addition to being instrumental.

To this point I have used the language of regime to talk only about constitutive matters. However, it is plausible to argue that any account of our aspirations should also include the more instrumental concerns of intelligent use of resources and attention to the sources of distributive outcomes. Our aspirations, then, should include getting some

---

4. James Boyd White, *When Words Lose Their Meaning*, 246.
5. Lon Fuller, *The Morality of Law*, chap. 2.

place as well as how we stand in relation to one another wherever we are going.

A complete account of our aspirations will cover how political institutions shall constitute us, how they shall be organized to make effective use of resources, and how they shall be organized to prevent systematic bias in the distribution of valued political outcomes. Our aspirations consist in major part of how our political institutions should be designed so as properly to combine these various concerns. A complete account of our aspirations is, in essence, a theory of political judgment for those devoted to the purposes of the American regime. It will be an analysis of the substance of rational political action for such people—that is, the rationality that should guide the choices necessary to bring us closer to the realization of our aspirations and prevent the corruption of what has already been achieved. The analysis in this book, then, may be understood as my account of those aspects of a theory of political judgment that concern cities. It is the account of a friend of the regime, of someone willing to exchange reasons about the content of our aspirations with others similarly inclined.

The essence of my account is that our foundational aspiration is to be a popular regime. We wish to be a popular regime first and foremost, even before we wish to be a commercial rights-bearing one. This being so, the workings of popular control are crucial to our aspirations, and I have specified three of its dimensions and analyzed the three kinds of failures that are associated with each. What is striking is the common thread that runs through the failures—the impact of property rights. Systematic bias is largely to be traced to the natural alliance between land interests and city officials, and the propensity to alliance stems from private control of the assets that city officials need to do their jobs and pursue their political ambitions. Land interests are similarly in a position to help restrict the civic agenda in ways that make it harder for citizens and officials to consider other methods of earning the city's keep than those presently pursued. And, finally, how city political institutions currently help to constitute us—and the principal barriers to the institutional changes necessary to help form the appropriate sort of citizenry—are intimately connected to the private control of assets. The conclusion of chapter 9— that is, that property rights are the Achilles' heel of a liberal regime— can thus be generalized. And to this may now be added the statement that the central task of political judgment for such a regime is how to combine a concern for property rights with our foundational aspiration.

The preceding chapters and the discussion above also suggest more general considerations about the content of the political judgment that is appropriate to this regime. First, when the three dimensions of political institutions are combined, the point of view should not be "external," from the outside, as if institutions had no life of their own and could be put together and decomposed at will, taking account only of goal achievement. When theorists argue that the value of institutions is in part "internal"[6]—as I have also said, at least with regard to the constitutive bearing of institutions—this is a way of indicating that the life of the institutions is, in part, what is valuable about them. The external viewpoint is inadequate both empirically and normatively—empirically because institutions cannot be combined and recombined at will and normatively because what makes it impossible to do this is, in part, what makes them valuable.

The danger to be avoided, then, is a kind of machine-shop rationalism in which political judgment is thought to consist of assembling institutions and regimes as if they were factories producing the outputs of policy goals. Political institutions are not severable from the regime, are not instruments to be deployed. In fostering particular political institutions, we are directly constructing the political way of life to which we aspire.[7] The reasoning appropriate to institutional design (or, more broadly, to fostering a regime) is best characterized as looking for good "fits," for how the parts may be made to fit together into a functioning whole. Political rationality is not primarily a matter of selecting means to ends.

A second general aspect of political judgment that has emerged is that a balance is required among procedural morality, political equality, and social intelligence. What this balance might look like is not easy to say, and I will not attempt here to address the question directly. It is, however, pertinent to note that the balance need not occur in every instance. To the contrary, in any given case, one or another consideration may well be dominant. In the case of cities, a good argument can be made that constitutive considerations should dominate because city political institutions (or perhaps local government institutions generally) are potentially the only ones that can constitute the citizenry in ways necessary to serve our aspirations to be a commercial republic. Balance refers, then, to an overall mix, across the full range of institutions of the regime.

It is also worth emphasizing that "balance" should not be construed as meaning that designing political institutions with an eye to conflictual, efficiency, and constitutive considerations involves wholly sep-

---

6. See, e.g., Alasdair MacIntyre, *After Virtue.*
7. See Elkin, "Regulation as a Political Question," and "Economic and Political Rationality," *Polity* 18, no. 2 (Winter 1985): 253–71.

arate domains; for example, what questions we must put to each other cannot help but have a direct bearing on how we should carry on conflict. A particularly important interconnection is that between constitutive and efficiency considerations. There is a common tendency to separate questions of proper political organization from those concerning how to achieve efficiency and then to see them as being in conflict. That such a tension occurs in some circumstances is no doubt true, but, as I have argued in chapters 5 and 9, the extent of conflict is at least exaggerated. One foundation for the belief that there is necessarily a conflict between the proper constitution of the citizenry and efficiency—and for the parallel belief that there is a necessary trade-off between equality and efficiency—is a conception of the ideal political institution as being one that is adept at calculation.[8] Such an institution will take inputs of resources and citizen preferences for particular outcomes and combine them in such a way that the resulting outputs (decisions) reflect the intensity of those preferences and the technical characteristics of those resources. The model political institution is much like an ideal market, "an analogue calculating machine."[9] To adapt Richard Nelson's phrasing to political matters, the political problem "is viewed as that of finding an allocation of resources to different technologies for the production of different goods and services so as to maximize consumer welfare, given prevailing preferences."[10]

With its emphasis on political institutions in effect doing socially what individual calculators do individually, this is a ratiocinative view of efficiency. If the ratiocinative view is replaced by a view that puts *interaction* (rather than calculation) at the center of social problem solving, then the presumed strong tension between good politics and the intelligent use of resources is lessened or disappears. This view of social problem solving as interaction is at the core of Charles E. Lindblom's thinking,[11] as I have noted earlier. To be sure, there are many steps between Lindblom's underlying point that interaction between political actors need not produce ineffective problem solving—and arguments about the compati-

8. See also the discussion below of those whom I will call aggregators, who take this view of political institutions to its logical conclusion.

9. Paul A. Samuelson, "The Pure Theory of Public Expenditure," *Review of Economics and Statistics* 36, no. 4 (November 1954): 388.

10. Richard R. Nelson, *The Moon and the Ghetto*, 132.

11. See, e.g., Charles E. Lindblom, *The Intelligence of Democracy*. In addition, see Victor P. Goldberg, "Regulation and Administered Contracts," *Bell Journal of Economics* 7 (Autumn 1976): 426–48; and Ian MacNeil, *The New Social Contract: An Inquiry Into Modern Contractual Values.*

bility of institutional arrangements that are preferable on constitutive and efficiency grounds.[12] Still, the objections to the supposed necessity of various kinds of trade-offs (objections canvassed in earlier chapters) suggest that there is a good deal of room to join the "economic" dimension of politics—that is, concern with the ends to which our resources are being put—to the "political"—that is, concern with what sort of people we shall be, as defined by our procedural morality. Political judgment may be less an exercise in defining trade-offs than is commonly supposed. It is more likely to be a search for proper combinations of institutional arrangements that takes as central the existence of cumulative advantages along the dimensions of equality, efficiency, and procedural morality.

SOME COMPARISONS

A principal temptation in defining the content of political judgment is, in effect, to disregard the question of how one might combine the various dimensions of political institutions and to assume that the only thing at issue is social efficiency or political equality. Urban policy during the postwar period has largely succumbed to this temptation, for the predominant approach has been to see cities as administrative units whose principal task is to carry out policy goals mandated either by federal law or by local decision. Sometimes the efficiency focus is direct, on the efficient achievement of policy ends, and sometimes it is indirect, seeking to promote the economic growth that is assumed to be necessary for the goals to be realized. Cities are thought of as administrative units, interchangeable with other candidates for the job. If cities prove to be deficient in alleviating poverty, promoting growth, or providing low income housing, so much the worse for cities. These jobs can be done elsewhere, and nothing is lost thereby. Quite the contrary: there is a gain in increased policy success. In short, there is no sense that city political institutions are intrinsically important for the ways in which they form the citizenry.

Much the same view can be found in the minor strand of urban policy in which cities are viewed as arenas of struggle between haves and have-nots. This was one of the informing principles of the War on Poverty, for example.[13] Again, the implication is that if the have-

12. See Elkin, "Economic and Political Rationality," for an additional discussion, as well as the discussions in chaps. 5, 9 above.
13. J. David Greenstone and Paul E. Peterson, *Race and Authority in Urban Politics: Community Participation and the War on Poverty.*

nots do poorly in cities and that little can be done to improve their competence in political struggle, then the problem of political imbalance is best attacked not in cities but elsewhere.[14] Here, too, cities are seen as interchangeable with other arenas.

Much of the spirit of postwar urban policy is nicely captured in the remarks of two well-known economists. They comment: "Most state and local taxes pay for services such as roads, police and fire protection. As consumers, we purchase many other goods and services for which no deduction [on federal taxes] is allowed: telephone, college educations and so on. Why should services provided by state and local governments be treated differently?"[15] The answer is that city political institutions are not only service providers and that, if their financial burdens are too great, they are unlikely to help constitute us in ways that are central to realizing our aspirations.

Another truncated version of political judgment appears in a more systematic form in the guise of what can be called an aggregative view of political institutions. In effect, its proponents focus only on social intelligence and, in fact, offer a restrictive view of what that entails and how it might be achieved. The aggregative view rests on an understanding of political institutions as aggregators of preferences.[16] Institutions are seen as devices to ascertain and combine preferences for the possible outcomes at stake in such a fashion that the extent of aggregate preference satisfaction among those concerned is increased and, ideally, is maximized.[17] As a stu-

14. This is explicit in Paul E. Peterson, *City Limits.*

15. Henry Aaron and Harvey Galper, "How to Tell if Reagan is in Tax Wonderland," *The Washington Post,* May 26, 1985.

16. For a parallel statement of an aggregative view of politics, see Edward C. Banfield, "Economic Analysis of Political Phenomena: A Political Scientist's Critique," working paper, University of Pennsylvania, n.d.

17. As one of its most sophisticated practitioners puts it in characterizing his own study, it is "concerned precisely with investigating the dependence of judgements of social choice and of public policy on the preferences of the members of the society." Amartya K. Sen, *Collective Choice and Social Welfare,* 1. It is worth noting that social choice theory proper, as it has grown out of the work of Kenneth Arrow, is concerned with choices among *social states,* not issues. See Kenneth Arrow, *Social Choice and Individual Values,* esp. 109. An aggregative view and much of the public-choice theory at its core is, in fact, concerned with issues. For some standard works employing an aggregative view, see Dennis C. Mueller, *Public Choice;* Robert L. Bish and Vincent Ostrom, *Understanding Urban Government: Metropolitan Reform Reconsidered;* Charles M. Tiebout, "A Pure Theory of Local Expenditures," *Journal of Political Economy* 64, no. 5 (October 1956): 416–24; Richard A. Posner, *Economic Analysis of Law;* and Elinor Ostrom and Vincent Ostrom, "Public Choice: A Different Approach to the Study of Public Administration," *Public Administration Review* 31, no. 2 (1971): 203–16.

dent of aggregative views' puts it, "society is rightly ordered and therefore just, when its major institutions are arranged so as to achieve the greatest net balance of satisfaction summed over all individuals belonging to it."[18]

The essential components of an aggregative view of political institutions include the following: (1) The total amount of preference satisfaction in the society is the definition of value on which judgments regarding institutional alternatives are based. There are alternative versions of what this means, the most common being some variety of Pareto judgment.[19] (2) Preferences are taken as given. They are exogenous in the sense that they are the stuff on which institutions are presumed to operate. These preferences may change, but the sources of change, including any effects of the institutional method of aggregating them, are deemed to be of little significance.[20] (3) Institutional arrangements are understood to be neutral instruments for the production of efficient outcomes; that is, they are judged in terms of their external consequences. Each, then, is a potential substitute for the other, with relative value being determined on the basis of which of them is the most efficient. (4) The preferred institutional arrangements are those that rely on exchange and economizing. These are thought to be the most effective in combining individual preferences into efficient collective outcomes.

The advantages of exchange processes, especially as they are revealed in markets, direct aggregators to collective or political

18. John Rawls, *A Theory of Justice*, 22. Rawls is here characterizing utilitarianism. An aggregative view has deep affinities with utilitarianism, but the bodies of theory also differ, not least because, in some of its branches, the aggregative view started out as an effort to avoid the interpersonal comparisons of utility, a notion that is central to utilitarianism. See, e.g., Jules Coleman, "Economics and the Law: A Critical Review of the Foundations of the Economic Approach to Law," *Ethics* 94, no. 4 (July 1984): 649–79.

19. E.g., a judgment of Pareto superiority means that a change has been made that leaves at least one person better off and no one worse off. The literature is now enormous. See, e.g., Coleman, "Economics and the Law"; Kenneth J. Arrow and Tibor Scitovsky, *Readings in Welfare Economics;* and Guido Calabresi and Philip Bobbitt, *Tragic Choice.* The first and the last especially discuss the range of paretian judgments.

20. As an acute student of aggregative views puts it, to treat the origins of preferences as outside the question of how to design institutions "makes it natural to see existing wants as starting points when the aim is to try to promote desirable states of affairs, and to define desirable states of affairs solely in terms of the degree to which . . . these preexisting wants are satisfied." Michael S. McPherson, "Want Formation, Morality, and Some Interpretive Aspects of Economic Inquiry," in Norma Haan et al. (eds.), *Social Science as Moral Inquiry,* 110.

institutions in which exchange is also central. Aggregators prefer,
then, regulatory institutions that rely on tax and incentive schemes,
and voting bodies in which log-rolling is encouraged. In these institutions, the bargains or exchanges struck are said to be mutually
beneficial and thus productive of an increase in aggregate preference satisfaction. When aggregators think of institutions as acting
in an economizing fashion, they are moving within the domain of
"systematic analysis for social action."[21] The closer an institution
comes to acting like a factory with a well-defined production function, the better economizer it will be—and thus, *ceteris paribus*, the
more likely that its choices will produce increases in aggregate
preference satisfaction.

For aggregators, politics offers nothing special; it is simply the
extension of private life by other means. The central political task
is understood as the need to solve a kind of investment problem
in which scarce resources are to be allocated among competing
uses in the service of some measure of aggregate preference satisfaction. From this perspective, political institutions are like complex bits of machinery that take fixed inputs, perform computations
on them according to a set of operating rules, and serve up a
series of decision products that, if the proper rules are at work,
will increase social efficiency. A society designed by an aggregator
would likely include a large arena for private exchange in which
common and statutory law would minimize transaction costs and
assign spillover effects, courts that would attempt to mimic the
outcome of perfect markets, legislatures that would rely heavily
on vote trading, regulatory agencies that would harness market
processes, and any other devices that would tend to reduce the
distance between collective decision making and exchange in the
marketplace.

The conception of political judgment implicit in aggregative views
is one dominated by a concern with efficiency and conflict. Aggregators want to finesse the coercion that they see in political conflict
by focusing on efficiency. In so doing, they lose sight of any other
role that political institutions can play—for example (to cite a role
considered in the present discussion), that of helping to constitute
the procedural morality of a people. And with this loss goes appreciation of the value of political institutions, for an exclusive
concern with conflict and efficiency is likely to bring in its train the
view that political institutions are fundamentally devices by means

21. Alice Rivlin, *Systematic Thinking for Social Action*. See also the classic
work by Charles J. Hitch and Roland McKean, *The Economics of Defense in
the Nuclear Age*.

of which some impose their preferences on others—in short, politics as unfreedom.[22] A concern for efficiency, with its strong emphasis on individual preference satisfaction, is likely to lead to a suspicion of all collective decision making,[23] whereas a focus on conflict will reveal political institutions as conferring powerful systematic advantages in the struggle over valued outcomes. Political judgment truncated in these ways will fail to appreciate that the central political problem of a free people is that *we* would like to act but are divided. If no attention is paid to giving substance to the we who are to act, the result will be either domination or inaction. Similarly, if attention is only paid to efficiency, the result is likely to be a mere aggregation of individuals.

There is little mystery in this neglect of the connection between regime and the constitutive impact of institutions, even though the latter is not foreign to our understanding of political judgment. At work is the fact that questions of conflict and distribution, of resource use and social efficiency, seem to be relatively concrete matters. Questions of procedural moralities and constitution, however crucial, seem more elusive. In addition, our very attachment to a regime characterized by popular control and commerce makes the theme of the distribution of valued outcomes and the theme of efficiency particularly comprehensible, for they are, respectively, among the central concerns of those who speak for the demos and for businesslike behavior.

CONCLUSION

An appreciation of the constitutive bearing of political institutions is crucial to serving our aspirations to be a liberal democratic regime. This is the point perhaps most likely to be neglected in discussions of political judgment. Much contemporary thought about how and why liberal democracies flourish is, in fact, insensitive to the crucial role of political institutions in forming the citizenry. To aggregators may be added the more traditional positions that consider competition and bargaining among elites, pluralism in the basis of political conflict, or adherence to democratic norms by political leaders as central. None of these schools of thought suf-

22. George A. Kelly, "Who Needs a Theory of Citizenship," *Daedalus* 108, no. 4 (1979): 21–36.

23. For an extreme version, which sees the state as a convenience that we should do without if we could, see James M. Buchanan and Gordon Tullock, *The Calculus of Consent: Logical Foundations of Constitutional Democracy.*

ficiently appreciates that a fundamental political task is the definition of citizenship, for that is what the constitutive nature of political institutions is finally about—How shall we stand in relation to one another, given our aspirations for a particular political way of life? The principal conclusion of the last half of this book can, in fact, be restated in citizenship terms: to have liberal citizenship, there must also be democratic citizenship. Our aspirations imply a *mixed* citizenship.

It is formulations such as these that must be at the center of efforts to have a political science that is helpful to citizens who wish for a political life worthy of them. Such a political science will be a practical science, oriented toward decision and action. The present descriptive and explanatory bent of political science will be harnessed to the marriage of theory and practice that is at the core of political judgment.

At its best, this practical science ought to resist the now widespread temptation to conceive of the central problem of political judgment as being the examination of the logical consistency of political principles. Such efforts are addressed to the wrong people—namely, to others with a taste for exercises in logic—and are of limited use to political actors and to friends of the regime. These latter must cope with the complex interconnections and tensions within and among political institutions. Their task is to combine such institutions, and those with experience in thinking about such matters will likely assent to Bernard Williams' doubt that "the virtues of an intellectual theory, such as economy and simplicity, translate into a desirable rationality of social practise." [24]

Instead, the task of political science as practical science is to offer to those who wish to reason about a political way of life that is worthy of them an account of how the various institutional pieces can be made to fit. And the core of this account must be an effort to hold fast to two principles that are not easy to reconcile: (1) that the basic organizing principles of the society must, in some form, be subject to political decision and (2) that the state must not be allowed to arrange the daily lives of individuals. To deny the first is to betray the democratic heritage; to deny the second is to betray the liberal heritage. A liberal democratic regime is the successful accommodation of these two impulses—one popular and communal, the other private and individualistic. Its appeal lies in its contradictions—and so do its difficulties.

24. Bernard Williams, "Auto-da-Fe," *New York Review of Books,* April 28, 1983.

Bibliography

Aaron, Henry, and Harvey Galper. "How to Tell if Reagan is in Tax Wonderland." *The Washington Post,* May 26, 1985.

Abbot, Carl. *The New Urban America: Growth and Politics in Sunbelt Cities.* Chapel Hill: University of North Carolina Press, 1981.

Ackerman, Bruce. *Private Property and the Constitution.* New Haven, Conn.: Yale University Press, 1977.

———. *Reconstructing American Law.* Cambridge, Mass.: Harvard University Press, 1984.

Alt, James E., and K. Alec Chrystal. *Political Economics.* Berkeley and Los Angeles: University of California Press, 1983.

Altshuler, Alan. *The City Planning Process: A Political Analysis.* Ithaca, N.Y.: Cornell University Press, 1965.

Anderson, Charles. "Pragmatic Liberalism: Uniting Theory and Practice." In Alfonso J. Damico, ed., *Liberals on Liberalism.* Totowa N.J.: Rowman & Littlefield, 1986.

Anderson, Martin. *The Federal Bulldozer: A Critical Analysis of Urban Renewal, 1949–1962.* Cambridge, Mass.: MIT, 1964.

Anton, Thomas J. *Federal Aid to Detroit.* Washington, D.C.: The Brookings Institution, 1983.

Appleby, Joyce. *Capitalism and a New Social Order: The Republican Vision of the 1790's.* New York and London: New York University Press, 1984.

Aranson, Peter, and Peter Ordershook. "Public Interest, Private Interest, and the Democratic Polity." In Roger Benjamin and Stephen L. Elkin eds., *The Democratic State.* Lawrence: University Press of Kansas, 1985.

Arendt, Hannah. *On Revolution.* New York: Viking Press, 1963.

Aristotle. *Nicomachean Ethics.* Edited by Martin Ostwald. Indianapolis: Bobbs-Merrill, 1962.

———. *Politics.* Edited and translated by Ernest Barker. Oxford: Oxford University Press, 1946.

Arrow, Kenneth J. *Social Choice and Individual Values.* New York: Wiley, 1963.

Arrow, Kenneth J., and Tibor Scitovsky. *Readings in Welfare Economics, Selected by a Committee of the American Economic Association.* Homewood Ill.: Richard D. Irwin, 1969.

Bailyn, Bernard. *The Ideological Origins of the American Revolution.* Cambridge, Mass.: Belknap Press, Harvard University Press, 1967.

Banfield, Edward C. *Big City Politics*. New York: Random House, 1965.
———. "Economic Analysis of Political Phenomena: A Political Scientist's Critique." Working paper. Philadelphia: University of Pennsylvania, n.d.
———. *Political Influence*. Glencoe, Ill.: Free Press, 1961.
Banfield, Edward C., and Martin Meyerson. *Politics, Planning, and the Public Interest: The Case of Public Housing in Chicago*. Glencoe, Ill.: Free Press, 1955.
Banfield, Edward C., and James Q. Wilson. *City Politics*. Cambridge, Mass.: Harvard University Press, 1963.
Barber, Benjamin R. *Strong Democracy: Participatory Politics for a New Age*. Berkeley and Los Angeles: University of California Press, 1984.
Barber, Sotirios A. *On What the Constitution Means*. Baltimore: Johns Hopkins University Press, 1984.
Barta, Carolyn Jencks. "The Dallas News and Council-Manager Government," M.A. thesis, University of Texas, 1970.
Benjamin, Philip S. "Gentlemen Reformers in the Quaker City, 1870–1912." *Political Science Quarterly* 85, no. 1 (March 1970): 61–79.
Bernard, Richard M., and Bradley R. Rice. *Sunbelt Cities: Politics and Growth Since World War II*. Austin: University of Texas Press, 1983.
Bish, Robert L. *The Public Economy of Metropolitan Areas*. Chicago: Markham, 1971.
Bish, Robert L., and Vincent Ostrom. *Understanding Urban Government: Metropolitan Reform Reconsidered*. Washington, D.C.: American Enterprise Institute for Public Policy Research, 1973.
Block, Fred L. "The Ruling-Class Does Not Rule—Notes on the Marxist Theory of the State." *Socialist Revolution* 7, no. 33 (1977): 6–28.
Boast, Thomas M. "Urban Resources, the American Capital Market and Federal Programs." In Douglas Ashford, ed., *National Resources and Urban Policy*. New York: Methuen, 1980.
Bobbitt, Philip. *Constitutional Fate: Theory of the Constitution*. New York: Oxford University Press, 1982.
Bock, Betty, Harvey J. Goldschmid, Ira M. Millstein, and F. M. Scherer, eds., *The Impact of the Modern Corporation*. New York: Columbia University Press, 1984.
Bradbury, Katherine L., Anthony Downs, and Kenneth A. Small. *Urban Decline and the Future of American Cities*. Washington, D.C.: The Brookings Institution, 1982.
Bridges, Amy. "Boss Tweed and V. O. Key Head West." In Clarence Stone and Heywood Sanders, eds., *The Politics of Urban Development*. Lawrence, Kansas: University Press of Kansas, 1987.
Brown, Richard D. "Collective Bargaining and Public Employee Strikes." *Texas Business Review* 52, no. 9 (September 1978): 179–81.
Browning, Rufus P., Dale Rogers Marshall, and Paul Tabb. *Protest is Not Enough: The Struggle of Blacks and Hispanics for Equality in Urban Politics*. Berkeley and Los Angeles: University of California Press, 1984.
Bryce, Lord. *The American Commonwealth*. London: Macmillan, 1889.

Buchanan, James M., and Gordon Tullock. *The Calculus of Consent: Logical Foundations of Constitutional Democracy.* Ann Arbor: University of Michigan Press, 1962.

Calabresi, Guido, and Philip Bobbitt. *Tragic Choice.* New York: Norton, 1982.

Carnoy, Martin. *The State and Political Theory.* Princeton, N.J.: Princeton University Press, 1984.

Caro, Robert. *The Power Broker: Robert Moses and the Fall of New York.* New York: Knopf, 1974.

———. *The Years of Lyndon Johnson.* New York: Knopf, 1982.

Chappell, Henry W., Jr., and William R. Keech. "A New View of Political Accountability for Economic Performance." *American Political Science Review* 79, no. 1 (March 1985): 10–27.

Cicero, Marcus Tullius. *The Republic.* Translated by C. W. Keyes. Loeb Classical ed. London: Heinemann, 1961.

Clavel, Pierre. *The Progressive City: Planning and Participation, 1969–1984.* New Brunswick, N.J.: Rutgers University Press, 1986.

Cohen, Joshua, and Rogers, Joel. *On Democracy: Toward a Transformation of American Society.* New York: Penguin, 1983.

Coleman, Jules. "Economics and the Law: A Critical Review of the Foundations of the Economic Approach to Law." *Ethics* 94, no. 4 (July 1984): 649–79.

Commons, John R. *Legal Foundations of Capitalism.* Madison: University of Wisconsin, 1959.

The Congressional Quarterly, June 15, 1985.

Crecine, John P. *Governmental Problem-Solving: A Computer Simulation of Municipal Budgeting.* Chicago: Rand McNally, 1969.

Crenson, Matthew A. *Neighborhood Politics.* New York: Basic Books, 1983.

Crick, Bernard R. *In Defense of Politics.* Chicago: University of Chicago Press, 1972.

Cropsey, Joseph. "The United States as Regime." In Robert Horowitz, ed., *The Moral Foundations of the American Republic.* Charlottesville: University Press of Virginia, 1977.

Dagger, Richard. "Metropolis, Memory, and Citizenship." *American Journal of Political Science* 25, no. 4 (November 1981): 715–31.

Dahl, Robert A. "The City in the Future of Democracy." *American Political Science Review* 61, no. 4 (December 1967): 953–70.

———. *Dilemmas of Pluralist Democracy: Autonomy versus Control.* New Haven, Conn.: Yale University Press, 1982.

———. *A Preface to Democratic Theory.* Chicago: University of Chicago Press, 1956.

———. *Who Governs?* New Haven, Conn.: Yale University Press, 1961.

Davis, Allen F. *Spearheads for Reform: The Social Settlements and the Progressive Movement, 1890–1914.* New York: Oxford University Press, 1967.

Dewey, John. *The Public and Its Problems.* Denver: Swallow, 1954.

Diamond, Ann Stuart. "Decent, Even Though Democratic." In Robert A. Goldwin and William A. Schambra, eds., *How Democratic is the Constitu-*

tion?. Washington, D.C.: American Enterprise Institute for Public Policy Research, 1982.

Diamond, Martin. "The Declaration and the Constitution: Liberty, Democracy, and the Founders." *The Public Interest* 41 (Fall 1975): 39–55

———. "Democracy and *The Federalist:* A Reconsideration of the Framers' Intent." *American Political Science Review* 53, no. 1 (March 1959): 52–68.

Diesing, Paul. *Reason in Society.* Urbana: University of Illinois Press, 1962.

Diggins, John P. *The Lost Soul of American Politics: Virtue, Self-Interest, and the Foundations of Liberalism.* New York: Basic Books, 1984.

Dillon, John M. *Commentaries on the Law of Municipal Corporations* (5 ed., 1872–1911), vol. 1 (1911 ed.).

Dworkin, Ronald. *Law's Empire.* Cambridge, Mass.: Belknap Press of Harvard University Press, 1986.

"Dynamic Men of Dallas, The." *Fortune,* February 1946.

Ebner, Michael H., and Eugene M. Tobin, eds. *The Age of Urban Reform: New Perspectives on the Progressive Era.* Port Washington, N.Y.: Kennikat, 1977.

Elkin, Stephen L. "Between Liberalism and Capitalism: An Introduction to the Capitalist State." In Roger Benjamin and Stephen L. Elkin, eds., *The Democratic State.* Lawrence: University Press of Kansas, 1985.

———. "Castells, Marxism, and the New Urban Politics." *Comparative Urban Research* 2 (1979): 22–32.

———. "Cities without Power: The Transformation of American Urban Regimes." In Douglas Ashford, ed., *National Resources and Urban Policy.* New York: Methuen, 1980.

———. "Economics and Political Rationality." *Polity* 18, no. 2 (Winter 1985): 253–71.

———. "Pluralism in Its Place: State and Regime in the American Republic." In Roger Benjamin and Stephen L. Elkins, eds., *The Democratic State.* Lawrence: University Press of Kansas, 1985.

———. "Political Structure, Political Organization, and Race: English-American Comparisons." *Politics and Society* 8, no. 2 (1978): 225–51.

———. "Regulation as a Political Question." *Policy Sciences* 18, no. 1 (March 1985): 95–108.

———. "Twentieth Century Urban Regimes." *Journal of Urban Affairs* 7, no. 2 (Spring 1985): 11–28.

Ellickson, Robert. "Cities and Homeowners' Associations." *University of Pennsylvania Law Review* 130, no. 6 (June 1982): 1519–1608.

Elster, Jon. *Sour Grapes: Studies in the Subversion of Rationality.* New York: Cambridge University Press, 1983.

Erie, Steven P. "Rainbow's End: From the Old to the New Urban Ethnic Politics." In Joan W. Moore and Lionel A. Maldonado, eds., *Urban Ethnicity: A New Era.* Vol. 28. Beverly Hills, Calif.: Sage, 1984.

Etzioni, Amitai. *Capital Corruption: The Attack on American Democracy.* San Diego: Harcourt Brace Jovanovich, 1984.

Fainstein, Norman I., and Susan S. Fainstein. *Urban Political Movements: The Search for Power by Minority Groups in American Cities*. Englewood Cliffs, N.J.: Prentice Hall, 1974.

Fainstein, Susan S., Norman I. Fainstein, P. Jefferson Armistead. "San Francisco: Urban Transformation and the Local 'State.'" In Susan S. Fainstein, Norman I. Fainstein, Richard Child Hill, Dennis Judd, and Michael Peter Smith, eds. *Restructuring the City: The Political Economy of Urban Redevelopment*. New York: Longmans, 1983.

Federalist, The. Edited by Jacob E. Cooke. Middletown, Conn.: Wesleyan University Press, 1961.

Feldstein, Martin S., ed. *The American Economy in Transition*. Chicago: University of Chicago Press, 1980.

Fenno, Richard. *Home Style: House Members in Their Districts*. Boston: Little, Brown, 1978.

Fiorina, Morris. *Congress, Keystone of the Washington Establishment*. New Haven, Conn.: Yale University Press, 1977.

———. *Retrospective Voting in American National Elections*. New Haven, Conn.: Yale University Press, 1981.

Fitch, Robert. "Planning New York." In Roger A. Alcaly and David Mermelstein, eds., *The Fiscal Crisis of American Cities: Essays on the Political Economy of Urban America With Special Reference to New York*. New York: Vintage, 1977.

Fosler, R. Scott, and Renee A. Berger, eds. *Public-Private Partnerships in American Cities: Seven Case Studies*. Lexington, Mass.: Lexington, 1982.

Fossett, James W. *Federal Aid to Big Cities: The Politics of Dependence*. Washington, D.C.: The Brookings Institution, 1983.

Fox, Kenneth. *Better City Government: Innovation in American Urban Politics, 1850–1937*. Philadelphia: Temple University Press, 1977.

"From Private Enterprise to Public Entity: The Role of the Community Development Corporation." *Georgetown Law Journal* 57, no. 5 (May 1969): 956–91.

Frug, Gerald E. "The City as a Legal Concept." *Harvard Law Review* 93 no. 6 (April 1980): 1053–1154.

Fuller, Lon L. "Means and Ends." In Kenneth I. Winston, ed., *The Principles of Social Order: Selected Essays of Lon L. Fuller*. Durham, N.C.: Duke University Press, 1981.

———. *The Morality of Law*. New Haven, Conn.: Yale University Press, 1964.

Fullinwider, John. "Dallas: The City With No Limits?" *In These Times*, December 1980, 17–23.

Galbraith, John Kenneth. *The New Industrial State*. Boston, Houghton, Mifflin, 1971.

Galston, William. "Defending Liberalism." *American Political Science Review* 76, no. 3 (September 1982): 621–29.

Gans, Herbert. "The Failure of Urban Renewal." In James Q. Wilson, ed., *Urban Renewal: The Record and the Controversy*. Cambridge, Mass.: MIT, 1966.

Gaventa, John. *Power and Powerlessness: Quiescence and Rebellion in an Appalachian Valley*. Urbana: University of Illinois Press, 1980.

Geertz, Clifford. *Negara: The Theatre State in Nineteenth-Century Bali*. Princeton, N.J.: Princeton University Press, 1980.

Gere, Edward A., Jr. "Dillon's Rule and the Cooley Doctrine: Reflections of the Political Culture." *Journal of Urban History* 8, no. 3 (May 1982): 271–98.

Glaab, Charles N., and Theodore A. Brown, *A History of Urban America*. New York: MacMillan, 1967.

Goldberg, Victor P. "Regulation and Administered Contracts." *Bell Journal of Economics* 7 (Autumn 1976): 426–48.

Gosnell, Harold F. *Negro Politicians: The Rise of Negro Politics in Chicago*. Chicago: The University of Chicago Press, 1935.

Greenhouse, Steven. "New Threat to Smokestack America." *The New York Times*, May 26, 1985.

Greenstone, J. David, and Paul E. Peterson. *Race and Authority in Urban Politics: Community Participation and the War on Poverty*. New York: Russell Sage, 1973.

Greer, Scott A. *Urban Renewal and American Cities: The Dilemma of Democratic Intervention*. Indianapolis: Bobbs-Merrill, 1966.

Griffith, Ernest S. *A History of American City Government: The Conspicuous Failure, 1870–1920*. New York: Praeger, 1974.

Gutman, Amy. "Communitarian Critics of Liberalism." *Philosophy and Public Affairs* 14, no. 3 (Summer 1985): 308–22.

Habermas, Jurgen. *Knowledge and Human Interests*. Translated by Jeremy J. Shapiro. Boston: Beacon, 1971.

Haefele, Edwin T. "Towards a New Civic Calculus." In Lowdon Wingo and Alan Evans, eds., *Public Economics and the Quality of Life*. Published for Resources for the Future and the Centre for Environmental Studies. Baltimore: Johns Hopkins University Press, 1977.

Hall, John Stuart. "Case Studies of the Impact of Federal Aid on Major Cities: City of Phoenix." Washington, D.C.: Brookings Institution, 1979.

Halperin, Morton. *Lawless State: The Crimes of the U.S. Intelligence Agencies*. New York: Penguin, 1977.

Harre, Rom. *Social Being: A Theory for Social Psychology*. Totowa, N.J.: Rowman & Littlefield, 1980.

Hartman, Chester H. *The Transformation of San Francisco*. Totowa, N.J.: Rowman & Allenheld, 1984.

Hartog, Hendrik. *Public Property and Private Power: The Corporation of the City of New York in American Law*. Chapel Hill: University of North Carolina Press, 1983.

Hays, Samuel P. "The Changing Political Structure of the City in Industrial America." *Journal of Urban History* 1, no. 1 (November 1974): 6–38.

———. "The Politics of Reform in Municipal Governments in the Progressive Era." *Pacific Northwest Quarterly* 55, no. 4 (October 1964): 157–69.

Heclo, Hugh. "Issue Networks and the Executive Establishment." In Anthony King, ed., *The New American Political System*. Washington, D.C.: American Enterprise Institute for Public Policy Research, 1978.

Herman, Edward S. *Corporate Control, Corporate Power: A Twentieth Century Fund Study.* New York: Cambridge University Press, 1981.

Hill, Richard Child. "Crisis in the Motor City." In Susan S. Fainstein, Norman I. Fainstein, Richard Child Hill, Dennis Judd, and Michael Peter Smith, eds., *Restructuring the City: The Political Economy of Urban Redevelopment.* New York: Longman, 1983.

Hirsch, Fred. *Social Limits to Growth.* Cambridge, Mass.: Harvard University Press, 1973.

Hirschman, Albert O. *The Passions and the Interests: Political Arguments for Capitalism.* Princeton, N.J.: Princeton University Press, 1977.

Hitch, Charles J., and Roland McKean. *The Economics of Defense in the Nuclear Age.* Cambridge, Mass.: Harvard University Press, 1960.

Hofstadter, Richard. *The Age of Reform.* New York: Knopf, 1955.

Hoover, Edgar M., and Raymond Vernon. *Anatomy of a Metropolis: The Changing Distribution of People and Jobs in the New York Metropolitan Region.* Cambridge, Mass.: Harvard University Press, 1959.

Horwitz, Morton J. *The Transformation of American Law, 1780–1860.* Cambridge, Mass.: Harvard University Press, 1977.

Howland, Marie. "Property Taxes and the Birth and Intraregional Location of New Firms." Urban Studies Working Paper no. 1. Institute for Urban Studies, University of Maryland, January 1985.

Huntington, Samuel. "The Democratic Distemper." *The Public Interest* 41 (Fall 1975): 9–38.

Inglehart, Ronald. "Post-Materialism in an Environment of Insecurity." *American Political Science Review* 75, no. 4 (December 1981): 880–900.

Jacobs, Jane. *Cities and the Wealth of Nations: Principles of Economic Life.* New York: Random House, 1984.

Jencks, Christopher. "How Poor Are the Poor." *New York Review of Books,* May 9, 1985, 41–49.

Jones, Bryan, and Lynn W. Bachelor. *The Sustaining Hand: Community Leadership and Corporate Power.* Lawrence: University Press of Kansas, 1986.

Kalecki, M. "Political Aspects of Full Employment." *Political Quarterly* 14, no. 4 (1943): 322–31.

Kateb, George. "The Moral Distinctiveness of Representative Democracy." *Ethics* 91, no. 3 (April 1981): 357–74.

———. *Hannah Arendt: Politics, Conscience, Evil.* Totowa, N.J.: Rowman & Allenheld, 1984.

Katznelson, Ira. *Black Men/White Cities: Race Politics, and Migration in the United States, 1900–1930, and Britain, 1948–1968.* London: Oxford University Press, 1973.

———. *City Trenches: Urban Politics and the Patterning of Class in the United States.* New York: Pantheon, 1981.

Keller, Morton. *Affairs of State: Public Life in Late Nineteenth Century America.* Cambridge, Mass.: Belknap Press of Harvard University Press, 1972.

Kelly, George A. "Who Needs a Theory of Citizenship." *Daedalus* 108, no. 4 (1979): 21–36.

Key, V. O. *Public Opinion and American Democracy.* New York: Knopf, 1961.

Kolko, Gabriel. *The Triumph of Conservatism: A Reinterpretation of American History, 1900–1916.* New York: Free Press, 1963.

Kotler, Milton. *Neighborhood Government: The Local Foundation of Political Life.* Indianapolis: Bobbs-Merrill, 1969.

Kramer, Gerald H. "Short-Term Fluctuations in U.S. Voting Behavior, 1896–1964." *American Political Science Review* 65, no. 1 (March 1971): 131–43.

Kramnick, Issac. "Republican Revisionism Revisited." *American Historical Review* 87, no. 3 (June 1982): 629–64.

Krasner, Stephen D. *Defending the National Interest: Raw Materials Investment and U.S. Foreign Policy.* Princeton, N.J.: Princeton University Press, 1978.

Lane, Robert E. "Autonomy, Felicity, Futility: The Effects of the Market Economy on Political Personality." *Journal of Politics* 40, no. 1 (February 1978): 2–24.

———. "Interpersonal Relations and Leadership in a Cold Society." *Comparative Politics* 10, no. 4 (July 1978): 443–59.

———. "Markets and the Satisfaction of Human Wants." *Journal of Economic Issues* 12, no. 4 (December 1978): 799–827.

———. "Market and Politics: The Human Product." *British Journal of Political Science* 1, no. 1 (January 1981): 1–16.

———. "Government and Self-Esteem." *Political Theory* 10, no. 1 (February 1982): 5–31.

———. "Market Justice, Political Justice." *American Political Science Review* 80, no. 2 (June 1986): 383–402.

Lindblom, Charles E. *The Intelligence of Democracy: Decision Making Through Mutual Adjustment.* New York: Free Press, 1965.

———. *Politics and Markets: The World's Political Economic Systems.* New York: Basic Books, 1977.

Lippman, Walter. *The Public Philosophy.* Boston: Little, Brown, 1955.

Long, Norton. *The Polity.* Chicago: Rand McNally, 1962.

Lowe, Jeanne R. *Cities in a Race with Time.* New York: Random House, 1967.

Lowi, Theodore J. *The End of Liberalism: The Second Republic of the United States.* New York: Norton, 1979.

———. "Machine Politics: Old and New." *The Public Interest* 9 (Fall 1967): 83–91.

Lubove, Roy. *Twentieth-Century Pittsburgh: Government, Business, and Environmental Change.* New York: Wiley, 1969.

Lukes, Steven. *Power: A Radical View.* London: Macmillan, 1974.

Lustig, Jeffrey R. *Corporate Liberalism: The Origins of Modern American Political Theory: 1890–1920.* Berkeley and Los Angeles: University of California Press, 1982.

Maass, Arthur. "Benefit-Cost Analysis: Its Relevance to Public Investment Decisions." *The Quarterly Journal of Economics* 80, no. 2 (May 1966): 208–26.

———. *Congress and the Common Good.* New York: Basic Books, 1980.

McClosky, Herbert, and Alida Brill. *Dimensions of Tolerance: What Americans Believe About Civil Liberties.* New York: Russell Sage, 1983.

McClosky, Herbert, and John Zaller. *The American Ethos: Public Attitudes toward Capitalism and Democracy.* Cambridge, Mass.: Harvard University Press, 1984.

McConnell, Grant. *Private Power and American Democracy.* New York: Vintage, 1970.

McDonald, Forrest. "The Constitution and Hamiltonian Capitalism." In Robert A. Goldwin and William A. Schambra, eds., *How Capitalistic Is the Constitution?* Washington, D.C.: American Enterprise Institute for Public Policy Research, 1982.

————. *Novus Ordo Seculorum: The Intellectual Origins of the Constitution.* Lawrence: University Press of Kansas, 1982.

MacIntyre, Alasdair. *After Virtue: A Study in Moral Theory.* Notre Dame, Ind.: University of Notre Dame Press, 1981.

McManus, Susan, *Federal Aid to Houston.* Washington, D.C.: Brookings Institution, 1983.

————. "State Government: The Overseer of Municipal Finance." In Alberta M. Sbragia, ed., *The Municipal Money Chase: The Politics of Local Government Finance.* Boulder, Colo.: Westview Press, 1983.

MacNeil, Ian. *The New Social Contract: An Inquiry Into Modern Contractual Values.* New Haven, Conn.: Yale University Press, 1980.

McPherson, Michael S. "Want Formation, Morality, and Some Interpretive Aspects of Economic Inquiry." In Norma Haan et al., eds., *Social Science as Moral Inquiry.* New York: Columbia University Press, 1983.

McQuade, Walter. "Urban Renewal in Boston," In James Q. Wilson, ed., *Urban Renewal: The Record and the Controversy.* Cambridge, Mass.: MIT Press, 1966.

MacRae, C. Duncan. "A Political Model of the Business Cycle." *Journal of Political Economy* 85, no. 2 (April 1977): 239–63.

Malbin, Michael. *Unelected Representatives: Congressional Staff and the Future of Representational Government.* New York: Basic Books, 1980.

Mansbridge, Jane J. *Beyond Adversary Democracy.* New York: Basic Books, 1980.

Mayhew, David R. *Congress: The Electoral Connection.* New Haven, Conn.: Yale University Press, 1974.

Meltsner, Arnold J. *The Politics of City Revenue.* Berkeley: University of California Press, 1971.

Michelman, Frank I. "Political Markets and Community Self-Determination: Competing Judicial Models of Local Government Legitimacy." *Indiana Law Journal* 53 no. 2 (1977–78): 145–206.

————. "State's Rights and State's Roles: Permutations of 'Sovereignty' in *National League of Cities v. Usery." Yale Law Journal* 86, no. 6 (May 1977): 1165–95.

Miliband, Ralph. *The State in Capitalist Society.* London: Weidenfeld & Nicholson, 1969.

Mill, John Stuart. *On Liberty.* Baltimore: Penguin, 1974. (Originally published 1859.)

Miller, Gary J. *Cities by Contract: The Politics of Municipal Incorporation*. Cambridge, Mass.: MIT, 1981.

Miller, Kenneth H. "Community Development Corporations and the Community Self-Determination Act." *Harvard Journal on Legislation* 6 (1969): 413–61.

Miller, Stephen. "The Constitution and the Spirit of Commerce." In Robert A. Goldwin and William A. Schambra, eds., *How Capitalistic Is the Constitution?* Washington, D.C.: American Enterprise Institute for Public Policy Research, 1982.

Mladenka, Kenneth. "The Urban Bureaucracy and the Chicago Political Machine: Who Gets What and the Limits of Political Control." *American Political Science Review* 74, no. 4 (December 1980): 991–98.

Mollenkopf, John H. *The Contested City*. Princeton, N.J.: Princeton University Press, 1983.

———. "The Post-War Politics of Urban Development." *Politics and Society* 5, no. 3 (1975): 247–95.

Molotch, Harvey. "The City as Growth Machine." *American Journal of Sociology* 82, no. 2 (September 1976): 309–32.

Monroe, Kristen R. "Political Manipulation of the Economy: A Closer Look at the Political Business Cycle." *Presidential Studies* 13 no. 1 (Winter 1985): 37–49.

Montesquieu, Charles de Secondat. *The Spirit of the Laws*. Translated by Thomas Nugent. New York: Hafner, 1949.

Mueller, Dennis C. *Public Choice*. New York: Cambridge University Press, 1979.

Muir, William K. *Legislature: California's School for Politics*. Chicago: University of Chicago Press, 1982.

Nedelsky, Jennifer. "American Constitutionalism and the Paradox of Private Property." Paper presented at the annual meeting of the Law and Society Association, Toronto, 1982.

———. "Private Property and the Formation of the American Constitution." Unpublished paper, Princeton, N.J.: Princeton University, n.d.

Nelson, Richard R. *The Moon and the Ghetto*. New York: Norton, 1977.

Nordhaus, W. D. "The Political Business Cycle." *Review of Economic Studies* 42, no. 2 (April 1975): 169–90.

Novak, Michael. *The Spirit of Democratic Capitalism*. New York: Simon & Schuster, 1982.

Oakeshott, Michael. *Rationalism in Politics, and Other Essays*. New York: Basic Books, 1962.

O'Connor, James R. *The Fiscal Crisis of the State*. New York: St. Martin's, 1973.

Offe, Claus. *Contradictions of the Welfare State*. Edited by John Keane. Cambridge, Mass.: MIT, 1984.

Okun, Arthur. *Equality and Efficiency: The Big Tradeoff*. Washington, D.C.: The Brookings Institution, 1975 .

Orlebeke, Charles J. *Federal Aid to Chicago*. Washington, D.C.: The Brookings Institution, 1983.

Ostrom, Elinor, and Vincent Ostrom. "Public Choice: A Different Approach to the Study of Public Administration." *Public Administration Review* 31, no. 2 (1971): 203–16.

Page, Benjamin. *Who Gets What From Government.* Berkeley and Los Angeles: University of California Press, 1983.

Pateman, Carole. *Participation and Democratic Theory.* Cambridge: Cambridge University Press, 1970.

Pease, Otis A. "Urban Reformers in the Progressive Era: A Reassessment." *Pacific Northwest Quarterly* 62, no. 2 (April 1971): 49–58.

Peattie, Lisa; Stephen Cornell; and Martin Rein. "Development Planning as the Only Game in Town." *Journal of Planning Education and Research* 5, no. 1 (Autumn 1985): 17–25.

Peterson, Paul E. *City Limits.* Chicago: University of Chicago Press, 1981.

Petshek, Kirk. *The Challenge of Urban Reform: Politics and Programs in Philadelphia.* Philadelphia: Temple University Press, 1973.

Pitkin, Hanna Fenichel. "Justice: On Relating Private and Public." *Political Theory* 9, no. 3 (August 1981): 327–52.

———. *Wittgenstein and Justice: On the Significance of Ludwig Wittgenstein for Social and Political Thought.* Berkeley: University of California Press, 1972.

Piven, Frances Fox and Richard Cloward. *Regulating the Poor.* New York: Pantheon, 1977.

Plattner, Marc F. "American Democracy and the Acquisitive Spirit." In Robert A. Goldwin and William A. Schambra, eds., *How Capitalistic Is the Constitution?* Washington, D.C.: American Enterprise Institute for Public Policy Research, 1982.

Pocock, J. G. A. *The Machiavellian Moment: Florentine Political Thought and the Atlantic Republican Tradition.* Princeton, N.J.: Princeton University Press, 1975.

Polsby, Nelson W. *Community Power and Political Theory.* 2d ed. New Haven, Conn.: Yale University Press, 1963.

Posner, Richard A. *Economic Analysis of Law.* Boston: Little, Brown, 1972.

Poulantzas, Nicos. *Political Power and Social Classes.* Translated by Timothy O'Hagan. Atlantic Highlands, N.J.: Humanities, 1975.

Protho, James W., and Charles M. Grigg. "Fundamental Principles of Democracy: Basis of Agreement and Disagreement." *Journal of Politics* 22, no. 2 (May 1960): 276–94.

Ravitch, Diane. *The Great School Wars.* New York: Basic Books, 1974.

Rawls, John. "Justice as Fairness: Political Not Metaphysical." *Philosophy and Public Affairs* 14, no. 3 (Summer 1985): 223–51.

———. "Kantian Constructivism in Moral Theory." *Journal of Philosophy* 77, no. 9 (September 1980): 515–72.

———. *A Theory of Justice.* Cambridge, Mass.: Belknap Press of Harvard University Press, 1971.

———. "Two Concepts of Rules." *Philosophical Review* 64, no. 1 (January 1955): 3–22.

Reedy, George. "Discovering the Presidency." *The New York Times Book Review,* January 20, 1985.

Rees, John. "Manufacturing Headquarters in a Post-Industrial Urban Context." *Economic Geography* 54, no. 4 (October 1978): 337–54.

Reich, Charles A. "The New Property." *Yale Law Journal* 73, no. 5 (April 1964): 733–87.

Reich, Robert B., and John D. Donahue. *New Deals: The Chrysler Revival and the American System.* New York: Times, 1985.

Riordan, William L. *Plunkitt of Tammany Hall.* New York: Dutton, 1963.

Rivlin, Alice. *Systematic Thinking for Social Action.* Washington, D.C.: The Brookings Institution, 1971.

Rodrique, George. "The Best Laid Plans." *D,* September 1981.

Rohr, John A. *To Run a Constitution.* Lawrence: University Press of Kansas, 1986.

Rousseau, Jean Jacques. *The Social Contract, and Discourses.* Translated with an Introduction by G. D. H. Cole. New York: Dutton, 1950.

Salamon, Lester M., and John J. Siegfried. "Economic Power and Political Influence: The Impact of Industry on Public Policy." In Thomas Ferguson and Joel Rogers, eds., *The Political Economy: Readings in the Politics and Economics of American Public Policy.* New York: Pantheon, 1981.

Salisbury, Robert. "Urban Politics: The New Convergence of Power." *Journal of Politics* 26, no. 4 (November 1964): 775–97.

Salkever, Stephen. "Virtue, Obligation and Politics." *American Political Science Review* 68, no. 1 (March 1974): 78–92.

Samuelson, Paul A. "The Pure Theory of Public Expenditure." *Review of Economics and Statistics* 36, no. 4 (November 1954): 387–89.

Sanders, Heywood. "The Politics of City Redevelopment." Ph.D. diss., Harvard University, 1977.

Sayre, Wallace S., and Herbert Kaufman. *Governing New York City: Politics in the Metropolis.* New York: Russell Sage, 1960.

Sbragia, Alberta M. "Politics, Local Government and the Municipal Bond Market." In Alberta M. Sbragia, ed., *The Municipal Money Chase: The Politics of Local Government Finance.* Boulder, Colo.: Westview, 1983.

Schattschneider, E. E. *The Semisovereign People: A Realist's View of Democracy in America.* New York: Holt, Rinehart, & Winston, 1960.

Schiesl, Martin J. *The Politics of Efficiency: Municipal Administration and Reform in America, 1800–1920.* Berkeley: University of California Press, 1977.

Schmandt, Henry J., George D. Wendel, and Allan E. Tomey. *Federal Aid to St. Louis.* Washington, D.C.: The Brookings Institution, 1983.

Schumpeter, Joseph A. *Capitalism, Socialism, and Democracy.* 3rd ed. New York: Harper, 1950.

Schurmann, Franz. *The Logic of World Power: An Inquiry into the Origins, Currents, and Contradictions of World Power.* New York: Pantheon, 1974.

Scott, James C. *Comparative Political Corruption.* Englewood Cliffs, N.J.: Prentice-Hall, 1972.

Searle, John. *Speech Acts: An Essay in the Philosophy of Language.* London: Cambridge University Press, 1969.

Selznick, Philip. *Law, Society, and Industrial Justice.* New Brunswick, N.J.: Transaction, 1980.

Sen, Amartya K. *Collective Choice and Social Welfare.* San Francisco: Holden-Day, 1970.

Shefter, Martin. "The Emergence of the Political Machine: An Alternative View." In Willis Hawley et al., eds., *Theoretical Perspectives on Urban Politics.* Englewood Cliffs, N.J.: Prentice-Hall, 1976.

————. "Party Organization, Electoral Mobilization, and Regional Variations in Reform Success." Working Papers on Political Economy, Program on Urban Studies, Stanford University, 1978.

————. *Political Crisis/Fiscal Crisis: The Collapse and Revival of New York City.* New York: Basic Books, 1985.

Shklar, Judith. *Ordinary Vices.* Cambridge, Mass.: Belknap Press of Harvard University Press, 1984.

Siena, James, ed. *Antitrust and Local Government: Perspectives on the Boulder Decision.* Cabin John, Md.: Seven Locks Press, 1982.

Smart, John Jamieson, and Bernard Williams. *Utilitariansim: For and Against.* Cambridge: Cambridge University Press, 1973.

Soltan, Karol. *A Causal Theory of Justice.* Berkeley and Los Angeles: University of California Press, 1987.

Steib, Steve B., and R. Lynn Rittenoure. *Case Studies of the Impact of Federal Aid on Major Cities: City of Tulsa.* Washington, D.C.: Brookings Institution, 1980.

Stigler, George. *Citizen and the State: Essays on Regulation.* Chicago: University of Chicago Press, 1975.

Stone, Clarence N. *Economic Growth and Neighborhood Discontent: System Bias in the Urban Renewal Program of Atlanta.* Chapel Hill: University of North Carolina Press, 1976.

Stone, Clarence N., and Heywood Sanders, eds. *The Politics of Urban Development.* Lawrence: University Press of Kansas, 1987.

Stone, Harold, Don K. Price, and Kathryn H. Stone. *City Manager Government in Nine Cities.* Vol. 8. Published for the Committee on Public Administration, Social Sciences Research Council Studies in Public Administration. Chicago: Public Service Administration, 1940.

Storing, Herbert J. "American Statesmenship: Old and New." In Robert A. Goldwin, ed., *Bureaucrats, Policy Analysts, Statesmen: Who Leads?* Washington, D.C.: American Enterprise Institute for Public Policy Research, 1980.

————. *What the Anti-Federalists Were For.* Chicago: University of Chicago Press, 1981.

Sullivan, William. *Reconstructing Public Philosophy.* Berkeley and Los Angeles: University of California Press, 1982.

Swanstrom, Todd. *The Crisis of Growth Politics: Cleveland, Kucinich, and the Challenge of Urban Populism.* Philadelphia: Temple University Press, 1985.

————. "Semi-Sovereign Cities: The Political Logic of Urban Development." Paper presented to the American Political Science Association, Washington, D.C., 1986.

Syed, Anwar. *The Political Theory of American Local Government.* New York: Random House, 1966.

Teaford, Jon C. *The Unheralded Triumph: City Government in America, 1870–1900.* Baltimore: Johns Hopkins University Press, 1984.

Thernstrom, Stephan. *Poverty, Planning and Politics in the New Boston: The Origins of ABCD.* New York: Basic Books, 1969.

Thomas, Keith. "Politics as Language." *New York Review of Books* 33, no. 3 (February 27, 1986): 36–39.

Thometz, Carol Estes. *The Decision-Makers: The Power Structure of Dallas.* Dallas: Southern Methodist University Press, 1963.

Thompson, Wilbur R. *A Preface to Urban Economics.* Baltimore: Johns Hopkins University Press, 1965.

Tiebout, Charles M. "A Pure Theory of Local Expenditures." *Journal of Political Economy* 64, no. 5 (October 1956): 416–24.

Titmuss, Richard M. *The Gift Relationship: From Human Blood to Social Policy.* New York: Pantheon, 1971.

Tocqueville, Alexis de. *Democracy in America.* Translated by Henry Reeve. New York: Vintage, 1945. (Originally published 1835, 1840.)

Tribe, Laurence. "Technology Assessment and the Fourth Discontinuity: The Limits of Instrumental Rationality." *Southern California Law Review* 46, no. 3 (June 1973): 617–60.

Tufte, Edward R. *Political Control of the Economy.* Princeton, N.J.: Princeton University Press, 1978.

Tussman, Joseph. *Obligation and the Body Politic.* New York: Oxford University Press, 1960.

Useem, Michael. *The Inner Circle: Large Corporations and the Rise of Business Political Activity in the United States and United Kingdom.* New York: Oxford University Press, 1984.

Verba, Sidney, Norman H. Nie, and Jae-on Kim. *Participation and Political Equality: A Seven Nation Comparison.* New York: Cambridge University Press, 1978.

Vogel, David. "How Business Responds to Opposition: Corporate Political Strategies During the 1970s." Paper presented to the American Political Science Association, Washington, D.C., 1979.

Walker, David. B. *Toward a Functioning Federalism.* Cambridge: Winthrop, 1981.

Walzer, Michael. "Liberalism and the Art of Separation." *Political Theory* 12, no. 3 (August 1984): 315–30.

———. *Spheres of Justice: A Defense of Pluralism and Equality.* New York: Basic Books, 1983.

Waskow, Arthur. *From Race Riot to Sit-In, 1919 and the 1960s: A Study in the Connections Between Conflict and Violence.* Garden City, N.Y.: Doubleday, 1966.

Weiler, Conrad. *Philadelphia: Neighborhood, Authority, and the Urban Crisis.* New York: Praeger, 1974.

Weinstein, James. *The Corporate Ideal in the Liberal State, 1900–1918.* Boston: Beacon, 1968.

White, James Boyd. *When Words Lose Their Meaning: Constitutions and Reconstitutions of Language, Character, and Community.* Chicago: University of Chicago Press, 1984.

Wiebe, Robert H. *Businessmen and Reform: A Study of the Progressive Movement.* Cambridge, Mass.: Harvard University Press, 1962.

————. *The Search for Order, 1877–1920.* New York: Hill & Wang, 1967.

Williams, Bernard. "Auto-da-Fe." *New York Review of Books,* April 28, 1983.

Wills, Garry. *Explaining America: The Federalist.* Garden City, N.Y.: Doubleday, 1981.

Wilson, James Q. *The Investigators: Managing FBI and Narcotics Agents.* New York: Basic Books, 1978.

————. *Negro Politics: The Search for Leadership.* Glencoe, Ill.: Free Press, 1960.

————, ed. *The Politics of Regulation.* New York: Basic Books, 1980.

Wirt, Frederick M. *Power in the City: Decision Making in San Francisco.* Berkeley: University of California Press, 1975.

Wolfe, Alan. *The Limits of Legitimacy: Political Contradictions of Contemporary Capitalism.* New York: Free Press, 1977.

————. *America's Impasse: The Rise and Fall of the Politics of Growth.* New York: Pantheon, 1981.

Wolfinger, Raymond. *The Politics of Progress.* Englewood Cliffs, N.J.: Prentice-Hall, 1974.

Wood, Gordon S. *The Creation of the American Republic, 1776–1787.* Chapel Hill: University of North Carolina Press, 1969.

Yates, Douglas. *The Ungovernable City: The Politics of Urban Problems and Policy Making.* Cambridge, Mass.: MIT, 1977.

Yearley, C. K. *The Money Machines: The Breakdown and Reform of Governmental and Party Finance in the North, 1860–1920.* Albany: State University of New York, 1970.

Index